SHIRLEY

SHIRLEY

AN APPRECIATION OF THE LIFE
OF SHIRLEY BASSEY
MURIEL BURGESS

CENTURY

First published by Century in 1998

Copyright © Muriel Burgess 1998

Muriel Burgess has asserted her right under the Copyright,
Designs and Patents Act, 1988, to be identified as the author of this work

First published in the United Kingdom in 1998 by
Century, 20 Vauxhall Bridge Road, London SW1V 2SA

Random House Australia (Pty) Limited
20 Alfred Street, Milsons Point, Sydney,
New South Wales 2061, Australia

Random House New Zealand Limited
18 Poland Road, Glenfield,
Auckland 10, New Zealand

Random House South Africa (Pty) Limited
Endulini, 5A Jubilee Road,
Parktown 2193, South Africa

Random House UK Limited Reg. No. 954009

A CIP catalogue record for this book
is available from the British Library

Papers used by Random House UK Limited
are natural, recyclable products made from wood grown in
sustainable forests. The manufacturing processes conform to
the environmental regulations of the country of origin.

ISBN 0 7126 7918 9

Typeset by MATS, Southend-on-Sea, Essex
Printed and bound in the United Kingdom by
Biddles Ltd, Guildford and Kings Lynn

In loving memory of my brother Alan Burgess

PREFACE

I HEARD A slim young girl called Shirley Bassey sing on television for the first time in 1957. I was captivated by the way she looked and her extraordinary voice. And then my memory went back two or three years and I realised Shirley was no stranger. I had known a girl who had held her in her arms when she was a baby. I'd seen the very house in Bute Street, where she was born. Here was little Shirley Bassey of Tiger Bay.

In the cosmopolitan, pre-Suez, society of Alexandria, a tall, half Egyptian woman was rather a mystery to us foreigners. She was a friend of the royal princesses who had stayed on in Egypt after their brother Farouk had abdicated. Her name was Hinda Battanouny.

She told me she was from a place in Cardiff called Tiger Bay down by the docks. She had fallen in love with a naval cadet and followed him out to Egypt. The Bassey family were neighbours in Tiger Bay and she had known Shirley as a baby. When she grew older, Hinda's brother, Annis, used to take Shirley out. I felt a link with the little Bassey girl.

Years later in the nineties I was writing a book about Marlene Dietrich. Bernard Hall, my collaborator said one day. 'Marlene was always jealous of Shirley Bassey. She didn't like it when I toured with Shirley.'

'Tell me more,' I said. 'Let's forget Marlene.'

Muriel Burgess,
August 1998

Contents

Prologue

It is June 1998. Shirley Bassey has arrived in London to conclude another of her famous 'Diamond' tours of Europe. The Royal Festival Hall is packed to the rafters with adoring fans waiting, many for the twentieth time, to see, hear and applaud their diva.

Bassey takes the stage to an ecstatic reception. She glitters in lamé and feathers; she commands with those dramatic movements of sweeping arms and expressive hands; she sparkles with 'naughty' repartee, teasing her audience even as she invites them to adore her. Above all, she opens her mouth and sings.

Full-throated and magnificent, she goes through the trusted routines, revealing strength and vulnerability, humour and sadness, through that God-given instrument which soars, swoops, trembles, and vibrates. There is nothing subtle about Bassey's voice or stagecraft; rather, it overwhelms with power, drama, sex appeal and the expertise of long practice.

By the end of the evening, ecstasy has become hysteria as the fans and the flowers crowd to the stage. Shirley has not disappointed. It was all there: 'Goldfinger', 'Big Spender', 'Something', 'This is My Life' and, from Sondheim's *Follies*, 'I'm Still Here'.

And she *is* still here, a seemingly indestructible and dazzling symbol of glamour and excitement. The Maria Callas of popular music, she ranks alongside legendary performers such as Judy Garland, Lena Horne and Frank Sinatra. She is, incredibly, sixty-one years old.

If the voice was God-given, the rest of her uniquely exciting armoury was fought for with determination, discipline and passion. Shirley Bassey is indubitably a great star, but that stardom, which remained intact for over four decades, has been bought at the cost of much personal pain and sacrifice. Only her indomitable will and a driving hunger for success have helped her to overcome the obstacles of her humble origins, and the exploitation of her talent by those who stood to benefit from it.

The extraordinary tale of how Shirley Bassey, the girl from Tiger Bay, rose from rags to riches, and from obscurity to become a famed icon of the age, is told in these pages.

I

TIGER BAY

LEGEND HAS IT that a Portuguese seaman gave the name Tiger Bay to this corner of the Cardiff docks. He swore that his voyage up the estuary had been so terrible, so wild and so dangerous that it was like entering a bay of tigers. It remained Tiger Bay for more than 150 years until, in the Sixties, the Cardiff council decided to do some slum clearance and tidy up the area. It is now named Cardiff Bay, but the locals have always referred to it as simply The Bay.

When the bulldozers moved in to the little streets with pretty names (called after the daughters of the Earl of Bute), the humble houses were destroyed, to be replaced by council buildings. Many people were broken-hearted as they watched their past being obliterated. Estranged from their familiar landscape, they felt they were paying too high a price for bathrooms and inside toilets. By the 1990s the docks had gone, and one of the few remaining landmarks on the headland over the Bay is the white Norwegian Church for Seamen, now a tea-room.

In 1937, when Shirley Bassey was born, Bute Street was the heart of the real Tiger Bay, forming the main thoroughfare from rigid Presbyterian Cardiff at the top to unruly Tiger Bay at the bottom. In those days Tiger Bay was a successful mixed-race community that had come into being thanks to coal – the black gold of Wales. Foreign seamen sailed into the docks to load their cargo of coal, seamen from Africa, Arabia, Egypt and parts of Europe. There was plenty of work here, and the lure of pretty girls encouraged some of the men to slip over the side of their ships and find a friend or relative in Bute Street. Indeed, most families in Tiger Bay could trace their origins to a foreign seaman jumping ship, and many of these families continued to live there for generations.

Henry Bassey, a member of the Efik tribe, hailed from Calobar in Nigeria. Had he been born in the vicinity of Lagos, inside the British colony, he would have been a British subject with rights of entry to the United Kingdom. Unfortunately, however, Calobar was only a protectorate and its inhabitants were not classed as British subjects. Henry Bassey jumped ship in the Twenties and went to live in Bute Street. As with many of the defecting sailors, he had no legal documents and lived permanently in the shadow of possible deportation should anything go wrong.

Henry Bassey's wife, Eliza, was English, from North Shields on the Tyne Estuary. Her neighbours talk of her northern accent and describe her as an intelligent woman who 'did her best' for her children. One of Shirley's older sisters has said that she thought her mother's family disapproved of her marriage to the Nigerian Bassey and, because of this, she never went back to Tyneside. A next-door neighbour of the Basseys knew the area where Eliza came from and used to chat to her about her home. She had grown up in a busy fishing port. The harbour at North Shields was ringed with fishing boats, and fishwives sold the catch down at the docks.

Any resemblance between North Shields – its houses grey and austere, its surroundings the wild moors – and Tiger Bay began and ended with the fact that they were both dockside hamlets. Life, as Eliza Bassey discovered, was certainly more pleasant and happy-go-lucky in South Wales than in the north of England; and in Tiger Bay one was surrounded by friendly brown faces and a lot of music.

The Bassey home was one of the many two-storey terraced houses that were later demolished, but when Shirley was a toddler, Bute Street was a friendly and lively place. The entrance to 182 was through a side door off the main road. Down the road was the Maria Street police station, where the bobbies lived with their wives and children. Then came the butcher's shop, the grocer, the milk bar, the fish-and-chip shop and, if you walked far enough, the Chinese laundry and a Chinese restaurant.

There were pubs everywhere, from the Golden Cross at the top down to the Ship and Pilot near the docks. The food shops catered to many tastes and to the dietary laws of the several religions that co-existed in the mixed community that was Tiger Bay – Caribs from the West Indies, Greeks, Slavs, Spaniards and Portuguese, Russians, Jews, West Africans, Arabs and Chinese, as well as a good sprinkling of native Welsh men and women. Despite having grown into a melting pot of differing peoples, Tiger Bay, situated beside the docks and surrounded by green hills and countryside, was a coherent and integrated hamlet.

Although the community was a friendly one, its members obeyed their own rules of silence and discretion. They didn't readily open their hearts to strangers, and wouldn't tolerate interference from the snooty welfare workers from St David's city who came poking around. Nobody forgot 1919, when the men of Tiger Bay, armed to the teeth, stood sentry at the corner of every one of the Bay streets while white rioters rode through Cardiff on their way to the Bay, protesting against black men taking their jobs. The line of police at Custom House, above Bute Street, parted as the mounted protesters thundered towards them, and warned them that they would proceed at their peril, for the men of Tiger Bay were ready for them.

At the summit of Bute Street, scuffles and fights broke out, but the protesters did not pass the barricades. Not a single horseman rode down Bute Street itself. After this confrontation, several families in Tiger Bay took heart and decided to buy 99-year leases on a house from the Earl of Bute, who owned the freehold of the properties. Up in Cardiff, the rumour took hold that it wasn't safe to venture down to Tiger Bay and, to this day, traffic wardens warn lone women drivers to be careful. The Bay people laugh at these allegations.

During the Twenties and Thirties, Henry Bassey was the tenant at 182 Bute Street. It would never have occurred to him to buy a house. He was not a good provider although he was, as they say in Nigeria, one of the 'savvy' kind. When he wasn't stoking boilers at sea, he could always turn his hand to pocketing a bob or two by some other means, sometimes renting a bed to a sailor who needed a roof over his head.

This was the world into which Shirley Veronica Bassey was born on 8 January 1937, the last of seven children, six of them girls. Her siblings, in descending order, were Gracie, Ella, Iris, the twins Eileen and Henry, and Marina. Shirley's birth certificate names her father as Henry Bassey and her mother as Eliza Bassey, formerly Metcalfe.

The new baby came into a family where she would sleep three in a bed with two of her sisters, and be clothed in hand-me-downs that had been passed from sister to sister and were old and shabby by the time they got to her. Bella Freeman, who Shirley knew as Auntie Bella and always remembered as having been kind to her, recalls how Eliza Bassey would visit with Shirley in tow. While the little girl played with Bella's daughter, Iris, Mrs Bassey would sit in Bella's front room, quiet and worn out. Bella 'worried about that little girl, because when the time came for them to go I could see that little Shirley sometimes looked frightened. I knew that Shirley was very close to her mother, but it was as if there was something in their house that little Shirley didn't like.'

Nobody can account for Bella Freeman's impression of a child in fear. Certainly, the Basseys' former next-door neighbour, Mr Wesley from Sierra Leone, recalled happy times in Henry's household. 'Henry was a man who loved a party and he liked to make something on the side. We called them dancing classes in those days, but they were a kind of street party where everyone paid their share, and if the party was held in your house you were paid for the trouble. Each week or so, the dancing class moved from house to house and it was a good cheap way to have fun.'

Henry Bassey used to get the children to put rags over their feet and polish the old floorboards in the front room until they shone. If there was a piano handy the neighbours would carry it over the doorstep, then a couple of guitar players from the Ship and Pilot pub down by the harbour would arrive. Drinks would be lined up for sale, a jar of poteen from the Irish community, ouzo from the Greeks, wine from the Italians and the Spaniards, and the home-brewed 'boozo' of Africa.

When the party started, everyone was there: young girls, sailors from the ships in port, wives and husbands. Those husbands that didn't dance played dice in the next room, while the older women looked after the babies and gossiped in a corner. The children would gather, the boys keeping a lookout for a nosy bobby, and little Shirley Bassey would crawl under the table, pull the chenille cloth down until she was hidden, and prepare to sing the night away. Shirley's mother later said, 'I think she got her singing from her father. He was always so fond of music. He never stopped playing gramophone records. Shirley used to sing with them as a tiny girl.' Shirley's sister Gracie always knew she was different, recalling that 'She sang as soon as she could talk. The neighbours liked to listen to her.'

Eventually the little girl, who was too shy to come out from under the tablecloth, would fall asleep and be put to bed. From the time she was born Shirley heard the sound of music. After all, this was Wales, and in Tiger Bay in particular there was always music. Guitars and drums sounded from the Ship and Pilot pub, piano lessons could be heard through the open windows of summer, and gospel singing and the Blues, Paul Robeson's voice from radios and gramophones, and the sound of the little Bassey girl joining in.

Tiger Bay had its brothel for the sailors and when during the war, the need for its services increased, a couple more sprang up. The pretty girls with lovely clothes who worked in the original brothel were well-liked by the local children. The girls were free in handing out the sweets that the sailors brought them from foreign shores, and the kids called them all 'auntie'. Now and then the police would raid the brothel and the horrified children would watch their 'aunties' being loaded into a Black Maria.

There were other, more conventional, places of amusement in Bute Street. At the Annexe, which rather resembled a mission hall, the Saturday night dances that were held for the young and the unmarried were often wild, and at the Old Vestry they had the sixpenny hops. But what the children of Tiger Bay loved best of all were those 'dancing classes' where they were put to polishing the dance floor.

Shirley Bassey was not yet three when trouble hit her family. Like most of the seamen who had jumped ship, Henry Bassey had never bothered to legalise his position and that was one of the reasons he was deported back to Nigeria. After his departure the Council, for reasons best known to themselves, thought it better to move Eliza Bassey and her children out of Tiger Bay, and relocated them to a place bearing the unprepossessing name of Splott. The next suburb along the Cardiff coast, Splott was only a short bus ride from the top of Bute Street, but it was a world away in every other respect. A steel town, whose inhabitants were very definitely white, the place had only a small quota of poor inhabitants, mainly Irish labourers who'd come to work in the mills.

Eliza Bassey was given a terraced house at 132 Portmanmoor Road – in the shadow of the giant Dowlais Steel Mills whose orange flames illuminated the night sky – and two pounds ten shillings a week National Assistance. It was a paltry sum, but food was cheap in those days. Farthings were still currency then and a small loaf of bread cost a halfpenny, while a shilling in the gas meter kept you warm in the winter. The two elder Bassey girls, Gracie and Ella, were out at work in Cardiff and their wages helped. And Tiger Bay did its best. Old Nora, who'd always been the best of neighbours in Bute Street, would come and help look after the younger children, other former neighbours contributed sheets and blankets to the household and, as they all reminded the Basseys, 'You're only a penny bus ride away.'

But life wasn't the same in Splott. In the Bay everyone waved or stopped to chat, everybody knew everything about everybody else. And all the children looked the same. Shirley didn't understand what her new life was all about, though her mother tried to explain. She had told the child truthfully that her father had gone away, nonetheless reassuring her that Henry was 'a good man and he always loved you. He used to call you Sharon. He said that was the pet name for the Queen of Sheba.'

Ifor Harry, a Welshman who was the Basseys' neighbour in

Portmanmoor Road, felt sure that the move did great harm to Shirley. Until the age of five, when she began at Moorland Road Junior School, the child had been oblivious to racial jibes. Then, when she went to her new school, for the first time in her life somebody called her 'nigger'.

The Bassey children were treated as foreigners in Splott, singled out and tormented because of the colour of their skin. One of her schoolmates remembered Shirley's early days at Moorland Road school. 'At first Shirley didn't understand what the other kids meant when they called her names. When she did, she went for them. What a fighter she was. I hoped she'd learned it in Tiger Bay. Anyone who called her "darkie" or "nigger" got a real walloping from Shirley. In our infants class she became a real heroine.'

Shirley and her sister Marina, walking hand-in-hand to school, were often stopped by jeering boys. Out of her front door would come Eliza Bassey and fly up the road, handbag at the ready to swing at the boys, swiping them around their heads and using language nobody would have guessed she even understood. Everyone who tormented her daughters got the same treatment.

'I really admired Mrs Bassey, she was a remarkable lady,' Ifor Harry recalled. 'You see, it was an all-white school and we know that children can be cruel. Mrs Bassey tried her best, but I think it was a nasty shock to the little girl. I watched her grow up and I could tell. I do blame those first years in Splott. If ever I read of Shirley behaving badly, when she seems to be hard and not care, I think it all began when she had to learn to be tough and act as if no-one could hurt her.'

The steel-mill workers were not poor. Their wartime wages were good and their children, who went to Moorland Road school, too, were rather better dressed than the little Bassey girl. Nigerian seamen who knew Shirley's father would call on the Basseys, bringing sweets and little presents for the children. They were all distressed at what had befallen the family. Eventually, one of these Nigerians, named Mr Mendi, became Mrs Bassey's lodger, his rent a welcome supplement to her income.

Mr Mendi, smartly dressed and well read, was a very different person to Henry Bassey, but when he'd been lodging with the family for some time, Shirley began to call him Dad. He would bring her wonderful presents back from his voyages – shoes, for example, which could only be bought in Wales with ration coupons. His gift of a pair of black patent strapped sandals led to an unhappy incident when a teacher told Shirley they were unsuitable footwear for school.

'My dad brought these back from New York,' growled Shirley. 'I have to wear them 'cause I haven't got any more.'

Mrs Bassey and Mendi got along very well, and were soon recognised as a couple. In keeping with the local custom, everyone began to call her 'Mrs Mendi', and it was only a matter of time before that was what she officially became.

Ifor Harry ran a barber shop in the front of his house at 128 Portmanmoor Road and remembered that, while cutting the customers' hair, he often heard Shirley and her brother Henry singing next door. 'They were always singing, those two. They had such good voices, and you know that in Wales we love good singers.'

Although the younger Bassey children went to school in Splott, most of their friends were in Tiger Bay, and they made their way there at every opportunity. The Rainbow Club in Bute Street had been started as a charity for the poor children of Butetown (as it had been officially known), and going there was like going back home.

Academically, Shirley didn't shine at school. Some children are lucky in finding a gifted teacher who takes a special interest in them, but this didn't happen to her. She'd had a bad start and she remained a rebel, ready to fight her way out of any situation.

Margaret Baird, one of her classmates through both junior and secondary school at Moorland Road, admired Shirley but thought her rather more recklessly brave than sensible. On one occasion, a teacher was showing Shirley up in front of the class and the girl, who hated being teased, picked up an inkwell and poised it ready to throw at her tormentor. 'If she had thrown it,' commented Margaret, 'she would certainly have been expelled. It was a very dangerous thing to do.'

Sports were a different matter. Shirley was very good at games, especially baseball – not the American kind, but the Welsh version where a soft leather ball is used. Down in this part of Wales there was a little pocket of good baseball and Shirley was part of it. Perhaps the fact a star of Welsh baseball, Jim Sullivan, had been born near the Basseys in Dowlais Cottages might have spurred her on.

As a little girl Shirley, no matter how well she sang, was always drawn to dancing and tried hard to shine at it. The original Rainbow Club was housed in empty shop premises in Bute Street, and Shirley began going there as a skinny seven-year-old. It served as a social club, and the kids played games as well as entertaining each other with song and dance. Most of them were little show-offs and they loved it. Everyone agreed that, for one so young, Shirley had a marvellous voice, but her dancing was less well received. 'Forget the dancing,' said the lady who ran the club. 'When you sing, Shirley, you're better than anyone else.' In the end, Shirley had to accept that in Tiger Bay she had best concentrate on singing. Nonetheless, in later years, Bernard Hall, Shirley's friend, sometime road manager and fervent admirer, who was a leading professional show dancer, said that Shirley was an incomparable ballroom dancer and an absolute delight as a partner. However, because she refused to bow to the strict disciplines that dance requires, the constant exercise and rehearsal, she was never able to turn professional.

In due course the Rainbow Club moved from the shop to better premises at the top of Bute Street where it became a worthwhile charity for the underprivileged children of Tiger Bay. At the new Rainbow Club, the kids had a real stage for their shows and competitions and made keen use of it. Television had not yet arrived, and most of the kids had their eye on show business, films or the stage. Some of their parents, including the piano-teaching mother of Louise Benjamin, had gone to London years previously to appear in the Paul Robeson film, *Sanders of the River*. All the locals went to see the movie and watch 'Uncle' Willy Needham leaping about in a loincloth. Tiger Bay was fair game for any film with an exotic background that needed a shoal of colourful extras. ('We have everything here, take your pick'.) The rich pickings for movie companies didn't fade with the years, and one of the more famous films serviced by the locals was *The Inn of the Sixth Happiness* in which Ingrid Bergman strode through the hills of Wales, which stood in for China, accompanied by about a hundred toddlers from Liverpool and Tiger Bay.

Shirley Bassey's career started the hard way. Her schoolmate Margaret Baird recalled how, at the age of thirteen, she began singing in dockland pubs and clubs. 'It could be tough. They threw things if they didn't like you and the applause was rare. And even if they did like you they didn't clap, they just didn't throw anything.' But her young school mates thought she was great. Another schoolmate was Doreen Bentley, whose father fitted up a microphone in the Bentley's front room where Shirley and Doreen used to practise harmonising together.

At thirteen, Shirley began earning the odd pound as a vocalist with a trio – piano, guitar and saxophone – formed by three local boys. By then, she knew all the words of every popular song through listening to radio and records. If she'd been caught singing in pubs at her age, she would have been in trouble, and the boys were assiduous in watching the door for a passing policeman, whereupon their teenage vocalist would swiftly crawl out of sight.

There was no shortage of natural talent in Tiger Bay. A group of girls got together, taught themselves to dance and to sing in harmony and, calling themselves the Bay Girls, performed for charity at the Rainbow Club. Not surprisingly, Shirley became a Bay Girl, and it was this association that eventually led to an audition in London and her first professional show.

Throughout her school years, she longed for the day she would turn fifteen and be legally free to earn money. The occasional ten bob or a pound earned under the counter went no way to satisfying her hunger for new clothes. She hated the hand-me-downs from her sisters, the shrunken jerseys and the shoes that needed paper stuffed into the toes to keep them on. It was doubly humiliating in the company of her schoolmates who were well turned out in smart pleated skirts and blouses and cardigans.

Years later, Shirley Bassey gave a radio interview in Australia in which the humiliation she had suffered through poverty was expressed. 'I always buy too many clothes nowadays,' she confessed to a Sydney radio audience. 'I buy shoes and coats and hats, not because I need them but because I swore to myself that one day I'd never wear other people's cast-offs ever again. Everything I wear has to be brand-new.'

In 1951, Shirley was a fourteen-year-old with no decent clothes and no money. It was a tough time for teenagers in Wales. Although the war had been over for five years, rationing was still in force, and without sufficient clothing coupons a girl could buy very little. Shirley was the only one of the Bassey offspring yet to earn her own money. Sixteen-year-old Marina had already been working at Curran's factory for over a year, and Henry, her only brother and the sibling to whom she was closest, was out working in a local factory.

Henry was a talented boy with a good voice. Neighbours recall him singing as he pegged out the washing in the back yard, and when he was still around, he and Shirley harmonised together for hours on end. The room in which they sang was virtually bare of furniture but for Henry's record player and a piece of worn carpet, and lit by a solitary bulb which dangled from the ceiling on a long piece of flex. Some time later, when Shirley was beginning to win public recognition, Henry invited a local journalist to see these unpromising surroundings where his sister practised her singing.

'Where's the furniture?' asked the newspaperman. Henry, amused by the question, replied, 'You don't need furniture to sing.'

In 1956, when Shirley's second record had just been released, another local journalist wrote, 'This Cardiff girl has the mysterious stuff of which stars are made. She has a style of her own, but do I hear, in "Born to Sing the Blues", a slight trace of Frankie Laine here and there?'

He was right. Sitting on the worn piece of carpet under the harsh light bulb, Shirley and Henry used to harmonise to Frankie Laine records. One of their favourite duets was sung to his recording of 'Girl in the Wood'. And they harmonised not only to Frankie Laine, but to Billy Eckstine, Sarah Vaughan, Lena Horne, Judy Garland and Johnny Mathis, all there in the pile of records that Henry used to buy. If there was indeed a flavour of these stars in Shirley's early renditions, it was hardly surprising since this was how she taught herself. She couldn't pay for lessons during her teenage years, and fell back on copying the greats of her time.

Michael Sullivan, Shirley's first manager, pushed her to develop her own individual style, but she still loved listening to records. Wherever she travelled, her portable record player went with her, and when she was already a star, orchestra leader Kenny Clayton was surprised when she directed him to listen to a Mathis recording in order to get her desired key for his accompaniment. Sorting out keys was not a skill that Shirley had any intention of acquiring – what was good enough for Mathis was good enough for her.

Talking of her childhood in an interview, Shirley recalled that, when younger, she didn't seem too popular with her older sisters. She always seemed to be underfoot when they didn't want her around. Then, one night, one of her sisters, quite unexpectedly, took her to a Billy Eckstine concert at the Cardiff's New Theatre. 'It must have been fate,' she said, for joining the throng of autograph seekers at the stage door afterwards, and seeing the ecstatic reception Eckstine got from his fans when he emerged, made a deep impression on her. She began to realise that singing, which to her was as natural as breathing, could make people feel important.

This thought was a revelation. After all, she, like Billy Eckstine, could sing, too. 'I had never been interested in show business until that point,' she said. A few days later, Henry came home with a recording of Judy Garland's signature tune, 'Somewhere Over the Rainbow' which they played over and over again until they could sing along with Judy. In that same interview, Shirley was paid the highest of compliments when the reporter suggested that, 'You may be the nearest thing to Judy Garland still going.'

Shirley's appreciation of the greats, and her perception of their rewards – fame, adulation, money – ignited the single-minded determination which has characterised her career. When she started out professionally, in two slightly tacky Joe Collins revues, one of the caustic comments made by her fellow performers was, 'Who does she think she is? The star?' Right from the beginning, Shirley Bassey knew where she was going: somewhere where she'd be important and the centre of attention, just like Billy Eckstine and Judy Garland, and her sisters would never again shout at her, 'Have you been messing with my lipstick?', because she'd have her own.

In the summer of 1951 Shirley's class from Moorland Road school went to Porthcawl Camp for a week's holiday. A group of girls from Albany Road school, more or less the same age, went too. The Albany Road girls considered themselves a cut above the Moorland Road girls, and were rather snooty.

It was a good holiday nevertheless, though there wasn't much to do in the evenings. Someone might play the piano and the girls danced together, but everyone was a little bored until the night when Shirley Bassey got up on the small stage and sang. Her harmonising chum, Doreen Bentley, recalled that 'Shirley was dynamite. She was only fourteen, but that night she told us what love was all about.' The girls, young and impressionable, were just longing to grow up, fall in love, and find out what they were missing. 'Shirley sang, and she really put her heart into it,' Doreen said. "Over the Rainbow" was the song she sang first, which was one we used to sing together in my front room, but that night Shirley's lovely voice told us what we were waiting for. It gave us promises and dreams.

'The girls from Albany Road school were a bit toffee-nosed compared to us, but everyone fell in love with Shirley that night. She absolutely took us by storm. The applause was deafening. The rest of that week was great, we had lovely evenings. Shirley could be a great organiser if she thought people liked her and she took us all in hand.'

Doreen Bentley has also told how 'Years later I was at one of her concerts, one of these huge affairs with more than a thousand people, and I had exactly the same feeling all over again. The audience were showering Shirley with their love. And I thought that even then, when she was fourteen, Shirley must have felt our love. So this is how Shirley gets her fix, I thought. This is how she gets all the love she needs.' It was an acute observation.

Shirley's last term at school ended just before Christmas of 1951. She would turn fifteen a couple of weeks or so later, on 8 January 1952. One of her classmates, Jeanette Cockley, recalled how Shirley 'went into every classroom and sang "This is My Mother's Day". That was the last time I saw her. I knew she went off to London with the Bay Girls, and I did hear that one of these girls was killed.'

All Shirley Bassey's friends and contemporaries from her schooldays have related their memories without envy, and with a certain sadness, as if they knew that someone, somewhere had failed Shirley, and that she paid dearly for everything she achieved. One of the girls from Moorland Road has related how, 'When I see her on television I cry and think how lucky I am to live in this small house in this little corner of Wales. I wouldn't change my happiness for everything material Shirley has earned for herself.'

2

CAN'T STOP SINGING

ONCE SHIRLEY BASSEY left school and became a working girl, life was a lot more fun. Her first job was at Curran's factory in Tiger Bay. Curran's was the workplace of large numbers of men, and all of them were aware of Shirley Bassey. 'What's she got?' wondered the other girls in the packing shed. 'Why do these silly buggers moon over her?'

On the surface, it was an understandable reaction for, to all outward appearances, she was just another ordinary working-class teenager striving to be 'grown-up'. She was pretty, but her looks only hinted at the striking style and glamour that was to become one of her trademarks.

To the young men at Curran's, however, she had that most powerful of qualities, sex appeal. She could positively radiate sex appeal, seeming to switch it on at will when certain men appeared with another load of saucepans to be packed. And she could sing;

she could sing all day while parcelling chamber pots, and she was the centre of attention. It was a far cry from the misery of school, despite the fact that when the girls sang along with *Music While You Work*, Shirley's voice was invariably the loudest and would cause the manager to come in and yell, 'Bassey! Pipe down!'

Curran's Enamelware factory was situated in a mean back street of Tiger Bay, where the sun seldom shone and gloomy shadows were cast over the factory buildings. The side of the Curran's building that faced on to the street was long and low, with a pointed roof that somewhat resembled a Methodist chapel. Two square windows provided the only exit for the fumes. Round the back were the workshops where the machines were manned, machines which dipped the pans into cream enamel and finished them off with a green edging. When they were dry, brawny men would wheel them into the packing shed where the girls were stationed.

The enamelware was packed the old-fashioned way, in boxes with lots of paper. Because she was young and it was a bit of fun, Shirley sometimes slipped her name and address into parcel. Now and then, she received a reply: 'I got your name in the chamber pot, Miss Bassey.'

Music blared out for most of the day in the packing shed. When it wasn't music it was *The Archers* or *Workers' Playtime* or *Welsh Rarebit*. The girls talked and laughed together, and there was plenty of teasing banter when the young men trundled in. Courtship began this way, and sometimes led to engagements and weddings. Many of the girls married boys from Curran's.

Sometimes Shirley wondered when and whether something dramatic would happen to change her life, something better than going to Newport for a song contest. Here she was, over fifteen and free to sing anywhere. She'd won many song contests, trekked to so many little towns around Cardiff at weekends, and won a certificate here or a medal there, but that wasn't what she wanted. Singing in pubs and working men's clubs had grown monotonous, though her first professional engagement had been in the Bomb and Dagger, on her own doorstep in Portmanmoor Road.

The venue, in reality was the Splott Social and Athletic Club, but it had been dubbed the Bomb and Dagger because the club had played host to radical left-wing speakers on a couple of occasions, and some wag stuck a label, 'The Bomb and Dagger', on the door. And on the front page of the *Daily Express*, as Lord Beaverbrook's warning to his readers to beware of subversive left-wing elements, there was always a picture of a little chap in a wide-brimmed hat and cloak, carrying a bomb and dagger.

One Saturday night, Shirley and a few of her more rowdy friends stationed themselves outside the club and sang, until the manager came out and put a stop to it. However, he recognised Shirley from down the road, whom he'd heard had won a medal or two for her singing, and he subsequently asked her if she'd like to sing at one of their weekend nights when the members' wives were invited.

This was how Shirley started doing the rounds of the clubs in Cardiff and its suburbs, and became well-known to the locals. But her growing reputation on her home turf still only earned her a pound or two for her efforts, and, beneath the defiant smile, she was beginning to feel dissatisfaction at the thought that she might spend the rest of her life singing in pubs.

During this period, one of the girls at Curran's said to her, 'You ought to sing on the radio yourself, Shirley. You know this programme *Welsh Rarebit*? They put on Welsh people who can sing. Why don't you try and get an audition?' The other factory girls embraced the idea with enthusiasm, alternately goading and persuading Shirley to try and get on the programme, made by the BBC Wales and consisting of bits and pieces supplied by local talent.

Shirley knew a dare when she heard one and wasn't one to ignore the challenge, which is how she found herself walking down a long corridor at the BBC offices in Cardiff in 1952, telling Wyn Calvin, the programme's link man, 'I've been singing in pubs since I was thirteen. If a bobby came in, the boys in the trio had to hide me and I crawled away on my hands and knees.' Wyn Calvin had taken one look at Shirley waiting in Reception, and known exactly where she was from and what she was. She had Butetown, the docks, Tiger Bay written all over her. Her mother, he guessed accurately, was white, her father black, and they were poor. She was the first girl from Tiger Bay who'd applied for an audition and he was determined to help her all he could if she had any talent, because God knows, if anyone needed help, it was a girl from Tiger Bay.

Wyn Calvin escorted Shirley to the audition studio, introduced her to the pianist, checked the microphone position, and waited for the producer, Miss Mai Jones, to give the signal from the control box. Mai Jones was a highly respected senior producer. A gaunt, forty-ish blonde, she was serious about music and liked to surround herself with up and coming young musicians, many of whom, such as Garaint Evans and Harry Secombe, became luminaries in the entertainment field.

Shirley Bassey had confidence in her natural gifts and considered them sufficient for the task – an attitude that remained largely unchanged throughout her career, although she learnt to hone her attributes to perfection. Her attitude to music was somewhat different to that of the formidable Miss Jones, who had two problems with this young unknown: Firstly, 'Stormy Weather', which was Shirley's chosen audition song, was not to the producer's taste; secondly, Shirley couldn't read music.

Wyn Calvin, however, was impressed with the girl the moment she opened her mouth and began to sing. 'She was young and raw,' he later recalled, 'but here was brilliance.' Although Shirley's voice was untrained, Wyn Calvin immediately detected its purity and responded to its warmth and emotion, and the voice needed to acquire some polish, Shirley hit the high notes without faltering. Listening to her, he hoped against hope that Mai Jones would give this kid from Tiger Bay a chance, but when he saw the expression of faint distaste on Miss Jones' face, he knew she would not. He guessed that Shirley had failed to impress, not because of her performance, but because she didn't fit in with his producer's ideas for *Welsh Rarebit*, which displayed pretensions to more highbrow material.

Wyn Calvin saw Shirley out, telling her that he thought she had a wonderful voice, and that the BBC would be writing to her. He tried to soften the blow of what he knew would be rejection, by telling her that if she were turned down, it would be on the grounds of the Corporation's age policy. After all, she was only fifteen. 'Get all the experience you can,' he advised her, 'then come back, will you?'

Watching Shirley leave, Wyn Calvin felt depressed on her behalf. He had grown up in white, middle-class Cardiff but he knew all about Tiger Bay, with its mixed-race community of people living in economic hardship. As a boy, he would cycle to the docks to see the big ships, and remembered his mother's warnings to be careful of the dangers that lurked in Tiger Bay. Recalling now the Halal butchery with its stringy meat in the window, the men playing dice on the pavement, the shabby pubs on every corner, and the children darting between the slag heaps in the dock area, Wyn Calvin knew that this girl deserved far better.

After her audition, Shirley's life appeared destined to settle into the same old routine, factory work by day, singing in the working men's clubs on weekend nights, securing her limited reputation. That reputation, among the older girls of Tiger Bay was sometimes less than enthusiastic. One of Marina Bassey's friends was fed up with 'That girl Shirley Bassey'. As she told it, 'Here we are in this nice, well-run dance hall in Cardiff then Shirley and this gang from Splott comes in and spoils it all. You know Shirley, it's "look at me, look at me", and then someone started a fight over her, and then they all got thrown out. I felt ashamed coming from Tiger Bay because of her antics. We all got tarred with the same brush.'

But Shirley's mother was confident that her daughter was destined for better things, and had always expressed the belief that one day she would be famous. There was never a less typical stage mother than Eliza Mendi, a quiet woman except when roused beyond endurance – as when any of her children were insulted. Modest and unassuming, she nevertheless knew instinctively that Shirley was different, one in a million, and she wasn't going to sit by and watch her packing chamber pots and saucepans for much longer. Not that she had any clear idea of how to change things for her daughter. She certainly had no desire to see Shirley go away or travel abroad. As she told everybody, she wasn't one for travelling herself, and once she had landed up in Tiger Bay, that was as far as she intended to go. The move to Splott had marked the end of her travels.

It was in a working men's club in Paradise Street, Cardiff that something at last began to happen for Shirley. She had a booking to sing there one Saturday night, and when she arrived the club steward came over to her. 'There's someone here called Georgie Wood,' he told her. 'He's a Cardiff man, but he acts as an agent for films and shows and things. After your song I'll take you over to him and introduce you. It might be a good idea to pretend to be American. You know, a pretty dark girl from Harlem.'

Meeting Georgie Wood after her number, Shirley disregarded the steward's advice. After all, as she realised, Wood was probably from Tiger Bay himself and there would be little point in embarking on such a far-fetched charade. This totally unexpected meeting in a noisy, smoky workers' club went very well. Georgie Wood was impressed with Shirley's voice and told her so. She was one of the Bay Girls, wasn't she, he asked? That was good he said, because he was about to audition some of the Bay Girls for a show from London called *Memories of Jolson* and they wanted a nice chorus line from Tiger Bay. Naturally, there'd be a bit of singing involved and would Shirley be interested in coming to the audition next week at Frenchie's? Frenchie's studio in Bute Street? And after that would she be interested in coming to London?

Would she ever! Shirley left the club in a state of mixed excitement and disbelief wondering whether she was at last on the edge of the 'big break', that the Tiger Bay girls had talked and dreamed of for years. She needed to talk to somebody and despite the fact that it was midnight, she made her way over to her best friend Iris Freeman's house in Sophia Street, Tiger Bay. She didn't think, in the circumstances, that Iris would mind being woken. Nothing was stirring in Sophia Street, and for a moment it seemed that even the doorbell wasn't going to rouse anyone in the Freeman household. 'Iris', Shirley finally yelled up to the front bedroom window where her friend was sleeping, 'Iris, open the bloody door!'

Iris' head finally appeared at the window. 'For God's sake Iris, open the door! We've been discovered. We're going to London.'

Walter French, as he was christened, or Frenchie, as he was known, was, according to local gossip, 'a bit of a lad'. A thin, elegant black man from West Africa, he owned a nightclub in Bute Street that was frequented by visiting sailors in search of romance and a bit of a jive. The nerve-centre of Frenchie's little empire, however, was the Annexe, where he had his studio. Also on Bute Street, the

Annexe was a simple construction that looked like a pre-war village hall, but which was the venue for the most popular Saturday night dance in the district. Saturday night dances were held at the Big Apple and the Colonial Centre as well, but Frenchie's was the best, everything really 'happened' there. The American GI's had loved it during the war because the jiving was really wild, and then there was the Calypso, and a dance called the West African High Life which absolutely raised the roof. The Annexe was also used for auditions because Frenchie, in his own way, was also into show business, and Shirley Bassey had learned to tap-dance in one of Frenchie's classes.

Georgie Wood was a bona fide agent from Cardiff, who supplied film companies and London theatre managements with exotic extras, or chorus girls who could appear as Orientals or Africans or Americans from Harlem. In *Memories of Jolson*, the Bay Girls were going to fill a slot as Americans from Harlem. They hadn't known this when Frenchie rounded them for Georgie Wood's audition, but they weren't bothered; they were all delighted to have a chance to get into real show business. Only Shirley Bassey had been personally invited to audition. The other Bay Girls there – Iris Freeman, Mahalia Davies, Robina Ali, Maureen Jammett, and Margaret and Daphne Freeman – were to make up the chorus line. Though Shirley gathered that she, too, would be in the chorus, she assumed that she would be given solo songs.

All the Bay Girls were a cut above the average. They were pretty, and they could dance and sing with some proficiency. Their mothers were heard to declare that, when the girls used to march arm-in-arm down Bute Street, singing in harmony, they were just as good, or better than, 'those big American' groups. And they believed it themselves after the auditions, when Georgie Wood pronounced them good enough to go to London for the final audition. He filled them in on *Memories of Jolson*. 'I'm sure you've all heard of Al Jolson, the big American star who made a film called *The Jazz Singer*? The first ever talkie?' They hadn't, but tried to look as if they had. 'Well,' Wood continued, 'Al Jolson won't actually be in your show, but there's a British star called Eddie Reindeer who will. You've heard of these big American shows that come to London, and this will be that kind of show, and you girls will have to be very glamorous and look as if you're straight from the Cotton Club in Harlem . . .'

The agent was being somewhat economical with the truth. The London variety show producer Joe Collins had discovered that coloured shows, masquerading as American, were going down very well in the British provinces. They were cheap to mount and made good money on the road. They were part of the last gasp before television killed off this particular kind of variety 'spectacular' that had been touring the provincial towns for as long as anyone could remember.

The girls had believed every word of Georgie Wood's spiel. Rehearsals would start on a certain date soon to be announced and they must be ready to leave for London as soon as the call came. Shirley and her mother decided that, to be on the safe side, she should give in her notice at Curran's. A fortnight passed, then a month, and still no word came. A month turned into six weeks, Shirley was seriously out of work, and even Mrs Mendi was downcast. All the girls were growing anxious, devastated by the knowledge that the Tiger Bay community was beginning to enjoy a laugh at their expense. 'That'll teach the little madams to brag about their wonderful American show,' seemed to be the prevailing sentiment. What nobody had pointed out to worried girls was that the delay was absolutely typical of show business at that level, and that rehearsals rarely began on time.

And then the call came. The Bay Girls took a train to London and presented themselves for their final audition at rehearsal rooms opposite the Windmill Theatre in Soho. A black stage manager named Bennie marshalled the girls into a row and introduced Eddie Reindeer, the star of the show and the only white face in the entire company. Reindeer flashed his 'star' smile at the girls, and asked what they were going to sing.

Shirley, supposedly toughened by her years on the pub and club circuit, was the natural spokesman for the group. But tough or not, this was London and the big time, and she was scared to death. Nervously, she stepped forward and muttered that they would sing 'Walking My Baby Back Home'. She then had the difficulty of trying to sort out the key with the pianist, but at last they got under way and delivered the number.

Eddie Reindeer thought the group sounded a bit ragged, and asked to hear Shirley sing on her own. He pronounced her 'not bad' but, ironically in view of her future career in which she came to utilise arm movement to dramatic effect, said, 'Not so much of the arm movements dear, you're not directing the traffic.' To Bennie Reindeer said, 'Nice loud voice. We'll give her a song.'

The Bay Girls in a state of stunned disbelief mixed with euphoria, returned to Cardiff. They had one week at home before starting rehearsals and going on tour in a professional show. Shirley's mother, bursting with pride at the news that her daughter had been given her own song in a real show, decided to give a party. All the Bay Girls came, of course, several with boyfriends, and some of their families, and toddlers and 'aunties' and 'uncles'. By the time the party really got going and the toddlers were fast asleep in corners, the guests were so numerous that they overflowed and everybody went along to the Lord Wimborne pub. When the pub finally closed, those – including Shirley and her family – who still weren't ready for bed, moved on to the lounge of a nearby hotel and partied the night away.

There would be other nights and other parties all around the world for Shirley. But this one was special – the first and one of the best. She was surrounded by those who loved her, with her mother by her side. She had a glimpse of an exciting new life.

3

LOUSY HOUSES, STINKING DIGS, GET YOURSELF A BOY WHO'S RICH!

THE GRAND THEATRE, Luton, always had standing room only on Saturday nights. Both houses on Mondays were sparse, but things improved during the week and filled up by the weekend, when people were looking for a night out. Few houses in Luton had television in 1953, and a trip to the Grand was usually a good night out. You were guaranteed an orchestra with lots of brass, bright lights and pretty girls – a good show.

It was at the Luton Grand that Shirley Bassey fulfilled her first professional engagement, appearing twice nightly for a week in *Memories of Jolson*. The Luton people were full of this new show 'from America', noting that 'Al Jolson' wasn't a real darkie, 'he wears greasepaint.' The girls were good, too. Real American coloured girls.

The Ben Johnson Ballet had been engaged for the show, and the Bay Girls were delighted to discover that Louise Benjamin from Tiger Bay was in the ballet company. She had come to London some months earlier and found herself the job through an ad in *The Stage*. She already considered herself an old hand at touring, but it was Ben Johnson's wife, Pamela Winters, who was appointed to act as house mother for the Bay Girls.

The girls from Tiger Bay were novices, and everything was exciting to them. Even watching the tour bus being unloaded in Luton was a novelty. It was just as well. Anyone who knew anything about show business would have recognised what kind of a show *Memories of Jolson* was just from looking at the backdrops that were being hauled off the roof of the bus – old rubbish from bygone shows or pantomimes, bought cheap for their mediocre depictions of a palm-encircled South Sea isle, a hotel terrace in Monte Carlo, skyscrapers in New York and the Statue of Liberty.

The dress basket carrying the chorus costumes was carried to the communal dressing room where some wag had chalked a welcoming message in greasepaint on the mirror: 'Lousy houses, stinking digs, get yourself a boy who's rich.' Amusement was quick to dissipate when Maureen Jammett rushed in to the dressing room to announce that the girls couldn't use the toilets 'because some boys have made peepholes in the doors'.

The contents of the dress basket brought a further dampening of enthusiasm. The girls removed layer after layer of paper, but there wasn't a costume in sight. At the bottom of the basket lay a box of safety pins and nothing else. Somebody had forgotten to pack the Bay Girls' outfits. Pamela Johnson (professional name Winters) was well-schooled in the vicissitudes of touring, and nothing that happened on a Collins tour could surprise her, but she was sensitive to these young girls from Tiger Bay who were taking everything very seriously. 'They've done it again,' she told them with a despairing groan. 'But don't worry, they'll all turn up tomorrow, we'll all just have to wear our own clothes for tonight's performance.'

This solution didn't seem a happy one, especially to Shirley, who only had a skirt and jumper to offer from her own wardrobe. Pam reassured the girls, promising somehow to find them all something suitable. Reassurance, she knew, was vital, since they were bound to be in for another shock in Luton: the digs where they would be living for the next week.

Theatrical digs were, and are, the same all over Britain. Victorian houses, originally homes to the middle-classes, now converted into dingy bed-sits, flats or lodging houses. Creaky stairs, linoleum floors and, presiding over all comings and goings, a landlady in nylon overall, bedroom slippers and hair-curlers. Pam knew better than to rub these dragons up the wrong way. She was on her best behaviour on arrival at the digs, where the landlady glared in disapproval at the eager band of nubile girls.

In the double room that Shirley was to share with Iris Freeman, Pam assembled her charges and gave them a rundown of their situation. The landlady would provide breakfast, but that was all. She charged two pounds a week for an evening meal and nobody could afford that on their salaries of a fiver. 'We all pay ten shillings a week into a kitty,' Pam explained. 'I've got a primus and we'll cook in the bathroom every night.'

The already familiar Bassey rebellion asserted itself 'Count me out', said Shirley, who preferred cake and ice cream to baked beans and mash. And anyway, she thought, there were bound to be young men waiting at the stage door every night, only too pleased to take a pretty show girl out for a meal . . .

When the clothes skip arrived on Tuesday, the girls had another nasty surprise. The costumes were worn and shabby, and had obviously done the rounds of several chorus lines for some time. There were short, close-fitting black skirts and gaudy blouses that needed an abundance of safety pins to get them to fit, and even the floating chiffon dresses were torn and in bad shape. Only the feather bikinis fitted everybody.

For Shirley's solo number there was a heavy green satin dress, strapless, with an ankle length skirt and a wide belt to hold it all together. It was too big, and had to be pinned to the belt. 'Don't fling yourself about, or you'll lose the lot,' Pam warned her. But Shirley could never sing without using her body, and 'Stormy Weather' was going down very well with the audience. Totally involved in the music, Shirley flung up one arm, then the other and the skirt responded by beginning to slither down round her ankles. She clutched at the strapless top. The audience went wild. What a show! Striptease! The applause was stupendous, but Shirley hurried off the stage humiliated. She was a singer, not a bloody stripper.

It was the first of many hard lessons learned and, throughout her career, Shirley remained fiercely protective of her status. 'I sing. That's all. I'm a performer . . . Don't try and throw me in with the dinner like they do in Las Vegas. If people want to listen, I sing.'

Very quickly during this first tour of her career, Shirley was learning that she was different from the others. She enjoyed a lot of it, particularly Eddie Reindeer's comedy routines which had audiences, and the girls, in convulsions of laughter, but she found it difficult to muck in with the others to life on the road. Pam had told them, 'We've got to live like a family, we've got to give and take, share and share alike,' it was good advice because life on the road with a third-rate company could be grim without some collective enthusiasm and laughter.

Most of the Bay Girls were very happy. They'd escaped their mothers' clutches, and if there wasn't enough to eat, so what. Shirley, on the other hand, refused to kow-tow to much that the others went along with – the fearsome threat that the landlady might discover them cooking sausages illicitly in the bathroom late at night; Ben Johnson ordering everyone to come straight home after the show. Shirley liked Ben, admired his dancing and frequently pleaded with him to teach her, not nobody was going make her come straight home. Shirley Bassey had other ideas about her life. She hated the idea of being a chorus girl, and if she couldn't be a star, then she didn't want any part of it. The tour ground its way northwards, playing industrial towns like Coventry. Not posh dates, but places which welcomed the show and enjoyed it. They played Monday to Saturday at each venue, and spent Sundays travelling to the next stop.

The problems of communal living in digs blew up into trouble in Salford, where Ben Johnson and the ballet boys stayed in the same digs as the girls. This allowed Ben to do a nightly headcount to make sure they were all in when they ought to have been. Shirley had acquired a new boyfriend, a policeman, who took her out after the show each night. Iris stuffed a bolster next to her and Ben was fooled until, a couple of nights on, Iris fell asleep quickly only to be awakened by somebody next to her with an arm around her. Iris, a luscious sixteen-year-old, turned to find one of the boys from the show smiling at her.

The virginal and hitherto untouched Iris let out a deafening scream that brought Ben Johnson bursting into the room at two o'clock in the morning. Iris pointed to the boy whom she had kicked out of her bed and was now trying to hide under it. 'He tried to interfere with me.'

'Ben, I went to the toilet. Got into the wrong room coming back,' the now terrified dancer stuttered, at which Iris yelled, 'As God is my judge he's lying.'

By now, most of the company were up, crowding in at Iris and Shirley's door to see what the fuss was all about. As they stood there gawping, the landlady, outraged by the disturbance, appeared on the scene and demanded an explanation. Ben told more or less the same story as the boy, it had all been a mistake but, just as everybody heaved a sigh of relief the landlady noticed the other bed. 'Where's the other one?' she demanded. Right on cue, Shirley arrived, wearing a smart red coat which she'd borrowed from Pam's wardrobe without her knowledge. She looked, said Louise Benjamin who later recounted the story, untroubled, happy and full of her favourite things – fish and chips, cream cake and ice cream.

The landlady turned on Shirley. 'Two o'clock in the morning, my lady, is it? I will not have my respectable establishment turned into a bawdy house.'

Shirley drew herself up, the picture of outraged innocence. 'I'll have you know that my boyfriend is a policeman. He wouldn't like to hear you say that because tonight he took me home to meet his mother.'

There was a huge row later, but that was over Pam's red coat. Shirley, it would seem, had a little habit of borrowing something she liked while forgetting to ask the owner's permission. According to Louise, 'Pam was furious and so was Shirley. Shirley yelled at Pam that she was always telling us to behave like a family, but when she treated Pam like a sister she got shouted at.'

Pamela Johnson was actually an extraordinary person. The daughter of an English mother and a Somalian father, she was tall, graceful and beautiful. She was the mainstay of the ballet company, making their costumes from materials bought in local street markets, and allowing the dancers to stay in her home between jobs. She was Ben's wife, and the mother of a small daughter, Maria, who had either to be taken along on tour or farmed out to a suitable family. It was not easy for either the mother or the child.

Both Ben Johnson and Pam had once danced with the famously innovative Katherine Dunham company. The black American Katherine Dunham and her dancers first caused a sensation in Europe with their mixed classical and modern repertoire after World War II. Shirley Bassey was greatly influenced by the ballet dancers, whom she watched attentively, and whose grace and strength of movement she tried to emulate. However, her first touring shows did little to enhance her dancing prospects. The management had little respect for the young people they sent on the road and the life was sordid and akin to slave labour.

Nobody helped the Bay Girls, except Pam who had little time to spare. They had no instruction in how to apply theatrical make-up, the Leichner greasepaint sticks Nos 9 and 5 that used to be standard usage in the theatre. Without black eyeliner and plenty of shadow, the eyes would look dim and washed-out under the strong stage lights, but nobody explained any of this.

Memories of Jolson finally closed in November of 1953 after several arduous months. Neither Shirley nor Louise went back to Wales, but stayed instead at Ben and Pam's house in Harold Wood where, it was understood, the girls would baby-sit little Maria while Ben tried to organise some more work. Shirley managed to pick up a couple of engagements singing in hotels during this time and, shortly before Christmas, she went off to entertain the soldiers at a sergeant's mess in North London. All the troops were drunk, including the sergeant major, but she earned ten pounds for her pains and a kindly warrant officer gave her a bag full of goodies from the NAAFI and made sure she got home safely.

Then it was home to Splott for Christmas with her family. It was a wonderful interlude. She had presents for everybody and for her mother, who always said she was the most generous of present-givers, she had bought a charming locket.

Shirley turned seventeen in January 1954. She was in love, and even though he was married and his identity was a secret, she was happy. She wasn't sure what she was going to do next in the way of furthering her career or earning a living when Georgie Wood came up with an offer for another Joe Collins tour. It was called *Hot from Harlem* and was much the mixture as before. Iris Freeman and a couple of the other Bay Girls were engaged for the show, but Louise Benjamin had gone to work in another Joe Collins Show. The good news from Shirley's point of view was that, this time around, she would have two or even three songs, and the show would play the New Theatre in Cardiff.

Traipsing from theatre to theatre across the country in a broken-down bus no longer held any novelty, nor did slogging on stage twelve times a week hold any glamour or excitement. But it was work, it was experience, and the show did indeed arrive at the Cardiff New, where all of Shirley's friends, relatives, and neighbours past and present turned out in force to see it. Ifor Harry, the barber from next door to the Basseys in Splott, was unimpressed with the evening. 'It wasn't a very nice kind of show,' he said afterwards. 'A bit on the rough side if you know what I mean.' But he did acknowledge that 'Shirley sang very well on that box' while wondering 'what in God's name was Iris Freeman doing, floating around holding a candle and wearing something that looked like her nightie?'

Iris Freeman had wondered the same thing, and Shirley had had a hard time trying to get things across to Iris, who wondered why Shirley was standing on a box singing 'Ebb Tide'. Patiently, Shirley explained that it wasn't really a box, it was a rock, on which she was standing and looking out to sea, waiting for her lover to come back with the tide.

'Okay,' said Iris, 'You're singing "Ebb Tide", so what am I doing buggering about with a candle?'

'Jesus,' exclaimed an exasperated seventeen-year-old Shirley, 'I give up. You're the bloody lighthouse.'

This anecdote really sums up the level of a cut-price touring road show sent out by the Joe Collins management. It was tough, but Shirley had to complete the tour.

*

From Cardiff, *Hot from Harlem* headed north. On occasion, the company were transferred from their bus into a train, as happened one Sunday morning when they had to change at Crewe. During the Fifties, show business people dreaded the very thought of Crewe station, where you boarded the train to arrive at yet another God-forsaken town to perform in yet another abysmal theatre. The platforms at Crewe on a Sunday were littered with the large wicker skips of various touring companies and piles and piles of battered luggage. Elder performers trod carefully, smiled bravely, and tried to look as though they usually went by motor car.

Iris Freeman and Shirley Bassey were sitting on a wooden station seat, suitcases balanced on their knees, when somebody shouted 'Coo-ee'. They looked up from their thoughts to see the tall, willowy Louise Benjamin running towards them. 'Everyone meets at Crewe!' she cried, brimming with pleasure at running into her old friends. The three girls exchanged news for a few minutes until Louise had to rush off to get her train.

As she turned to go, Iris grabbed her arm and propelled her along the station, calling out to Shirley, 'I'll be back before your train gets in.' As they hurried along, Iris told the bemused Louise that Shirley was pregnant. 'Five months gone. She's going home to Cardiff. Left the show, walked out. Told no-one about the baby.'

Louise was aghast, not only at the bombshell about Shirley's condition, but at the threat to her professional reputation if she left the show. She raced back to the bench and, as she later described it, urged Shirley to reconsider, to go back to the company with Iris. 'If you leave the show without telling them, you're finished,' she said. Her efforts were to no avail. Shirley Bassey obeyed nobody but herself and her only response to Louise was to smile and say she knew what she was doing.

Despairing of her friend, who didn't appear to be in the least upset or worried, Louise rejoined Iris, who seemed rather more in need of comfort than the object of their concern had done. 'She thinks she might do radio,' Iris told Louise. 'The man in Cardiff told her to come back.'

'Why doesn't she marry the boy?'

'He's already married with two kids.'

The following October, four months after the meeting on Crewe station, Louise received a card from Shirley – always an inveterate sender of postcards – saying simply, 'Had the baby in September.'

Back home in Splott, Shirley Bassey telephoned Wyn Calvin, the *Welsh Rarebit* link man at the BBC. It was over a year since her unsuccessful audition, and he was surprised and pleased to hear from her. An appointment was made and she presented herself at the Cardiff studios once again. Calvin came to meet her in Reception, and noted that that she seemed quite grown up now, and much more attractive. She radiated eager anticipation, and hadn't forgotten the good-looking Welshman. They chatted like old friends, and Shirley, reminding him of his advice to go out and get some experience, told him that she'd been on the road in two shows, 'real London revues', for Joe Collins. Calvin, who knew of the popular appeal of the Collins shows, asked whether she had been given any solo numbers to sing.

'I had my own spots in my last show, *Hot from Harlem,*' she replied. I sang "Ebb Tide", and then I sang "Stormy Weather". Do you know, my two shows toured most of the English provinces, and I do believe we did every village in Wales.'

Shirley told Wyn that she had only left her show a week or two earlier, and was now seriously looking to get into radio. As he recalled, she was quite blunt about it, saying 'you told me to come back. Well here I am.' He was delighted by her attitude and her confidence, and saw no reason why she shouldn't audition again, but his optimism was short-lived. When Shirley moved to shake free her loose summer coat which had snagged on the chair, the well-rounded bulge of her advanced pregnancy was revealed, to Calvin's evident dismay. Quite unfazed by his expression, she smiled. 'It won't matter will it? No-one will see me because it's radio.'

It was a perfectly rational observation, but this was 1954 and the august establishment of the BBC was not ready for this, particularly not in the strict Presbyterian climate of Wales. An unmarried teenager foolish enough to fall pregnant was, in the custom of the time, expected to go into hiding at home and, if forced to go out, to cover her shame under voluminous garments. They were certainly not invited to audition for that model of rectitude, Miss Mai Jones.

Reluctantly, Wyn Calvin suggested that Shirley would do better to wait until after the birth of her child. He was terribly upset by the situation, by what he saw as the inevitable waste of a special talent. He made the assumption that this young girl would probably finish up pushing a pram round Tiger Bay, and living in one of those dismal houses down by the docks; that she would probably marry a factory worker, and there'd be more babies and more prams and a husband who would never know that his wife had thrown away a chance in a million.

Shirley, however, didn't strike Wyn as being in the least disappointed at being turned away, instead expressing her determination to return again at a later date. She never did go back for that audition, but they met again four years later when Shirley Bassey was a name, and Wyn Calvin had left the BBC to go on the stage himself. He was a natural comedian who eventually became known as one of the best pantomime dames in the business. On 13 May 1958, he found himself on the same bill as his former would-be protégée at the New Theatre, Cardiff. The billboards, in huge red lettering, announced 'Cardiff's own SHIRLEY BASSEY, direct from her success in Las Vegas and Hollywood. Phillips recording star.' Lower down, in smaller letters, 'Cardiff's own WYN CALVIN, Character for laughs.'

After her meeting with Wyn at the BBC in May 1954, Shirley walked down Frederick Street in the centre of Cardiff. She was telling herself that if radio was out for the moment, she had better find another job to support herself and her baby, when she saw a 'Waitress Wanted' card in the window of a small restaurant. It was the kind of place that has since completely disappeared, an establishment catering for the lunch break of office workers in the neighbourhood. From midday onwards, typists and filing clerks from the nearby offices would swarm in for a cheap and wholesome hot meal that cost about two shillings and sixpence – steak and kidney pudding or Shepherd's pie, followed by treacle tart or Spotted Dick. And a well-paid secretary would leave a threepenny tip under the plate.

Shirley went in to enquire about the advertisement and came out with a job. 'You'll need a black dress,' the Greek owner told her, 'and my wife will find you a nice white apron to wear. He smiled at her. 'You'll look good, *kala kala*.' She did look good, and many an office clerk slipped threepence under his plate for her. She picked up an Americanism and referred to her work as 'slinging hash'. Years later she said, 'I liked that job and I was very good at slinging hash in Frederick Street.'

Shirley Bassey's daughter was born in September 1954 and was christened Sharon. Shirley went back to work at the restaurant and remained there until the following February, leaving baby Sharon in the loving and capable care of her own mother. During the cold winter months, it was a particular pleasure to come home and sit with her mother and cuddle her baby by the warmth of the fire. It seemed to her a hundred times better than touring in a Joe Collins revue, freezing half to death in bleak digs on the sufferance of disdainful landladies who could barely contain their hostility to 'a crowd of coloureds from God knows where.'

The glowing coal fire was one of the best things about being home again, even though it meant constantly having to go out with a shovel in the freezing cold to refill the scuttle in the coalhouse. It was a chore which Shirley did gladly in order to spare her mother. She adored her mother. There was always a strong bond between them, and whatever Shirley did was all right with Eliza.

Three of Shirley's five sisters lived nearby. The two eldest had left Wales, Gracie to Milwaukee as a GI bride, Ella and her husband to London. The three who were left behind were all married: Iris, Eileen and Marina. Eileen and Marina both had children and Iris was eager to look after Sharon. The sisters often got together for a fireside gossip in their mother's front room, a simple room with a minimum of furniture. There was a sideboard with a round mirror into whose edges family snapshots were tucked, a table with a chenille cloth, a sofa, a couple of stools and two chairs by the fire.

Marina, the next youngest after Shirley, was the sister to whom Shirley was closest. They had walked to school together, hand-in-hand, and both had gone off to work at Curran's factory for three pounds a week. Marina was also the one who most resembled Shirley and, later on, when her baby sister was famous, people would stop Marina in the streets of Cardiff to ask whether she was Shirley Bassey.

During this time, Shirley's sisters found it difficult to understand why her career was on hold. She was the only one with this enormous talent yet, at the age of eighteen, she seemed to have given up on her future. The first offer that came to return the stage she had initially turned down flat. She had had a telegram from Ben, inviting her to audition in London for the job of girl singer with the Ben Johnson Ballet, who had a two-week booking in March at the Little Theatre in Jersey. She read the telegram and said an emphatic 'no'.

Her mother, whose faith in Shirley's destiny, had remained unshaken, was astonished and bewildered. Had she known how miserable Shirley had been in the Collins revues, how she had hated touring, how she had longed for her mother and the familiar warmth of home, Eliza Mendi would have understood. But, typically, Shirley had never confessed to her unhappiness, and her mother was shocked at her refusal. 'If you don't go to an audition how will one of these agents ever see you?' she asked. 'You need an agent.'

Shirley could have set her mother straight regarding the intentions of most agents. They were usually only interested in their percentage, but it would be a waste of time explaining this to Eliza, whose knowledge of the hard facts about show business could have been written on the back of a postage stamp. Instead, she detailed the expense that would be involved in going down to London – and, what about Sharon? How could she leave her?

'Go!' was her mother's urgent response. 'I'll look after the baby.' And so she went. Not because she wanted to, but to please her mother. For her own part, she had decided she was thoroughly disillusioned with show business. At the great age of eighteen, with only two third-rate tours behind her, she thought she knew it all: the big talk, the big build-up, the big let-down. As far as she was concerned, she was back where she started and she would rather have stayed at home with Sharon and put the theatre behind her.

Or so she thought.

4

A Promise of Fame

St Valentine's Day, 14 February, 1955, turned out to be a significant date in Shirley Bassey's life. Over the years several people in the entertainment industry have made the comment that if Michael Sullivan hadn't discovered her, somebody else inevitably would have done, but it is undeniable that theirs was a meeting of an unusual man and an unusual girl on that day. He had rare vision, she had great talent.

Michael Sullivan was an agent whose bread and butter was the booking of acts for the variety circuit. Fine-featured and good-looking, he had the cultivated speaking voice of a West End actor that impressed the managers of variety theatres. He'd built up his own theatrical agency, controlling the bookings for many venues, and had seventy-two acts on his books, but the agency was rapidly going down the drain thanks to the advent of television.

In early February, he'd had a call from a theatre owning client in

Jersey who was looking for a two-week ballet season for March. As the man had put it, 'Something sexy, you know the kind of thing. Pretty girls with long legs and a good-looking man or two to dance with them.' So Sullivan had done a quick tour of the West End nightclubs and had found exactly what he was looking for at Churchill's: a group of experienced coloured dancers whose men were dark and handsome and the women pale-complexioned and beautiful.

He went backstage after the show to find that the company was available and eager to take the Jersey booking, and quick to agree with Sullivan that as it was a theatre job, not a nightclub, they could hardly be expected to dance nonstop for two hours. What was needed was a singer to fill in during the scene changes. Did anybody know a girl with a strong voice, he asked.

It was Louise Benjamin from Shirley's old touring mates, the Ben Johnson Ballet, who suggested a friend of hers near Cardiff who had a good strong voice, and that was how Shirley was sent a telegram by Ben Johnson which, but for her mother's insistence, she would have ignored.

About a week later, Michael Sullivan climbed the two flights of bare wooden stairs, in a rickety building in Great Newport Street, which led to the Max Rivers Rehearsal Rooms, to hold an audition with Shirley. His mind was preoccupied with the kid from Cardiff, as he thought of her – he wasn't expecting too much, just enough to suit the package and keep the audience occupied during scene changes. All the girl had to do was stand there and sing.

He opened the door to the rehearsal room to be hit by the familiar odour of sweat from generations of dancers, and the smell of stale cigarettes from the countless butts stubbed out by chain-smoking rehearsal pianists. Sullivan glanced round the room where Pam and Ben Johnson and Louise Benjamin were limbering up at the barre, while pianist Stanley Myers was seated at the upright, waiting to play for the audition.

A girl dressed in tight black trousers and a shabby yellow sweater sat on the floor, legs outstretched, with the Johnson's toddler on her lap playing with the chain the girl wore around her neck. This, then, was the 'kid from Cardiff'. He was aware of her observing him with not overly friendly dark eyes; she, with the cynicism of a world-weary eighteen-year-old, was taking in the smart suit, the immaculate white shirt, the fashionable tie of the smart London operator.

The agent crossed over to her and, holding out his hand, introduced himself 'I'm Michael Sullivan'. She shifted the child on to her hip, and returning his gaze without a smile, shook his hand and muttered her name.

Sullivan wasted no time in small talk, but enquired briskly what she was going to sing. In a husky voice she told him 'Stormy Weather'. Inwardly, he blanched, convinced that she had chosen badly and that she would never cope with the complicated key changes of the Harold Arlen classic. Did the kid think she was Lena Horne? Well, if she could sing in tune, she'd be worth eight pounds a week and her hotel room.

The beleaguered agent had had a long, hard and none-too-successful day and was longing to relax in the pub with a stiff scotch and a cigarette. He left pianist Stanley Myers to run through the song with the girl while he went out for ten minutes. Shirley joined Myers at the piano, telling herself that it didn't matter if she didn't get the job. She'd stay the night with her sister Ella in Islington and go home to Splott in the morning.

Louise Benjamin remembered that Shirley did not look happy that day in Great Newport Street, and although she tried to cheer her up, saying they'd have a great time in Jersey, she was acutely aware that Shirley was very different from the rest of them. Louise loved everything to do with show business and as long as she had a stage to dance on, she was happy to join in with the company and endure the hardships of touring. Shirley, as she well knew from their time in the Collins revues, would never adjust to that life. As Louise saw it, 'Shirley *knew* she was going to be a star. She didn't need or want the camaraderie of showbiz.'

Taking a breather in the pub next door Michael Sullivan, who always chain-smoked when he was worried, lit another cigarette and reflected on his present difficulties. Variety shows, his mainstay, were already playing to half-empty houses and it was obvious to him that, as TV encroached further, half the provincial theatres would have to close. After all, people could now enjoy variety shows on the box in the comfort of their homes without paying the price of admission. One Hippodrome had already gone bust, owing him two thousand pounds, and despite the seventy-two acts he had painstakingly built up, he was broke.

Sullivan needed to find a star, and he needed it badly. Like all agents, he dreamed the impossible dream of discovering an unknown talent whom he could nurture and who would make them both a fortune. He was thirty-five and so far this million-dollar ticket had not turned up. Oh well, for the moment he'd better deal with the kid from Cardiff and pray to God she had enough competence to solve his immediate problem . . .

Back in the rehearsal room, he took a good look at the girl who was running through her paces with Stanley Myers. As soon as she saw him, she moved to a position behind the piano almost as if she were trying to hide, but not before the agent noticed that she'd got a good figure, and good legs under those dusty trousers. Still, she wasn't a patch on her friend Louise, who Sullivan considered a knock-out beauty.

By now Shirley, cowering behind the upright, looked patently frightened as if she were about to face the executioner. Making an effort to put her at her ease, Sullivan said, 'Just try your best, that's all we need' and gave Myers the go ahead to begin.

The opening bars sounded on the piano and the girl opened her mouth: 'Don't know why, there's no sun up in the sky, Stormy weather . . .' The voice was in tune. Well, that was something. And it was strong. 'Since my man and I ain't together, Keeps rainin' all the ti–ime . . .' Wait a minute, forget strong. This voice was unusually powerful. It soared, it grabbed a high note and held it, flawlessly changing key. Then it unleashed a storm of sound, passionate and exultant. It was quite extraordinary.

Michael Sullivan was suddenly scared of what he was hearing. Out of the blue he had a vision of a great orchestra playing. He could hear the strings, the brass, the drums in his head, and reaching above it all, the rich and thrilling sound of this girl's voice. He shivered, and shook himself back to reality, wondering if he was going a little crazy. He had never heard a voice in audition that affected him so powerfully.

Shirley followed 'Stormy Weather' with 'Jezebel'. No, he hadn't been imagining it, she sang the notes high, clear and true. Sullivan glanced round the room expecting to see the others sharing his reaction, but other than some vaguely encouraging glances from Ben, Louise and Pam, and a smile from Stanley Myers nothing happened. Pam fastened her little girl into a baby chair, and the three dancers returned to their exercises.

Sullivan was bemused and disappointed, but came down to earth as he realised that these Johnson ballet people had toured with Shirley, had heard her sing hundreds of times over and took it for granted. He hurried over to the singer, bursting with excitement but reminding himself to play it cool. He congratulated Shirley on having a good voice and told her the job was hers, then went over to Myers and said 'Great voice.' Stanley was one of the best musicians in London, and if anyone could judge the girl's potential, it was he.

'Yes. Good for a beginner, but needs a lot of work.'

Before the group repaired to the pub, Sullivan drew Shirley aside and told her he was certain he could help her with her career. She appeared strangely unresponsive and he later remembered saying to her, 'You act as if this doesn't mean a lot to you. Don't you want the job? Don't you want me to take you on?'

'You might change your mind,' she replied.

'What if I say that I'll fly out to Jersey for your first night?'

'All right.'

'What if I say that I'll pay you a salary while I teach you all the things you have to know?'

'What do you mean?'

'Like appearing on television, making a record, doing a top-notch variety tour with second billing.'

'You're kidding.' But Shirley was no longer unresponsive. Her large dark eyes were alert and sparkling, and Sullivan saw what beautiful teeth she had when she allowed herself to smile.

Later that night, walking down Shaftesbury Avenue towards the Mapleton Hotel, where he and his wife lived, his head was full of the sound of Shirley Bassey singing 'Stormy Weather'. Somebody had once told him that there were 674 theatrical agents in Britain and all but four of them were Jewish. Sullivan was a Roman Catholic and he'd certainly had to work hard to be one of those four. And now his dream was going to come true. Certain that he wasn't making a mistake or going out of his mind, he resolved that he would make Shirley Bassey into a star, no matter what it took. The first thing it would take was money, and, at that moment, he didn't have so much as the return fare to Jersey.

Looking back on this eventful day much later, Shirley Bassey said, 'I wasn't sorry when I had to leave *Hot from Harlem* and I wasn't sorry when I went to work in the Greek restaurant, but I was very sorry when I had to leave little Sharon and go to London for that audition. She was only six months old. I *hated* leaving her. When I got to London I spent all my money on phone calls to my sister to see if the baby was all right.'

Shirley's mother had held a conference with her daughters as to what they would do if Shirley got the job in Jersey. Her elder sister Iris loved the baby. It was decided that she and her husband, Bill, would take care of Sharon in Shirley's absence.

The decision was not an easy one for Shirley to take. She was worried that her sister might grow too close to the baby and not want to part with her. She was a lovely baby, and a good one. Shirley had named her Sharon in memory of her father's pet name for her, when as a baby herself, she had been his 'Sharon', the pet name of the Queen of Sheba. Shirley had settled in well to her new role as mother and breadwinner and, although she was on her feet all day in the Frederick Street restaurant, when she got home, her fatigue vanished.

Fame, it had seemed, was no longer the spur to Shirley's desires. The sleazy experience of touring with the chorus line of Bay Girls, who seemed to have little function other than to arouse and titillate male audiences with their 'exotic' sex appeal, had tarnished her dreams of show business. Now here she was again, about to join a show because she had auditioned only to please her mother.

This time, however, things just might be different She had met someone who appeared to be part of the 'real' entertainment business, an experienced agent who told her that she had a great voice and a real future, and seemed to mean it. He wasn't just a flash guy with a big car and the line that went, 'I'm worth a lot of money. I know someone who owns a nightclub in Soho and if I tell him to give you a job, he will.' This genuinely looked as though it might be the breakthrough, but Shirley had suffered so much dis-appointment so quickly that even now, in the midst of her excitement, she tried to protect herself, telling herself it would probably fizzle out as it had always done.

The morning after the audition, Michael Sullivan set about the business of turning Shirley Bassey into a star. It was going to be a long haul, and the first thing he needed was some ready cash. This he hoped to get from his friend and occasional business partner, Leonard Beresford Clarke, who lived in Reigate.

Berry, as he was called, was an accountant by profession, but was also completely stagestruck. During the wartime Blitz, Berry had worked in the Fire Service. One of his mates had owned a circus before the war and kept Berry enthralled with tales of circus life. The upshot was that Berry joined forces with his mate in running the circus after the war, and found it thrilling to be involved with 'the smell of the greasepaint, the roar of the crowd'.

Michael Sullivan, then a youngster of sixteen, joined the circus for a time and met Berry there. Sullivan was bursting with ambition to become an agent, and was full of ideas. In the years that followed, when Michael came up with a good proposition, Berry would finance it. Shirley Bassey was now the proposition that Michael would have to 'sell' to him.

Berry was honeymooning in Guernsey with his new bride, Sylvia, who was starring as Dick Whittington on ice at the local theatre there. Sullivan had produced and directed the show, and every chorus girl on ice had come to detest him. Sylvia, who admired his skill, nonetheless admitted that he was a very hard taskmaster, something Shirley would come to learn for herself. Meanwhile, Sullivan organised his trip to Jersey for Shirley's first night, planning to go on to Guernsey and sweet-talk Berry – always provided that his 'discovery' was as good as he anticipated.

While he made his plans, the Ben Johnson Ballet – Ben, Pam, Louise, Cynthia from London and American Elroy – plus their four musicians and their girl singer, arrived in Jersey. To Shirley's surprise and delight, they were driven to a decent hotel in St Helier, where there would be three proper meals a day and no cooking in the landlady's bathroom. She still, however, had to share a room, but she and Louise, both Tiger Bay girls, got along well enough.

Ben Johnson was a West Indian who had started his ballet company in 1951. Although run on a shoestring, the company was hardworking and artistic, Ben having – as he openly acknowledged – drawn much inspiration from two great inventive dancer-choreographers, Katherine Dunham and Robert Helpmann. The Australian Helpmann, a leading dancer with the Royal Ballet, had also famously danced in the films *The Red Shoes* and *Tales of Hoffman*; the American Dunham had not only opened new vistas for dance as an art form, but had forced open the doors that had been closed to black talent.

Shirley and the five dancers were, of course, old colleagues, having worked together in both *Memories of Jolson* and *Hot from Harlem*. But things were a little different now. Shirley was no longer a chorus girl with a solo spot in a downmarket revue, but the featured singer in the Ben Johnson Ballet, and because Shirley passionately loved dancing, Ben had decided to give her a dancing spot in the show, partnered by him. Shirley was delighted. She admired and respected the dancers, considering them true artists, and was awed by Louise's dedication. That didn't alter the fact that, while Louise's idea of heaven was the daily dance rehearsals called by Ben, Shirley considered them a pain in the neck.

She did, however, discover the joy and freedom that came from dancing the Ben Johnson way. In the show, she and Ben glided nightly round the stage to 'By the Light of the Silvery Moon', and she never tired of it. She was quite aware that Ben had taught her the simplest of steps so that he could always cover if she made a mistake, and that the others knew this. They felt that 'dancers do the dancing', but she didn't mind. This was how she had imagined show business would be, a chance to improve herself and to learn new skills. It was in watching and working with the ballet, that Shirley originated the sinuous movements of her solo stage performances later on.

Michael Sullivan arrived in Jersey, having decided to slip in to the first matinee, unannounced and unexpected. Shirley, who had few clothes, agreed to wear on stage her bridesmaid frock from one of her sisters' weddings. With its acid-green satin bodice and bouffant net skirt, the dress was a disaster, unappealing and doing less than nothing for its wearer's slim and graceful body – a body which, as several designers would learn, was an absolute dream to clothe.

When she made her first entrance that afternoon, Sullivan inwardly groaned. Visually, everything about this girl standing under the stage lights, was worse than he could ever have expected. It wasn't only the hideous dress, but she clearly had no idea about stage make-up. Her eyes had disappeared into her head, emphasising the ill-chosen gash of bright orange lipstick she wore. Worst of all, she had no stagecraft.

Standing alone and diffident in front of the microphone, Shirley appeared so raw and untrained, her gestures so stiff and contrived, that it hurt him to watch. Her exit, in his view, was nothing short of a calamity. She marched off the stage without even a smile to the audience, as though she were leaving the show forever. The voice, which had so overcome him in the London rehearsal room, was fine, but brought only lukewarm applause. His spirits sank.

The ballet numbers were good and the girls, in their flimsy, pretty gauze costumes, looked delightful. How, wondered Sullivan, could they have allowed Shirley to wear that terrible green dress? What he didn't yet know, was that Shirley had very much a mind of her own and since the Johnsons, whose costumes were run up by Pam on her sewing machine at home, had nothing to offer her from their wardrobe, there wasn't much they could do about her choice.

When, later in the programme, Shirley came on with Ben for their dance number, she was wearing one of Pam's flimsy creations. She looked very good and very professional as Ben guided her through the relaxed and intimate routine. Suddenly, the men in the audience sat up and took notice. Now that Shirley was properly on show, her sex appeal was obvious.

The applause for the dance number was generous and gave Shirley a boost. From then on, it was as though an ember had been reignited, and with each successive song, that unique voice grew in excitement, and so did the audience. Whatever she sang – 'Smile', 'Ebb Tide', 'The Sunny Side of the Street' – she was a sensation, and the applause was rapturous.

But Michael Sullivan was now suffering from doubt and conflict. Yes, the audience had loved Shirley, who had come through wonderfully for the Monday matinee crowd, retired pensioners who knew what they liked. But she could just as easily have failed to captivate them. She was so clearly untrained, with little idea of how to present or pace herself. The talent was there, waiting to be exploited, the voice was extraordinary, but he knew that she would be laughed off the stage in a top spot at a number one venue.

It was obvious that Shirley Bassey was no ordinary singer but, wondered Sullivan, had he jumped the gun? Was he really capable of taking on a beginner and teaching her everything? And did she want to learn? He was suddenly beset with worries about the enormity of the undertaking. Not only would he have to pay her a salary and teach her the tricks of her trade, but he'd have to find her somewhere to live, look after her, nursemaid her. He knew that stars didn't come ready gift-wrapped, but there were so many problems, not least the fact that he hated taking care of other people.

He decided to defer any decision until after the evening performance, to which he took his friend Sydney James, a professional booker who lived in Jersey, and whose opinion he valued.

Sullivan took a cold, hard, objective look at the second show. Yes, the green dress would have to go, but his wife, Juhni, a professional costume designer who had just dressed a show at the London Palladium, would know exactly how to dress Shirley to advantage. And the quality of that wondrous voice, which was what it was all about, was not in doubt. That evening, he began to realise that Shirley had several advantages, not least that she was young and fresh and every man in the auditorium fell in love with her. Each time she came on that evening, it was an occasion. She'd got that certain elusive and indefinable something given to few – star quality.

His indecision was over. By the time he'd finished with Shirley Bassey, she'd be stunning. The talent was all there, just waiting to be developed and unleashed on an unsuspecting world. It wouldn't, he realised, be a pushover; this girl was not going to be easy to control and he'd sensed the wariness, even suspicion, behind those liquid dark eyes of hers. No matter. His gut feeling told him that he was on to a winner.

Sydney James didn't share his friend's conviction. 'This is Jersey in the winter, they applaud anything,' he told him. 'I can't really be sure about this girl of yours. Personally, I'd be inclined to turn her down.' Sullivan was undeterred, his mind was made up.

Later that night, after he and the company had shared a drink or two, he sat down alone with Shirley in his hotel to discuss the serious business of her future. First, he needed to make sure that she no commitment to any other agent. Shirley told him that Georgie Wood in Cardiff had got her and the Bay Girls into the first show she had done, but reassured him that she was entirely free. He wasn't entirely convinced, he knew how careless these girls could be about contracts, and made a mental note to check out the Georgie Wood situation.

He then suggested that she might like to undertake a tour with a variety show. The very word 'tour' was enough to draw an emphatic no from Shirley, who had so hated being on the road, but Michael pressed on. There would be no such tour until she'd had at least three months of training, he told her.

'What training?' demanded Shirley, to whom it sounded far too much like school to appeal to her.

Carefully, he explained to her that she had much to learn about stagecraft and technique, without which her ambitions would never be realised, and then he took the plunge. 'I shall find you a hotel. I shall pay you a salary. I shall hire a rehearsal room and a pianist who'll teach you about music. Only when you're ready will we think about a variety tour. And then I shall pay all your expenses.'

Shirley was confused, overwhelmed and suspicious. This was not at all what she'd had in mind when the agent had offered to take her on. Her idea of stardom came from Hollywood movies and *True Romance* magazines. 'Why?' she asked. 'Why do I need all this, and why do you want to do all this for me?'

'Because I think you've got talent. Tomorrow I'm going to Guernsey to meet someone. I'm going to tell him you need a hundred pounds for dresses.'

'A hundred pounds! For me?' Suddenly she looked very vulnerable, young and unsure.

'If you work hard, Shirley, I promise I can make you a star.'

It had all been too much for the feisty but naïve eighteen-year-old who, only a matter of weeks before, had abandoned all thoughts of show business to sling hash in Cardiff by day, and spend her evenings at home in Splott with her mother and her own adored baby. Suddenly, she burst into tears. Touched by this Michael Sullivan put his arm around her and comforted her, as she wept on his shoulder.

As Michael wiped away her tears, she suddenly smiled at him. Not stopping to give the matter any thought, he obeyed his instincts and led her, unresisting, up to his hotel room. Years later, looking back on this time, he said, 'That was the first and last time I made love to Shirley.' After that, he decided to keep sex right out of their relationship, but he also said later that that was perhaps his biggest mistake, that he should perhaps have bound Shirley to him completely with a strong sexual relationship. This rather curious reasoning from a man who was married at the time, was said in the sad aftermath of his professional break from the star he had created.

In the event, until the parting of the ways came, Shirley acquiesced to most of Michael's demands. Although she could be as strong-willed as he, she knew she needed the benefit of his experience and expertise to advance her own quest for stardom. However, she certainly didn't seem interested in any other aspect of the man, and most people who knew them disagree that a sexual relationship would have achieved anything. Shirley, under her defiant exterior, was a sensitive girl who needed more tenderness and compassion than Sullivan would ever have been capable of giving.

In 1955, British show business was dominated by men like Michael Sullivan, hard men who took all the decisions. Sylvia Beresford Clarke, Berry's wife and one of the bystanders to the Bassey–Sullivan working partnership, has said, 'I shall never know how Shirley survived those years. How she came through it all.'

That night in Jersey, for better or worse, the die was cast. Shirley vacated her new manager's bed for her own. When she got back to her hotel, she demanded of her room-mate, Louise Benjamin, 'Where's my Wagon Wheel? Did you leave one for me?' One of Shirley's passions was for biscuits, and she often slept with a small packet under her pillow in case she felt hungry during the night.

Louise was eager to know what had transpired with Sullivan, and could hardly believe the news that he was going to provide a hundred pounds for dresses. To the girls from Tiger Bay, this was a small fortune. Louise remembered when Shirley didn't have a pair of knickers to her name, and her own aunt, Iris Freeman's mother whom Shirley called 'Auntie Bella', had had to lend the girl knickers so she could go sliding down the slag heaps with Iris.

The memory led on to reminiscences about their childhood in Tiger Bay and Louise pondered on the difficulties for children of mixed-race parentage. As a coloured girl from Tiger Bay, she had found life in London very difficult at first. London wasn't yet geared to multi-racialism, and she sometimes found herself wondering just exactly who she was. Years later, Louise said, 'The day I accepted that I was black everything fell into place and my life became easier.'

Shirley Bassey never seemed to have the problem. She told a journalist in an interview that, 'My mother was white so I never thought I was anything else.'

That night in Jersey, however, she had other things on her mind. Mr Sullivan had said, 'I promise I can make you a star.' For the first time in her young life she believed that here was a man who had spoken the truth.

5

A Star is Born

Before Michael Sullivan left Jersey for Guernsey and his meeting with his partner, Berry, he gave Shirley his Shaftesbury Avenue office telephone number and told her to ring him as soon as the Ballet arrived back in London. Unfortunately, he didn't tell her where he lived – round the corner from his office at the Mapleton Hotel – which led to a big mix-up when the unexpected happened.

Sullivan had caught influenza and instead of being at his office when Shirley arrived back from Jersey, he lay shivering in bed at the hotel. Shirley was staying at Harold Wood with Pam and Ben, from where she rang his empty office constantly. Meanwhile, Juhni, Sullivan's wife, was waiting in vain outside the office looking for a dark girl – answering her husband's description of Shirley. At last, in desperation, Sullivan telephoned Ben Johnson at the rehearsal rooms and asked him to send Shirley round to the Mapleton.

An hour later Juhni opened the door to Shirley, who looked dazzling in a vivid orange dress under a silvery see-thru plastic mac. She was very unsure of herself in this unfamiliar situation of coming to meet a man who was ill in bed – and a hotel bed at that. She had never met anybody who actually lived in a hotel.

She sat nervously on the edge of a chair, almost as if to ensure a quick getaway from this man who lay in bed coughing and sneezing, and who didn't at all resemble the polished ball of fire who had promised her one hundred pounds for her costumes.

Sullivan cleared his throat and told Shirley he had booked her a room at Olivelli's, a nearby Italian restaurant with accommodation above which was rented out to theatricals. He didn't tell her that he had asked Papa Olivelli, the owner, to keep an eye on her, and if he was ever concerned about her, to get in touch with him.

'You'll have breakfast there, if you want, and dinner at night. It's inexpensive,' Juhni Sullivan told the clearly apprehensive girl.

'How long do I have to stay there?' asked Shirley warily.

'At least three months,' Sullivan replied.

'So long!' Shirley looked worried. 'What do I have to do?'

'Work hard,' said Sullivan shortly. 'Every afternoon you'll be in a rehearsal room with a pianist. In the evening I'll teach you the things you have to know. You've got a lot to learn, and not just about singing. You've got to learn voice production, and we've got to get rid of that accent.'

'What accent?' asked Shirley.

Juhni interrupted. She could see the girl was getting agitated. 'You'll enjoy it. Every good performer has to go through this.'

'All right,' said Shirley, getting up. 'All right.'

'Sit down,' ordered Sullivan. 'Now we come to the important part. The contract. You're still a minor so your mother has to sign for you. I'm going to read it through to you carefully, clause by clause, until you understand it. Then you'll go home to Cardiff and let your mother read it. Then she'll sign it and you'll come back.'

'How long can I stay in Cardiff?' Shirley asked desperately.

'Don't worry,' said Juhni. 'We'll talk about it when I give you the return fare.'

'And ten pounds salary,' added Sullivan. You'll see in the contract that you get a salary of ten pounds a week.'

When Sullivan had finished explaining the contract, he was too hoarse to continue the meeting and Juhni took Shirley to the lift. She came back and, with some misgiving, asked her husband whether he genuinely believed he could turn this girl into a star.

Michael Sullivan had grown up in the era of the movie heroes and heroines of the 1930s and '40s, and had wanted to be a film director. Instead, he became an office boy to a man who booked variety acts, and, at weekends, he went down to Southend-on-Sea to help a man who owned a freak show. Sullivan was fifteen, he wore a straw boater and carried a cane, and earned a pound every Saturday.

The owner of the show helped him to train his voice. 'Now make sure they can hear you all over the fairground,' he instructed him. 'You've got to fill this tent at sixpence a go to see the five-legged sheep.' The young Michael succeeded in filling the tent, and although the sheep's fifth leg was only glued on, he made the customers laugh. But this was something different. Juhni was right, how the hell was he going to turn an eighteen-year-old girl from nowhere into a star?

Hundreds of kids went to RADA and other drama schools every year and how many of them became big stars? A mere handful. Okay, the raw material he had was good, he could polish the talent, but what the hell did he do finally with a beautifully polished singing bird?

His anxiety was not helped by recalling Joe Collins' words to him. He'd been to see him when he got back from Jersey because

Joe had been the management that sent Shirley's last show, *Hot from Harlem*, on the road. To his horror, Collins had said, 'Don't touch that girl with a barge pole.'

Joe Collins could be a difficult man, but he knew his stuff, and he made money. 'Shirley Bassey walked out of my show,' Joe told him. 'Left us flat without a girl singer. Don't touch her, she'll let you down.'

Sullivan began to feel ill again. What had he done? Signed up a girl for God knows how long at ten pounds a week. He was broke, and even if she didn't walk out and didn't let him down, he wasn't sure what was he going to do with her. He needed lessons himself. He'd have to find out how these men who dealt with star acts succeeded. He needed to know their secret.

Shirley returned from Cardiff with the contract duly signed by her mother. Sitting in an imitation zebra skin chair in Sullivan's rather opulent office she looked strangely subdued. She had been unnerved by her longed-for visit home to Splott. In a few short weeks she had become 'Auntie Shirley' to her own child, while her sister Iris, as she had feared, had taken on the role of Sharon's mother. 'I show her your picture every day,' said Iris, 'don't worry.'

But Shirley did worry. Three more months away from baby Sharon, at this crucial time of the child's life when she was bonding with those close to her, couldn't be right. She hardly heard Sullivan going on at her about her last show *Hot from Harlem*. Why had she walked out of the show, why had she let Joe Collins down so badly? Didn't she know it was a mortal sin? . . . A performer never walks out!

Shirley began to weep. She wept not because of Sullivan or Joe Collins but because she was losing her baby. Kindly but surely she was being taken away from her.

Sullivan was aghast. 'Don't take on like that. Just tell me why, that's all I ask.'

It all poured out, the pregnancy, the fears, the fact that she hadn't been able to get into her costumes because she was five months gone. But never mind all that, now she was going to lose her darling Sharon. 'She puts her arms around my sister,' wept Shirley, 'and says, "Mum, mum".'

'Will your sister adopt her?' Sullivan asked.

'No, never!' wailed Shirley, hearing her secret fear voiced for her.

Sullivan's instant reaction was concern that his plans for Shirley might be thwarted by gossip and scandal. He was not about to see the dream collapse into ruins, despite his anxieties and uncertainties, and his advice was ruthless and emphatic.

'You *must* keep your baby a secret,' he urged. 'If you become well-known, and I'm certainly going to try my hardest to make you famous, this is the kind of story that the newspapers love to sniff out. You have to listen to me on this. And what about your family? Can they be trusted to keep the secret?' Shirley nodded. 'Now what about Tiger Bay and that other place, Splott?'

'I know they won't talk in Tiger Bay,' said Shirley.

It was getting on towards seven o'clock in the evening when Sullivan drew the curtains, shutting out the life of theatreland below. Shaftesbury Avenue with its illuminated signs, the bright lights, the traffic, the noise, and the crowds of people going to the theatres. He took out two glasses, a bottle of rum and a bottle of lemonade. The rum was for him and the lemonade for Shirley. The first lesson began.

Lesson number one focused on getting rid of the Cardiff accent. Although Shirley's accent could be very appealing, he wanted to make her speaking voice as beautiful as her singing voice. He handed her a copy of worn sheet music, Cole Porter's 'I've Got You Under My Skin'. 'You are going to read this lyric to me,' said Sullivan, 'but first I want you to read it through once to yourself. Then read it through again, and finally read it to me. You will speak slowly, carefully, you are going to enunciate each word very clearly. Open your mouth, like this, round your lips, like this, then start. When you are ready I want to hear every word loud and clear.'

He was teaching her the old-fashioned way, the exclusive, expensive RADA way. Each word had to have a bell-like quality. He listened to her, corrected her, then made her go to the other side of the room and do it all over again.

'You've got to understand the meaning of words,' he told her. 'Do you understand what "under my skin" means? Have you ever been so in love that you feel your boyfriend has become a part of you? The smell of him and the feel of him, so that you can't get him out from under your skin. Well, have you? Do you know what I'm talking about?'

Shirley said she thought she did. Privately, she wasn't at all sure.

Sullivan explained that the song told a story, and that *she* must tell the story in the singing of it – every word must be heard as clearly as if it were a pinging bell. She must pour feeling into it. Doing her best to hold on to all these instructions, she sang the song for him, but it wasn't right.

'You're putting about as much emotion into the song as a plank of wood,' Sullivan told her. 'You're singing from your head, not your heart.'

'What's the difference?' asked the by now thoroughly confused Shirley.

'When you've loved a man and he doesn't love you, then you'll know,' was the rather unhelpful reply, before he produced another Cole Porter standard, the witty and implicitly suggestive 'Let's Do It'. He told Shirley that the song meant exactly what she might think it did, 'Now you've got to thrill me so much I can hardly sit still, but first you've got to study the lyrics.'

She drank some lemonade, Sullivan poured himself a large rum, then it was another song, another lesson, another break, after which she received her first lesson in how to project her voice properly. 'Where did you learn that Mr Sullivan?'

'When I was a kid and joined a circus for a month. Now, get over to the other side of the room and have a go. Imagine you're in a theatre, and send your voice right up to the upper circle.'

He had guessed that Shirley wasn't the type of girl who would sit in front of a mirror for hours on end, quietly practising – that would be too much like school – but he soon discovered that she was a quick learner. She had a knack for imprinting lyrics indelibly on her memory after what seemed like little more than a cursory glance at the page.

At home that night, he told his wife that Shirley was full of surprises. 'She's not at all like I thought she would be. She gives herself completely to what she's doing. She's unusual, and I'm really quite impressed.'

Although Juhni smiled and said how pleased she was to hear this, she still felt uneasy, almost frightened, of what he'd undertaken. Sullivan himself, however, was privately convinced that Shirley was like a beautiful vessel that he would fill with knowledge and expertise. She was going to be his star, his creation.

For her part, Shirley Bassey had much to think about. Her first lesson with her agent-teacher had been demanding and exhausting, but she realised that the new disciplines were the first step to fame and fortune. It should have been the most exciting realisation of her life, but she felt that had made a bitter down-payment on her future by leaving her baby in Cardiff. It nearly broke her heart.

For the next three months, Sullivan would book whatever available rehearsal room he could find, and Shirley worked continuously with the well-known pianist, Bob Wardlaw. He had agreed to stay the course with her, and to accompany her once Sullivan had booked engagements for her.

When Shirley told Sullivan that she had learned most of her songs by copying the recordings of famous American singers, he was aghast. She needed above all to acquire her own individuality. When she sang, people had to know immediately that they were listening to Shirley Bassey. Bob Wardlaw, he assured her, would help her to develop a style of her own. She must, he instructed her, forget about her American role models.

Michael Sullivan was giving Shirley a crash course – his version of what was taught at most stage schools. He was self-taught, but he'd been in the business all his life, he knew it all. In his opinion, she was getting the best, and on a one-to-one basis. If she slacked at all, he yelled at her to stop wasting his money. He had developed an excellent vocal technique himself, and when he lost his temper he could be heard halfway up Shaftesbury Avenue.

While Sullivan took care of interpretation, projection and stagecraft, Bob Wardlaw taught Shirley phrasing and breathing. Those bookers who wouldn't touch a beginner, who prided themselves on never hiring a flop, advised Sullivan that if he could get her on a Moss Empires or Hippodrome circuit, she'd learn something nobody could teach her – how to fight her way through her act.

Shirley's routine of lessons was relentless, but there were times when Michael would relax and take her out for a drink. On one of these occasions, he introduced her to TV producer Robert Hartford-Davis, around thirty years old, attractive and a man of the world. Shirley fell for him and always remembered him as the first man to take her to a 'real' restaurant, and to buy her her first bottle of perfume.

She was impressed by Hartford-Davis' sophistication, the fact that he knew his way around, and ignored the fact that she knew he had another girlfriend even while he was dating her. Shirley's affair with Bob lasted about eight months, until he went out to Africa. Shirley later confessed that she had been devastated at his departure and, for the first time, really understood Michael Sullivan's little lecture to her about being left by a man and suffering because she still loved him. Bob, she felt, really was 'under her skin, deep in the heart of her', and she cried her eyes out – but at last she knew how to sing Cole Porter's song with her heart rather than her head.

During Shirley's affair, Sullivan had not let-up on grooming his discovery. He taught her one of the most important techniques for an entertainer: how to get, and hold, an audience's attention. She must, he explained, mentally divide her audience into three sections, then 'work' each section in turn. 'Your eyes,' he told her, 'must go to the front of this section of the audience, then to the middle, and then the back. Let the audience feel you're with them, that each and every one of them is important to you and that you are looking at each individual. Then do the same with the next section, and the next. When you get a high note, throw your head back and hold it, then send it right up to the circle.'

To this day, this is basically how Shirley Bassey 'works' her audience.

Shirley had settled well into her working routine with Michael and Bob Wardlaw and, despite her preoccupation with Bob Hartford-Davis and her lessons, she also began enjoying the camaraderie at Olivelli's, making a couple of friends among the boys in show business who also stayed there. She grew to like most of her lessons, and found that her natural way of speaking, Welsh and precise, helped her in the phrasing of her songs.

But, as the weeks wore on, the thought that all her lessons and practice must eventually culminate in a public performance, began to worry her. 'I don't think I could do a solo act with a big orchestra. I'd be frightened,' she confessed to Sullivan.

He assured her that there'd be nothing to worry about come the big day. 'We'll be with you. Bob will be there in the orchestra, playing just for you, and I'll be in front listening and watching, and Juhni'll be waiting for you in the dressing room. You'll never be alone.'

The first big explosion between Michael and Shirley came over the dress she would wear when she actually performed before an audience. Shirley had made up her mind that it would have yards and yards of net in the skirt, and that it was going to be bright. Very bright. And when Shirley made up her mind, she was not to be budged.

A despairing Michael turned to his wife for help. As patiently and tactfully as she could, Juhni explained to Shirley that she had a beautiful body, that she was in the tall, slim, classical mould – the easiest, and the most exciting kind of figure to dress. She must wear something that was moulded to the lines of her body. It certainly couldn't be net, and a bright colour would not be sufficiently sophisticated to make an impact. She, Juhni, envisaged Shirley in black velvet, off the shoulder – 'because you have beautiful shoulders' – with just a tiny strap for safety.

'Black!' screamed Shirley. 'Never! Black is for widows.'

'Black,' echoed Sullivan firmly, 'tight-fitting and with a slit up the thigh.'

'I won't go on,' yelled Shirley. 'I won't go on in black.'

'Okay,' said Sullivan, 'then I rip up your contract.' This exchange of threats and counter threats was subtly being established as a routine between them.

Shirley stormed out but, by the following day, she'd thought better of it and agreed to have her first fitting for a black velvet dress. However, throughout the making of it – Juhni's mother, fortunately for the finances, was the dressmaker – Shirley affected lack of interest and contrived to miss a fitting whenever possible. She remained adamant that she hated black.

Not yet nineteen and very slim, Shirley needed some discreet padding on her hips so, to placate her, an arrangement of cerise satin was made that attached to the black dress without detracting from its line. A top-knot of hair was pinned on to her own to give her added height, and she was given long black gloves and gold gypsy earrings. Once dressed in her full regalia, she had to try and perfect the art of entrances and exits, to learn the necessary grace which was so far lacking.

At last, Michael Sullivan felt that sufficient preparation had been made. It now only remained carefully to plan Shirley's public debut. He felt that the best course would be to assemble, and make bookings for, a complete variety show, with Shirley slotted to close the first half – always the second best spot on the bill. The plan was not well received. 'No, no,' Shirley cried on being told of it. 'I want to be squeezed in somewhere easy. That way,' she argued, 'no-one will notice if there's a disaster.'

Sullivan was unmoved. 'We start the way we mean to go on. Stars don't "squeeze in" anywhere,' he told her.

The theatre that was finally chosen for Shirley's first venture into the big time, was the Hippodrome in Keighley, West Yorkshire. It looked a long way up the map of England but it was exactly the kind of venue that Michael Sullivan wanted. The town was neither too big nor too small, and the audiences were usually good. It was a number one provincial date and Shirley couldn't have done much better. She still hadn't mastered the art of getting off the stage gracefully so Sullivan decided that, at the end of her performance, she should stand behind the microphone facing the audience until the curtain was lowered.

That autumn Monday morning in 1955 after the train journey and a night's rest in their hotel, the Sullivan entourage entered the

Keighley Hippodrome for the band call – the run-through of the complete variety programme with the artists and full orchestra. The three of them, Sullivan, Bob Wardlaw and Shirley might have seemed calm, but inwardly their stomachs were churning. Shirley had plunged into a sudden crisis of confidence. She couldn't remember the lyrics of her songs, she said, and she didn't want second billing.

The cleaners were busy around them, their vacuum cleaners making a terrible noise. 'It isn't fair,' Shirley burst out again. 'I don't *want* second billing.' Sullivan ignored her. 'After this rehearsal with the band,' he told Bob, 'we'll have two more this afternoon. That'll steady her down. Come on, Let's get this one over with.'

As they walked through the theatre he conferred in a whisper with Bob. 'What shall we do? It doesn't look good.'

Wardlaw suggested they keep their fingers crossed and keep talking. 'Poor kid, she's terrified,' he remarked.

'So am I,' said Sullivan, 'but if we can keep her in one piece until six-fifteen for the first house, we might stand a chance.' He was anticipating the collapse of his grand plan, indeed, of his entire career. He had staked everything on Shirley Bassey and here they were, her first appearance in a number one theatre, second billing, closing the first half and she was refusing to go on. They'd laugh; no, they wouldn't laugh, they'd crucify him, and the manager of the theatre would go berserk. And he was already broke. Berry had even had to pay the rail fares up here and now Shirley wouldn't go on. He turned round and saw her behind him, looking lost and frightened. He waited until she caught up with him then he put his arm around her. 'Don't worry sweetheart,' he said, 'it doesn't matter, nothing matters. As soon as this rehearsal is over we'll go over to the pub and have a drink and we'll ask them to make you a nice cup of tea.'

Somehow Shirley got through the rehearsals, and it looked as if all might be well until, in the dressing room, Juhni started helping her dress. Then the panic returned, but this time it was even worse. She began trembling and couldn't speak. Juhni pinned the knot of curls on her head, fitted the gold earrings, pulled the long black gloves over her hands and up her arms and still Shirley didn't say a word. Juhni and Michael helped her walk to the wings. She was icy cold and they tried rubbing her hands, but her eyes looked glazed as if she was somewhere else.

The pit orchestra struck up the intro to her first number, 'I Can't Give You Anything but Love, Baby', and here came the voice over the loudspeakers: 'Introducing ... Miss Shirley Bassey ...' Sullivan gave her a gentle little push and Shirley pulled her hands together, straightened her back and walked on to the stage. She reached the microphone. Suddenly she smiled. She raised an arm, she spread her fingers wide, she opened her mouth in true Bassey fashion and, by God, she sang.

Tears began pouring down Juhni Sullivan's cheeks. She couldn't stop. Through her tears she turned to look for Michael but he had gone. He was through the pass door in a flash and standing out front. He mouthed each word Shirley sang, watching her, and nodding in silent approval, and relief. She was going well. She was holding her own. The applause when she finished was very good. And now here she was announcing her own next number very nicely, slowly and clearly. She sang very well, and the applause was even better.

Sullivan took a good look at the audience. It was a full house, some of them old, some of them young, but they liked Shirley all right. She was doing everything he had taught her to perfection. There she was, making full contact with the audience, one side at a time. But she was also doing something he had never taught her: she'd got the audience by the scruff of their necks, the real Shirley was coming through and she was magic. When she sang 'Stormy Weather' there wasn't a dry eye in the house.

Her act ended to tremendous applause and shouts of 'More, more!' And this was Yorkshire where they hated phonies. The matter-of-fact Yorkshire people were crazy about her.

Back in the dressing room Shirley couldn't stop talking, 'Was I all right? Did you hear me forget the first announcement? Did they like me? Did you hear them shout for more? I couldn't believe it.' She jerked off her gloves, 'I hate these things, I won't wear them again,' she said and, turning to Juhni and Michael who stood staring at her, asked anxiously, 'Was I really all right?'

'You were wonderful! We're so proud of you.' And then the three of them clung together, their arms wrapped tightly around each other, until they all broke down and cried.

After her success at Keighley, Michael Sullivan's original faith in Shirley Bassey was confirmed, particularly when the stolid manager of the Hippodrome, a true blue Yorkshireman, commented – after Shirley had stopped the show every night for a week with 'Stormy Weather' – 'I may have heard better, you know, but I have to admit that she goes over bloody well.'

Shirley now had two weeks off and Sullivan took this opportunity to change some of her songs and adjust the stage lighting for her act. Then it was off on an eleven-week Hippodrome tour of the provinces for impresario Bernard Delfont. This was not the famous Moss Empire tour, but another circuit which could claim a certain prestige. Sullivan had always had links with the three Grade brothers, future TV boss Lew, top agent Leslie, and Bernard Delfont, the middle brother – and was able to get a better deal for Shirley with them than he might have done elsewhere.

Although Sullivan did not go on the tour with Shirley, he kept tabs on her from a distance. Any word of criticism from one of the Hippodrome managers about Shirley's performance and he was up in arms. Juhni was worried that he was growing obsessed with Shirley and losing his sense of objectivity, so hostile was he to any hint of negative criticism.

Money was also short. Shirley was not Michael's only client, but she was his most important. She was earning thirty-five pounds a week, out of which he paid the train fares and twelve pounds a week to pianist Bob Wardlaw. Shirley received eighteen pounds. 'This is only the beginning,' he kept telling Juhni, and he was already making plans for what should follow after the Hippodrome tour.

A nice surprise awaited Shirley when she arrived for her week at Birmingham. The Hippodrome there was a smart little theatre in Hurst Street, with the trolley buses running outside, and so far, in spite of the advent of television, was still going strong with its twice nightly variety shows. As often happened on the vaudeville circuit, one of the acts had dropped out because of illness and had to be replaced at short notice. Michael Sullivan contacted Berry's wife, Sylvia Beresford Clarke, and despatched her, with her dancing partner as the 'fill-in' sister act at Birmingham. 'Give my love to Shirley,' he said. 'You'll share a dressing room with her.'

Sylvia, who loved her profession and all the excitement that went with it, welcomed the chance of meeting Shirley at last. The two girls, only two years apart in age (Sylvia was twenty) liked each other instantly although, as Sylvia recalled, there was one major difference between them. 'Shirley was out of her depth,' she said. 'She'd been thrown in at the deep end, and I realised straight away that she was only a kid, really.'

While Sylvia had her own family living in London, her mother and her sister; Shirley had nobody to turn to. She didn't understand money and had no idea of how much it was costing to build her career. As Berry's wife, Sylvia had heard many of the discussions between her husband and Michael Sullivan about Shirley's future, and was in the somewhat awkward position of knowing more about the plans for Shirley than Shirley herself did.

Michael, as Sylvia well knew, had wanted Shirley to do this Hippodrome tour in order to build her confidence, but he didn't intend her to remain in variety much longer. The way to stardom was to shine alone, not as part of a variety bill. In his view, cabaret should be the next step – a real class act, with songs especially written for Shirley.

Young as she was, Sylvia felt that Michael Sullivan was making a mistake – the first of several as it would turn out. He was accustomed to taking the decisions about Shirley's career without discussing things with her. She had accepted each *fait accompli* so far, but Sylvia felt badly on Shirley's behalf She worried that the girl was being over-controlled by two much older men in her husband and Michael Sullivan. Although she was fond of Sullivan and admired his several positive qualities – his energy and charm, his taste and vision – she knew that he could be absolutely ruthless, and wondered whether Shirley had any idea what she was in for.

She later said, 'I sometimes wondered how Shirley managed to get through it all. What happened to her would have broken a lot of girls. Men with power, especially in show business, can do terrible things to girls, sometimes without even knowing it. They can destroy a girl's self-esteem with their jibes, and it's easy to destroy fragile confidence. When I met Shirley, she was eighteen, and that's not old enough to have enough armour to protect yourself.

And, of course, what Sylvia didn't know was that, over-arching all other difficulties, was the shadow of a little girl named Sharon in Tiger Bay. Back there, everybody naturally speculated as to who the child's father might be, and most thought he must have been one of the boys who had worked with Shirley at Curran's factory. In the event, it took an unrelated court case over forty years later for Shirley to reveal any more about the identity of Sharon's father.

In January 1998, Shirley was sued by her ex-secretary who alleged that the star was anti-Semitic and had called her a 'Jewish bitch'. Shirley, who had many Jewish friends and business associates, passionately denied the charges. After winning the case, she let it be known that her daughter Sharon was half-Jewish. Her father, Shirley revealed, was Jewish and had been married with two children at the time of their liaison. He never knew that Sharon was his daughter. 'I have never told him,' Shirley said, 'it would hurt too many people.'

Back then, on the Hippodrome tour, however, Shirley followed Michael Sullivan's strictures, and the very existence of Sharon was a closely guarded secret. Her task was to nurture and develop what her new friend, Sylvia, agreed was a great talent. She used to watch her performance from the wings, and later said that, 'Unless you've watched Shirley close up, like in cabaret, you don't get the full impact of her performance and her magic.' Happily, audiences worldwide who have been to Bassey concerts in vast auditoriums, have been bowled over by that magic and power.

Looking back on those early days, Sylvia recalls with amusement how she loved show business but never expected to be a star, while Shirley, much of the time, hated the business but, sure as hell, she was going to be a star! She remembered saying to Shirley, 'You've done it all so quickly. Just four or five moths ago you were holding the curtain in Jersey.'

'You've got it wrong, Syl,' Shirley replied. 'I've been singing for fourteen years, ever since I was four. Real hard stuff, singing to rough audiences who were often paying for the privilege.'

*

Shirley Bassey might have imagined that her early experiences in the pubs and clubs of Tiger Bay had hardened her, but Glasgow proved to be her baptism of fire. She has since admitted that she was almost paralysed with fright as she stood in the wings waiting to go on for the kind of audience she'd never expected to encounter on a respectable Hippodrome tour.

Glasgow in the mid-Fifties was a city rife with roaring drunks. In the Gorbals, the slum district of Glasgow, fights to the death were a regular occurrence; bottles were smashed and throats were slit with the jagged edges. The place had a sinister reputation. On opening night, Shirley first realised this was going to be no ordinary performance when she heard a rumpus from the back of the stalls. Then the acrobats, who were on just before, came running off the stage giving her the thumbs-down signal.

There was nothing she could do but go on, of course, but she made her entrance shaking with nervous apprehension. Bob Wardlaw was at the piano as usual, but he wasn't giving her any signals. As soon as she appeared on the stage, the barracking started. The drunks in the stalls took one look at Shirley's figure in her tight black velvet dress and called for a striptease. 'Shake your chassis, Bassey! Ger 'em off!'

She was astounded by the crudity. The worst nights in Tiger Bay had been a picnic compared to this. What should she do? If *she* couldn't hear the music – and she couldn't – for sure nobody was going to hear her. Should she leave the stage? Anger and pride took over. 'Shurrup!', she yelled, at the top of her lungs, not bothering to censor her language. 'Lissen ta me. Whadda they call ya, behaving like this?' She had reverted to pure dockland Cardiff such as she'd heard in the docks of Butetown, but they hadn't thrown anything at her yet, and her knees had stopped knocking together.

Shirley held up a hand and yelled, 'All right. If you don't want to listen, I'm off.' A voice from the stalls piped up, 'Gie the lassie a chance' and, gradually, in the face of Shirley's verbal onslaught, the crowd quietened down, and she could hear the orchestra playing 'When You're Smiling'.

Bob Wardlaw gave Shirley the signal to begin, and begin she did, unleashing that powerful voice of hers at full throttle, 'working' that unruly Glasgow mob, section by section as Michael had taught her, until she held them in the palm of her hand. By the end of the opening number, she was worn out from the effort, but was given renewed energy by the unexpectedly deafening applause. The crowd who, moments before, had nearly driven her away, were hooting and whistling and clapping and stamping their feet, calling for more.

Shirley's act was twenty-five minutes long; that night, it felt more like twenty-five hours, but she got through the songs and gave them the full treatment. As the first-half curtain came down, a couple of scattered voices shouted 'Ger 'em off!', but Shirley Bassey didn't care. It was the interval, they could go to the bar and get even drunker, but she didn't give a damn because she wasn't afraid anymore. She had won.

6

Meet Me At The Astor

After Shirley's success on the Hippodrome tour, Michael Sullivan proceeded with the next stage in his plans: to find the right cabaret venue where he could introduce her remarkable voice to the West End. During the Fifties, London's nightclubs were doing good business. Wealthy foreigners were flooding in, the Americans were coming back, and the newly rich Arabs, donning Western dress but drinking orange juice in public, frequented the clubs to eye the pretty girls on show.

Sonny Zahl was a leading London light entertainment agent, successful, affable and a gentleman, and he loved the business. Sullivan knew it would be better for Shirley's image if a recognised specialist agent were to negotiate her cabaret debut, and he enlisted Sonny Zahl's help.

Michael told Shirley that he had his sights set on a Mayfair club for her after the provincial tour. She was happy with the plan; after all, it would be better than singing in a pub. Considerably better.

Sonny Zahl suggested the Astor, an exclusive club in Berkeley Square, owned by the well-known nightspot entrepreneur Bertie Green. Michael was over the moon. He knew Green, and there were few venues better suited to his purpose than the Astor. If her and Sonny could persuade Bertie Green to engage Shirley, it would enhance her prospects. In a fashionable showcase like that, Shirley Bassey would be bound to attract the notice of the press. She'd be on her way – and so, of course, would he.

The beautiful young ladies who worked as hostesses at the Astor were classy – unlike some of the other cabaret clubs in Soho where it was not unknown for girls of no more than fifteen to sometimes cater to the after-hours requirements of a very different sort of male clientele. The Astor was a serious cabaret club, where a quality singer was always featured as an element of the club's attractions.

Michael Sullivan made the first approach to Bertie Green, explaining that he was promoting a wonderful girl with an extraordinary voice. She was young and lovely and, though she was as yet unknown in London, she was a seasoned performer, even at that very moment on the last leg of a Hippodrome tour for Bernard Delfont.

'Has she anything special to sing?' asked Green. 'Does she have her own songs?'

The question stymied Sullivan, but not for long. He immediately contacted a Soho connection in the music business and asked who was currently considered the best songwriter in town. The answer was Ross Parker who, among other things, had composed 'There'll always be an England'. 'He's tops,' Michael was assured. Ross Parker turned out to be a large man with a very pleasant personality but, as he told Sullivan, his fee was three hundred pounds per song.

Michael didn't blink. He nodded, and arranged to take Parker to see and hear Shirley in her show, which was playing not too far from London at Chatham. Shirley was enjoying a good week in Chatham, where every sailor in port was eager to get an eyeful and earful of the singer.

Shirley was catching on fast. She was at her most enchanting when she met Ross Parker after the show. Wide-eyed and admiring. 'Oh, Mr Parker, are you really going to write a song just for me?' The trip to Chatham had done the trick; Sullivan would worry about the money later. Meanwhile, he and Parker began working together, meeting at the flat of Juhni's mother who had a piano. At their first session, Ross said, 'Just tell me what you want, Mike.'

Sullivan had already given the matter some careful and canny thought. 'Imagine that we're in a nightclub,' he said. 'Imagine beautiful girls, men wanting to sow a few wild oats looking at them; getting ideas, wondering. Staying up late. Burning the candle at both ends. That kind of thing.'

'What do you want to sell, Mike?'

'Sex.'

'I think Shirley Bassey has a very good voice and she's got a great future,' said Ross. 'Let's write her a very good song. Why don't we start with your idea about burning the candle. Lovely light. Fabulous flame. Let's think about heat . . . burning . . . sex. The girl needs help, the man needs help. Let's call this song "Who'll Help Me Burn My Candle". At both ends . . .'

Ross Parker was an inspired lyric writer. It took him a little time, but when the song was finished, it was full of wit and innuendo. Shirley would need to learn fifty lines, and she still had one last booking, in Hull, before her tour was over. On the whole, the tour had gone smoothly, but in Workington an almighty row had erupted between Shirley and Michael over money. Most of their rows were over money. Shirley, it turned out, owed forty pounds in back commission to her first agent, Georgie Wood, and had held on to one of the salary cheques in order to pay it.

'You've been using my money,' declared a furious Sullivan. 'You know you have to take your salary out and give the rest to me.'

'I earn the money,' argued Shirley. 'I pay you.'

Resentment and anger escalated on both sides and led to Shirley in tears, while Sullivan insisted that he paid her and she owed him money. He drew up a balance sheet demonstrating just how much she was in debt to him. He was promoting her, he told her, and if she didn't like the arrangement, he would tear up the contract there and then.

Never mind that she'd just had an unqualified rave review in Workington: 'Shirley Bassey has a magnetic personality. We want to see much more of her.'

Never mind that next week she would be second-billed on her home ground, the New Theatre in Cardiff, where she would be going home to Sharon and to her mother . . . and Shirley wept because she couldn't bear it if she didn't go.

And so they made up. The week at Cardiff was a complete sell-out. All the Bay Girls came to the show and to Shirley's dressing room afterwards, where she gave each of them a little keepsake that she had bought and wrapped. At last, Shirley Bassey was 'The Rose'. In Tiger Bay the most beautiful girl in the community had always been called The Rose. The label had connotations of grace and charm and elegance. It was a great honour, far more so than simply being called the most beautiful girl, and it was an honour that had never been accorded to Shirley.

Now, at the New Theatre, wonderfully lit in her beautiful dress and full make-up, Shirley Bassey brought prestige to the community. Now she really was 'The Rose of Tiger Bay'.

*

Ross Parker had gone up to see Shirley in Hull so that they could rehearse the new song and try it out in front of an audience. Shirley often remarked later in her career that, at first, she didn't understand half the words she sang in that song. That may have been so, but Ross was very pleased with her and agreed that he would act as her accompanist when she opened at the Astor club. Shirley relied on his guidance for the correct phrasing and emphasis – without his help, she still lacked the experience to put the song across to its best advantage. It was as important to Ross as to Shirley and Michael that his new song should be a success.

Shirley was having a new dress made for the Astor: rich white silk, moulded to the contours of her body down to the knees, then flared out in stiffened folds to the floor. White suited her wonderfully, and this dress for her London debut was a prototype for the sort of clothes that became her trademark. Not for her the diaphonous little numbers in flimsy chiffon that reveal more than they conceal, but something beautiful, dramatic, and discreetly alluring. Her dresses have often had to withstand twenty-eight per- formances in a two-week booking; over the years they were designed to remain perennially fashionable.

Every outfit that Shirley has worn since her first London appear- ance has been made by an expert designer who understands what can happen to the dress. They have always been lined and made of resilient fabric. In the early days, Shirley had two brilliant young men, who she called 'the two boys', who designed her stage clothes. She remained faithful to them and Douglas Darnell, who was one of those 'two boys', was still creating her outfits in the 1990s.

Agent Sonny Zahl, who negotiated the contract for Shirley's two-week engagement at the Astor, had done well for her. Her salary was sixty-five pounds a week, a very decent sum in 1955. But, as Michael Sullivan said to her, 'This is only a steeping stone Shirley, a stepping stone to something much better.'

*

One o'clock in the morning at the Astor club. By the pink glow of the shaded table-lamps, waiters are pouring champagne as music plays softly and couples in the red velvet banquettes hold hands. The cigarette girl, long legs in black fishnet tights topped by a lacy corset-style bodice, offers her tray of expensive cigars.

The background music ends, and Ross Parker slips into his seat at the piano. The orchestra plays an introduction and, floating across the heavily perfumed atmosphere, a disembodied voice announces, 'Miss Shirley Bassey'.

A slim dark girl in a dramatic white dress appears in the spotlight. She is very young. Her face still has the rounded contours of youth, but her expression is intriguing – half innocent, half knowing. This girl knows exactly what she is doing; she has been trained to give the illusion of sophistication. She raises a long, slender arm, displays a hand with long and graceful tapering fingers, and then she begins to sing.

The audience comes to attention. What a voice! By the time she performs her big number, 'Help Me Burn My Candle', everyone is held in her thrall. She is wicked, she is saucy; she invites every man in the room to 'burn our boats together' and, when she finishes, the room bursts into applause that seems as if it will never end. They don't want her to go. Eighteen-year-old Shirley Bassey is a sensation.

In the dressing room afterwards, Ross Parker hugs her, Michael Sullivan hugs her. Michael is ecstatic. He knows that this is a breakthrough, he knows he was right all along. This girl has magic, she can rise to any occasion, and she has a showcase at the Astor where she will be seen and heard by the right people.

Berry and Sylvia went to see Shirley at the Astor. Years later, Sylvia recalled how she looked around the room at the sophisticated audience of rich middle-aged men and beautiful women, and the glamorous hostesses weaving between the tables, and thought that it was an awful lot for a young girl to cope with. Then Shirley made her entrance and opened her mouth, and was everything Michael Sullivan had always said she would be.

Sullivan had already calculated his next move. He had learnt that Ross Parker was one of Jack Hylton's favourite songwriters, and that the two men liked each other. Jack Hylton was a very big name indeed, famous for his West End musical shows, and Ross had promised Michael an introduction next time Hylton came into the club.

Jack Hylton had been famous for a long time. During the Thirties he had beguiled the younger set with his own band which played on the radio. Then, during World War II, his music had given heart while the bombs were falling. He belonged to the big band era, when world-famous musicians such as Tommy Dorsey, Benny Goodman and Glenn Miller were at the height of their popularity, and Hylton's music was transmitted constantly on the BBC. Shirley had more than probably sung along with his band as she packed her saucepans in Tiger Bay.

Hylton, a shrewd Yorkshireman, had got out of the big band business and become an impresario, producer and theatre owner. He had bought the Victoria Palace and the Adelphi in the Strand, and had a lease on the Coliseum in St Martin's Lane, all of which were used mainly for musicals, family entertainment and comedy. Some of the Hylton shows were homespun, but he also presented big, glossy American musicals.

One evening, Jack Hylton arrived at the Astor, accompanied by the French comedian and cabaret producer Robert Dhery. Ross, as promised, introduced Michael sullivan to the short, middle-aged, bespectacled Hylton, who still spoke with a pronounced Yorkshire accent. The two men talked about TV, in particular the nightly show that Hylton had arranged to stage for Associated Television. Then Shirley made her entrance.

After the tumultuous applause which always greeted the end of her act, Hylton turned to Sullivan and said, 'She's very good, you know. Do you think she could open at the Adelphi tomorrow night?' Sullivan swallowed hard. This was too much too soon, even for him. 'I've got to find someone to fill a small spot,' Hylton continued. 'The girl I've got is in hospital with peritonitis, and I think this girl would do. It's only for two weeks until Tony Hancock can take over.'

Without pausing to consider any of the negative implications, Sullivan agreed.

'Be at my office tomorrow morning at ten o'clock, and we'll sort out her songs.'

Only then did the realisation dawn that Shirley would have to do three shows a night: two performances nightly at the Adelphi Theatre, and her cabaret at the Astor at one o'clock in the morning, but Sullivan refused to allow this to bother him. He knew what this chance offer could lead to – Jack Hylton was in television in a big way, and he had his own nightclub, the Albany, from where his late-night shows were televised. He was a very important man and, through him, Michael could realise his dream of introducing Shirley to an audience of millions through that little box which would soon be in every living room.

It did finally occur to him that Shirley would have to spend five hours every night at the Adelphi, even though her spot was in the first half. Jack Hylton was a stickler for the whole cast being present for both the opening of the show and the finale. Tomorrow would be a very exhausting day for his star-in-the-making.

Shirley had a strict rule that nobody should wake her before midday. Her friend Bernard Hall, a dancer who later toured with her as her road manager, recalled how he would go in to her at twelve noon and very gently touch her eyelids until they fluttered open. It was a way of ensuring a happy start to the day, but that was of no concern to Michael on that morning when work preparations had to be made for the Adelphi show. His phone call, nearer eleven than twelve, brought a furious response from Shirley. 'Eff off; I want to sleep. Go away!' At that moment she couldn't care less what Jack Hylton's demands were.

Sullivan, already carried away with visions of star-making headlines in the newspapers, knew this chance was too good to lose. He took a deep breath and yelled back, ordering her to get up and get ready; he'd be round to pick her up in ten minutes.

His biggest problem that morning, however, was to find Ross Parker who had apparently vanished. Without him, there wouldn't *be* a new star, because Hylton wanted Shirley to sing 'Burn My Candle' in the show, and there were no band parts for the Adelphi orchestra. There were no band parts for any orchestra. At the Astor, the number was sung to piano accompaniment only, and Parker hadn't got around to scoring it yet.

Eventually, Ross was tracked down to Brighton, where he had gone to relax for the day. The Adelphi orchestra's enterprising leader, Billy Ternant, had to copy down the scoring by phone, down which the composer sang it to him. The next problem was the gold lamé sheath dress that Hylton wanted Shirley to wear. It was too big for her and had to be safety-pinned up the back, which meant that she must remember never to turn her back to the audience. The six-fifteen opening of the first show was held back for quarter of an hour to give Shirley and the musicians enough time to rehearse.

When the pressure was on, Shirley would grow icy calm. No longer did she lose her temper or begin to panic as she would have done not that long ago. It was others who let her down. Comedian Dave King, for example who, though well-primed by Sullivan, forgot Shirley's name when he introduced her. But it didn't matter, Shirley overwhelmed the audience with another unforgettable performance.

Next morning the newspapers lived up to Michael's hopes and expectations: 'Shirley the Shy Bombshell . . . From Cardiff's Dockland to West End Triumph . . . Jack Hylton's newest discovery.' That last brought a wry smile from Sullivan. So Jack Hylton had discovered Shirley Bassey, had he? Oh well, you couldn't win 'em all.

On the Saturday when Shirley's two-week run ended at the Adelphi, Michael invited Shirley's mother and two of her sisters, Ella and Iris, to see the show. Afterwards in the dressing room he opened a bottle of champagne and invited them to witness the signing of Shirley's new contract with him. Shirley was guaranteed twenty-five pounds a week for the first year and sixty pounds a week for the second year. Thereafter, artist and manager would enter into a fifty-fifty partnership.

Sullivan's sights were really set on a contract he hoped to sign with Jack Hylton for Shirley to appear in Hylton's new show, *Such is Life*, that would open at the Adelphi in December 1955. A long run in a West End theatre would keep Shirley in the public eye and also save the money needed for travelling on tour. Jack Hylton did agree to sign Shirley, at sixty-five pounds a week – not a great deal – but Michael was sure he could find her lots of nightclub work.

That was another of Sullivan's mistakes. In his determination to make Shirley a star he had been pushing her to the limit for months. He treated her more as an automatum than as a young girl who could get tired and miserable and miss her mother and her baby. A girl who might one day explode through fatigue and resentment.

Rehearsals started and Shirley was given 'The Banana Boat Song', a number made famous by Harry Belafonte. Shirley's version would be completely different from Belafonte's calypso, far more sizzling and sexy. Her attractive costume was right for her, dazzling and provocative, yet simple enough in its design to reveal her fresh, youthful qualities. The dress was sleeveless, with a low round neck, and a long white bodice embroidered with a circular motif picked out in sequins. This joined a floor-length skirt, frilled and full, with each frill edged with the same sequin effect. On her head she wore a silk turban, ornamented with high plumes of multi-coloured feathers, leaving only a little of her hair still visible. Among the chorus of girls in white crinolines, lacy pantaloons and frilly bonnets, Shirley looked like an exotic flower.

When *Such is Life* opened, Shirley Bassey and her song stole the show. Later, in 1958, when she made a recording of 'The Banana Boat Song', it went straight to the top of the charts, out-selling Harry Belafonte's version.

The critics adored Shirley. 'She was all-electric and uninsulated,' they wrote, 'this eighteen-year-old from the Cardiff docks has hit rain-washed London like a freak heat-wave. This may be a revue for the coach trade, but Miss Bassey is in the limousine class.'

Shirley's social life took off. She was invited here, there and everywhere by a horde of interested males. Prior to her new-found popularity, she'd had a kind of steady boyfriend who had taken her to the movies in the afternoons for the past few months – Shirley was crazy about the cinema – then he'd take her home to Olivelli's and go up to her room for the farewells. He never went to the theatre with her, or took her out after the show. They were fond of each other in a youthful sort of way; Terence, or Pepe, as he was was known, was a year younger than Shirley, and the contrast with her former lover, Robert Hartford-Davis, couldn't have been more pronounced.

Pepe had a sister named Gloria, who got on well with Shirley, and comfortably off middle-class parents who lived in Bayswater.

Had Shirley not become popular so suddenly, or so desirable to other men, their affair might have gradually fizzled out, as these affairs do, but Pepe became violently jealous and the ground was gradually being laid for his own very dramatic and disastrous entry into the world's headlines.

The first inkling of what lay ahead came late one night when Pepe lurked in the shadows outside Olivelli's, waiting to see who brought Shirley home. He watched her say farewell to her escort, and when the taxi drove away he rushed up to her room. There was a lot of shouting and threatening on his part and then he punched her in the face.

The next evening in her dressing room at the Adelphi Theatre, Michael Sullivan, who had been alerted by Shirley's dresser, Helen Cooper, marched in. Shirley was sitting at her dressing table, patting make-up over her swollen jaw and cut lip. 'How did this happen?' he demanded. She explained what had happened and how Pepe had punched her. She was obviously very frightened and upset. She had never imagined he could be so violent.

'Why did he hit you?' Sullivan asked.

'I'd stood him up a couple of times, and he threatened to beat me up if I did it again,' Shirley confessed, before begging Michael to do something about it. She didn't want Pepe to come near her, and was more than willing that Michael should phone Pepe's mother and see that she kept her son away.

Not only did Sullivan telephone the mother of Terence Davies, but he went to Bow Street police station and had a word with a friendly detective who said he would give the boy a confidential word of warning. Sullivan was surprised that Shirley found the time and energy for such a full social life because he was piling on the personal appearances as much as he dared. She was doing TV spots for Jack Hylton at his club, the Albany, and a weekly local radio show. She rather liked opening new stores, especially those that sold dresses because she was always given a sample or two. Michael was eager to get her recording career started as soon as he could, and he always insisted that she make time for a lady journalist's interview.

There was real and steady money to be earned by appearing in midnight cabaret at industrial balls, like the Boiler Makers' Ball at the Dorchester Hotel in Park Lane, where Shirley had said, 'I don't think they like me. Did you see the way some of those women glared at me?'

'It's not you, they're glaring at love, it's their husbands. They like you too much.'

January 1956 brought Shirley's nineteenth birthday and a happy Sullivan, who felt they were at last beginning to make money. They had a guaranteed twelve-month run of *Such is Life* at the Adelphi, plus Shirley's late-night club act which should help his bank balance. He signed a contract for her to appear at the Embassy Club every night, and to please Jack Hylton he could always persuade her to squeeze in one more TV appearance on Jack's show at the Albany Club. 'It's a wonderful way to promote you. Everyone in the south of England knows the name Shirley Bassey because of TV.'

Together, they had rapidly scaled extraordinary heights. From a rehearsal room off Shaftesbury Avenue on St Valentine's Day in February 1955, to a featured spot in a big West End show and more high-class cabaret work than she could cope with within the space of a year, was quite an achievement.

Shirley, however, felt very differently about her place in Sullivan's scheme. She hated having to wait around every night until the end of the show to appear at the grande finale. She would then have to rush off to the Embassy nightclub, every time giving her best for the audience. It was a killing pace. She missed her friend Pepe, who had been someone to turn to, someone her own age. Everyone around her in this business was so much older than her. Life in the spotlight was proving an exhausting affair, and a lonely one.

Each and every person who ever worked for Jack Hylton hated his rule that all the cast must appear in the opening and the grande finale of his shows. Jack had a nasty little habit of arriving unexpectedly to sit in his box for the grande finale and count the smiling faces on the stage. He could immediately see which chorus boy had raced off to catch his train to Brighton, or whether Shirley Bassey was late again.

The finale of this particular show was very noisy and colourful. It was set on a Mississippi Showboat, and Al Read, the star, absolutely loved it. He was togged up in an immaculate white dress suit and large white top hat decorated with the Stars and Stripes. The girls in the cast wore white crinolines and bonnets and the men were in satin coats and striped white trousers. Shirley was told to stay in her 'Banana Boat Song' Creole costume, and because everyone was ordered to wear a tall minstrel hat, she wore hers on top of her turban. The idea was that every member of the cast would come running down the stairs and wave an ecstatic farewell to the audience. Shirley, who sang her heart out twice nightly, was forced to sit twiddling her thumbs in her dressing room and wait for that moment.

On one particular night, Michael arranged for Shirley to appear on one of Jack Hylton's TV shows at the Albany Club, which would take place straight after the finale at the Adelphi. She'd then have to do her stint at the Embassy Club. He'd ordered a taxi to wait for them outside the stage door and whisk them from venue to venue.

Shirley was fuming with anger as she hurried backstage for the finale. It wasn't as if she were making a fortune doing all this, she was getting a paltry twenty-five pounds a week and just a little extra for the club appearances. She arrived at the position where the stage manager lined up the company for the finale.

'Bassey, you're late again,' he shouted. 'So bloody what?' shouted Shirley back, and in moments they were going for each other, shouting every name they could think of. Shirley was the clear winner in the insults department and, after one particular taunt, the stage manage shouted, 'You can't say that to me,' and promptly smacked Shirley's face. She immediately gave him a hefty wallop back.

She was distressed when she arrived back in her dressing room, after the finale. 'He hit me,' she wailed. 'Just because I was late.'

'Did you hit him back?' asked Sullivan, knowing all about the Shirley of old who had learned how to pack a punch in Tiger Bay.

Shirley threw her turban and minstrel hat into the corner of the dressing room and burst into tears while Sullivan, who knew that an offended stage manager could seriously damage any girl's career, went in search of the injured man. He brought him back and negotiated a peace settlement. Shirley said she was sorry, he said he was sorry, they shook hands and that was that. The taxi was ticking away outside the stage door, and Sullivan asked the dresser to help Shirley change into her evening gown for the Albany. 'I can't go, I'm ill,' cried Shirley. 'I want to go home.'

As Michael moved towards her, she threw a jar of cold cream at him and then had hysterics. 'What do I do?' he asked the dresser.

'Calm her down,' she said. Michael again made a move towards Shirley, who screamed even louder, throwing at him everything she could find. He shouted that she was billed to appear on television and, by God, she was *going* to appear on television. His hand rose and he realised he had slapped her face. Immediately he felt guilty. The theatre manager came in to see what the ruckus was all about, and it was he who finally managed to quieten Shirley down. The dresser helped her change and, whispering words of comfort, led her to the waiting taxi.

Shirley sat beside Michael whimpering softly like a child recovering from a tantrum. Then the taxi drew up outside the Albany Club and Shirley realised she wasn't being taken home after all. 'You've conned me,' she shouted, in a fury all over again. Sullivan bundled her out of the taxi and into the club, where she started to yell for help. By now frantic, Michael bundled the struggling, protesting young woman into the ladies' room and kept her there, causing consternation with his presence, let alone Shirley's tantrum.

In the club, cabaret compere Ron Randell was doing his best to keep things going while he waited for Shirley to turn up, but down stairs in the ladies' loo all hell had broken loose. A short, thickset man with a comedy act, who always hovered around in case someone didn't show up for the TV programme and he could fill in, heard the noise that Shirley was making and walked in through the open door past the clutch of transfixed onlookers. 'I can deal with this,' he said to Sullivan. 'Stand back!' He looked the kind of man who was more used to controlling streetwalkers than highly-strung teenagers. He raised his hand and gave Shirley a good slap across the face. Her third in the space of an hour. She groaned, her head fell back, and she slumped against Sullivan.

'What are you doing to the girl?' a voice cried, and a small man pushed through the crowd that was now filling the cloakroom. 'Out!' he said to them all, 'Out!'

Jack Hylton sat Shirley on one of the sofas, let her head sink to his shoulder and began to comfort her. Somebody brought them a glass of water which Shirley sipped, then a glass of champagne which he called for. He knew how to look after a girl in trouble. They didn't move until Shirley had drunk the champagne. When Jack walked her into the club she was herself again, though tears glistened in her eyes as she sang.

After her number, she joined Jack Hylton's table and when

Sullivan approached, Jack told him to go away, he'd done enough damage for one evening. Sullivan realised that he was to blame for what had happened. Next day he cancelled as many of Shirley's commitments as he could. He hadn't become a considerate manager overnight, but he had been shocked into an awareness that there was only so much that Shirley could take.

In the Fifties young women in show business were often treated like cattle. Shirley told a story of how, when she first arrived in London, young journalists would proposition her. On one occasion, a hefty young man who worked for the *Daily Mirror*, pushed her into a telephone box, closed the door, and said to her, 'You do want your story and your picture in tomorrow's issue, right?'

Shirley stared at him, terrified of what might happen next.

'All right,' he said. 'Now that's understood, let's get down to business.' He made a grab at her. Shirley raised her knee – she wasn't from the Butetown docks for nothing – and got him where it hurt.

She'd learned a few things since that encounter, and the promise of stardom seemed closer to being fulfilled, but, so far, events in 1956 made her painfully aware of the price she might have to pay.

7

SHIRLEY MEETS BALLS

IN THE LIFE of every aspiring star there is at least one lucky break. Shirley Bassey nearly missed one of hers on that disastrous night at the Albany Club when she had been slapped almost senseless by three men. It was a night she would gladly have forgotten but, as it happened, about a mile and a half away from the Albany Club someone, quite by chance, heard her sing on television, an occurrence that was to start her on the road to international recording stardom, and eventually a collection of gold and silver discs on a wall in her fine house in Chester Square.

Johnny Franz, recording manager of Phillips Records in Bayswater walked into his flat late that night when Shirley was singing at the Albany Club, and on his way to the kitchen to make a cup of coffee switched on the television.

This was the Fifties and commercial television was very new. BBC producers were being poached by the score by Associated

95

Television because BBC TV had been going for a long time, operating for the few who owned TV sets even before the war. The public only stared buying television sets seriously around 1950 and it was a mini Gold Rush. Americans with know-how were being invited over and Sir Lew Grade made his famous remark about TV being a licence to print money. Everyone in the business saw that getting into TV fast was important.

At that time TV musical shows had little of the present-day glitz. They were filmed in black and white: merely a face, half of the body, a voice, a microphone, and now and then a dancer or two in the background. Even so, Jack Hylton's show from the Albany Club, with its new talent, was one that Johnny Franz – being in the recording business – tried never to miss.

On his way back from the kitchen Johnny could sense there was trouble at the Albany. Compère Ron Randell stood at the microphone, obviously covering up for some latecomer. He ad-libbed and joked, but all the time he was keeping a watchful eye for the missing girl singer. Then the latecomer, the rather tearful Miss Shirley Bassey, suddenly appeared. The music began, and the young girl took Ron's place in front of the microphone. She flicked away a tear and started to sing.

Johnny Franz, coffee cup in hand, stared and listened. He was right, the girl had been crying, she still had tears in her eyes, but what a voice! The song she had chosen was 'Stormy Weather' and her voice went right to his heart. Instinctively he knew he could make this girl into a recording star.

That night marked Shirley's last appearance at the Albany Club. Her contract was over. If, as she had wanted, she had gone home and failed to appear Franz would not have heard her sing and her entrance into the world of British recording would have been, at the very least, delayed. Johnny Franz was exactly the right man to take on the fledgling star and shoot her to the top of the hit parade, which he achieved some months later with 'The Banana Boat Song'.

Even before he heard that Johnny Franz wanted to audition Shirley, Michael Sullivan had decided that he had to change his attitude towards her – his investment.

He was ashamed of the scene at the Albany Club. Jack Hylton had said, 'You've done enough harm to the girl. Leave her alone!' After her song, Shirley had sat at Jack Hylton's table, sipping champagne and giving Sullivan, so he thought, a look of triumph – and who could blame her?

Most of the trouble between Sullivan and Shirley was his fault after all. He still treated her as the scruffy kid from Tiger Bay he had auditioned. Yet, in less than a year, she had become a huge success. She was now a desirable young woman who would soon flower into a beauty, but Michael had never taken into account how much she had changed. He still treated her like a wilful apprentice, yet she was earning a lot of money for both of them. He took the lion's share, and she was often too tired to appreciate what was left. Two shows a night at the Adelphi, one-night stands in cabaret around the Park Lane hotels for the annual balls of various unions and federations, social clubs in outlying suburbs and anywhere else where they could pay her price.

Sometimes there had been a hiccup in Sullivan's schemes. A booking he made with the Savoy Social Club in Rushey Green, for example, where Shirley was to sing for twenty minutes at their dance for one hundred and seventy-five pounds, went wrong. When she arrived, she was horrified to learn that she was expected to sing with an unknown band without rehearsal.

Shirley tried out her specially written arrangements with the band but found they were not capable of playing them. She tried them with a bass and drums accompaniment alone, but they couldn't keep time. At that point she was stopped from continuing the rehearsal and the band was ordered to play dance music.

'I eventually sang three songs to the best of my ability,' she said. The only three I *could* sing without a proper band accompaniment.'

The club was annoyed that she gave only a ten-minute performance instead of the twenty they had expected. They would pay her proportionately less. However, she did receive prolonged applause from the members, and the club officials would have done well to frame Sullivan's bill for future members – a memento of the night Shirley Bassey, sang not for thousands of pounds, but for seventeen pounds ten shillings a minute.

Sullivan had kept Shirley working late into most nights, promising her a white Jaguar car as a reward. There must have been times when she thought that if she ever really saw that Jaguar – and she didn't trust him to keep his promise – she'd get into the driving seat and drive away for good.

Shirley appreciated that Michael Sullivan had done a great deal for her, but she must have often thought that there should be more to life than a room over an Italian restaurant and late-night suppers with a succession of admiring strangers. She needed romance and tenderness and Pepe Davies, his jealousy notwithstanding, had given her these. Now he'd been pushed out on to the fringes of her life because she was afraid of his violent tendencies.

In the early Spring of 1956 a young man named Bernard Hall came into Shirley's life. Typically, Shirley, who liked giving people nicknames, soon changed his name. She called him Balls, because she said, in the vernacular of the time, that he was 'a ballsy guy'. He was good looking, talented, and in the same profession as herself.

Bernard Hall was twenty-seven, tall, and with the typical muscular figure of a dancer. He was born in Golders Green, north London, but lived in Monte Carlo, and when he met Shirley, he was in London to find English dancers for performances to celebrate the wedding of Grace Kelly and Prince Rainier. For him, Shirley was love at first sight.

He knew all about Olivelli's the restaurant in Storr Street, just off the Tottenham Court Road, he'd often eaten there. Every theatrical knew you could get a good meal there after the show or, if you needed a bed in a hurry, Papa Olivelli would do his best to oblige. Papa, however, ran his establishment quite strictly and never rented a room to anyone unless they could prove they were bona fide show people; he permitted no vagabonds or fly-by-nights. The rent was cheap – between two and three pounds a week, with breakfast thrown in and supper at a special low price.

Papa Olivelli, overweight and smiling, with a large paunch, stood inside the basement restaurant to welcome the clientele, while in the kitchen behind a wide counter worked Mama Olivelli, cooking spaghetti bolognese, lasagne, gnocchi, or whatever else you fancied. When the dish was ready, she would plonk it on the counter, put her head through the opening to the restaurant and yell, 'Pronto Angelina!' to the Italian serving girl, another of her nieces 'brought over from Italy to learn the language'. It could be hot and smoky in the restaurant but there was always a delicious smell of real Italian cooking.

One night, Bernard Hall was dining at Olivelli's with two friends, Dr Carl Lambert and his blonde wife, Grace, who was leading lady to the Crazy Gang at Jack Hylton's Victoria Palace. The three hadn't met for some months and had much to talk and laugh about. Before Bernard had left to live in France, he had once played the juvenile with Grace in the Crazy Gang. Through her, he had met her husband Carl, a well-known Mayfair psychiatrist, and a close friendship had developed between the two men.

They had begun their meal at Olivelli's when Carl noticed a pretty girl sitting alone at a corner table. Bernard had noticed her as soon as he sat down, and he and she had already made eye contact across the room. 'I know who she is,' said Carl. 'She's appearing at the Adelphi in *Such is Life* with Al Read. Her name is Shirley Bassey.' Because Carl's wife, Grace, worked in show business and was never free until the end of the second house, Carl spent a lot of his evenings going to other West End shows. 'As soon as we finish our ravioli,' he said, 'I shall go over and tell her how much I enjoyed her performance. She has an extraordinary voice, by the way, and I'll ask her to join us for a glass of wine and a cup of coffee.'

Bernard doubted that the girl would join them, she looked so young and shy. Living in France, he had never heard of Shirley Bassey. But she did accept Carl's invitation, she did come over to their table and Bernard was delighted. Shirley seemed very pleased to meet him and Carl was all smiles at having engineered this meeting of the two young people. 'Now you three have a lot in common,' Carl told them. 'You all work, or have worked, for Jack Hylton. How do you like him?'

Bernard said he liked Jack Hylton. He was tough, but he was fair. Bernard had been dancing in Jack's show, *Call Me Madam* at the Coliseum when he got the chance to go to Paris with The Debonairs, an American dance group who needed a replacement dancer in a hurry. 'He could easily have refused to let me go,' said Bernard, 'but he didn't.'

Shirley said that Jack had looked after her when she was in trouble. 'I'm under contract with him until the show closes at the end of the year.' Bernard assured her that he'd come and see her show at the Adelphi just as soon as he'd finished his arrangements for auditioning the dancers and showgirls.

Bernard fell in love with Shirley that first evening, and over coffee he was quickly trying to work out where he could take her afterwards.

Fortunately Carl and Grace understood, and when the second bottle of wine was finished, they took their leave. 'I know you're going to be a big star, Shirley,' Carl said to her in farewell. Bernard remembers that he was mystified by the fuss Carl made about Shirley. To him, she was a sweet, shy, seventeen-year-old, wide-eyed and unspoiled. He'd got her age wrong, she was nineteen, but that was how he thought of her. She stroked the arm of his jacket and said, 'It's so soft. What's it made of?'

'Cashmere,' he told her. 'What's that?' she asked. So he told her. He was delighted by her. She was so pretty and desirable, and there was a strong sexual chemistry between them. When he asked her if she would leave with him she told him it wasn't necessary because she had a room upstairs.

He always afterwards wished that their love affair had started in more glamorous surroundings than Shirley's modest little room at Olivelli's with its single bed, washbasin in the corner, and creaky wardrobe, but everything else was perfect that night. Neither of them realised it, but their love affair was one that would endure over the years. They were both performers and they toured wherever there was work to be had. As Bernard described it, 'Whenever she saw me, no matter in what part of the world, Shirley would throw up her arm and shout, "Balls, I love you."'

Like Shirley's, Bernard's career had started when he was fifteen, but he'd gone to the Italia Conti school in Soho, which trained its students well, and booked professional engagements for them in between classes. He'd done repertory, radio, television, cabaret and musical theatre, and his standards were high. He went to see Shirley's performance at a matinee, without telling her he was there. In retrospect, he realised he went to see the girl he was in love with, not the artist, but at that time he thought she needed to learn more about stagecraft. He recognised that she had a very good voice but he felt she was still a beginner. Remembering his hard work when he was young in the business, he thought Shirley lacked the confidence of a real pro.

In France and Monte Carlo Bernard Hall was well known and he earned much more money than Shirley, but he fell in love with the girl and not the performer. When he saw her act again in another venue some months later, he realised that he had been wrong. She had stardom written all over her.

On the personal level he remembered something that surprised him at the time: Shirley was constantly telephoning her home in Cardiff. Later, when he found out about her baby Sharon, who at that time was less than two years old, he of course understood the reason for all those calls. He recalled that Shirley didn't talk very much about her family or her earlier life, which is why those phone calls puzzled him, but Shirley could be a very private person.

Their love affair that year in London lasted for about a month. Bernard always remembered the end of that time, when they'd been to a party given by someone who lived in Dolphin Square. At the beginning of the evening, Shirley seemed shy but, as the evening went on, relaxed, and laughed and talked to everyone. He felt proud of her and so much in love, but he knew that after they left he had to tell her he was leaving early the next morning for Monte Carlo, to prepare for the royal wedding. They'd walked down to the Thames embankment, Shirley was wearing a smart blue redingote with handbag to match and her usual high-heeled shoes. She clung to his arm as they walked and, when they reached the wall, they stood with their arms round each other, looking down at the river. Then he drew her closer, and told her when he was leaving. Shirley was furious. She hit him with her handbag. He tried to protect himself but she kept hitting him until he caught her arm and kissed her. He told her that this was *not* the end, they would write to each other. Shirley, still angry, told him he only deserved postcards.

Before he left for Monte Carlo, Bernard said to Carl, 'I feel you had a lot to do with this'. He meant that Carl had somehow stage-managed his meeting with Shirley. Carl smiled. 'I did it with good intentions.'

Meanwhile, in London, one of the most important events of Shirley's career was taking place – her very first recording session with John Franz of Phillips, one of the most respected producers in the British recording industry. But Johnny Franz was also a charming man and very kind, especially to this young newcomer, Shirley Bassey. Michael Sullivan was, of course, very impressed, absolutely delighted that Johnny had taken Shirley on; the recording industry would soon make enormous fortunes for the lucky few.

Before each session Michael and Shirley would go to Johnny Franz's flat and talk over what she was going to record with Johnny, and with Oliver, who was the orchestrator. It was decided that her first recording should be the song Ross Parker had written for her debut at the Astor club, 'Burn My Candle'. Johnny soon found that Shirley had exceptional gifts; not only a powerful voice, but a photographic memory, and the priceless ability to interpret what the composer and lyricist had in mind. She could change key in the middle of a song – something few singers can do – and she listened and absorbed quickly.

Compared to modern recording studios, the Phillips studio in Bayswater in 1956 would seem old fashioned, but at the time and of their kind they were very good. It was a large studio and a full orchestra of excellent musicians was always engaged. When her song was being recorded Shirley sat alone in a soundproof box so that she could not hear (as she sang), how her song was going.

At the end of a take the two men in charge would go over to her. Johnny would say, 'Come in softly, then build it up in volume. Okay Shirley?' And Oliver would say, 'Now how about a bit of light and shade here. Can you do that, Shirley?' They recorded take after take until they got it right. Johnny Franz had unlimited patience.

Shirley's first two recordings were very successful and the second was a best-seller. On Phillips P.B. 598, Shirley sang 'Born to Sing the Blues' on one side and on the other, 'The Wayward Wind.' She was applauded for her original style. Here was a home-grown singer who didn't turn herself into a carbon-copy of American stars. Critics observed that Shirley might still have been a bit of a rough diamond but this Cardiff girl singer had the mysterious stuff of which stars are made.

With praise like this Shirley and the recording team were delighted, but Johnny wanted her to record something that would really soar in the charts, which the other songs had not quite done. Shirley didn't care for the number he chose. It was a calypso; she didn't want to be known as a calypso singer and she sang it every night in *Such is Life*. It was, 'The Banana Boat Song', but Johnny persuaded her into it and it rocketed right to the top of the charts.

Everyone said that Johnny Franz died too soon; he was well loved in the industry and his life ended tragically early. He would have been so pleased to know that his protégée, Shirley Bassey, would become one of the biggest recording stars in the world.

Shirley assumed that all record producers would be as kind and understanding as Johnny Franz. She was very wrong. Months later, when Shirley was invited to make a recording at the Columbia Studios in New York she was treated very differently. In New York it was tough professionalism. Time was money over there and Mitch Miller, the American producer, one of the world's greatest with pop records, whose artists included Sinatra, told Michael Sullivan in no uncertain terms that if Shirley couldn't get the phrasing right, the recording had better be cancelled. It was only when Sullivan soothed him, and then hissed at Shirley, 'This guy expects the very best, for God's sake, get it right this time,' that the song was finally recorded.

Afterwards, on the way back to their hotel, Shirley wept in the taxi. 'I'm not used to this; Johnny took me through every song several times.' Although it was too late and the recording was not a real success it had been a hard and valuable lesson, and Shirley realised that she still had a lot to learn if she was going to be big on record.

But this was in the future – America had yet to come. Only a year had gone by since Shirley had climbed out of obscurity, and Sullivan knew that she needed one more big break. Something that would *really* get her name in the papers; something better than a conventional nightclub engagement, or appearing as a soubrette in revue. He wanted a big-name venue where foreign stars climbed over each other to get a booking – something that could herald her entrance into American show business.

The Café de Paris in Piccadilly Circus on the way to Leicester Square was his next goal. It had just reopened after being blown up in the war when many of the revellers and dancers had died. An eccentric little man, Major Donald Neville Willing, ex ENSA, was in charge now. He was a touchy fellow who wouldn't appreciate the tough approach Sullivan had used with Bertie Green and Jack Hylton. Noël Coward and Marlene Dietrich were the Major's idea of stars, not Shirley Bassey from Tiger Bay.

The nightclub at the Café de Paris had an air of luxury. The excellent restaurant downstairs circled the dance floor and boasted an abundance of attentive waiters; the orchestra was soft and melodic, and leading down from the balcony was a beautifully carved staircase. Down this staircase came some of the biggest names in international showbiz.

Sullivan began a slow and careful courtship of Major Donald, who was an elfin little man with a monocle. Every now and then he slipped in a mention of this fabulous singer he represented. The Major shook his head, 'Sorry, dear boy, but I'm fully booked.' Sullivan went round to see him often, because he lived nearby. 'I'll pay,' Sullivan kept whispering, 'wonderful costume, new songs, jewellery . . . and she's beautiful and so sexy.' The little major shuddered. 'Leave it with me, dear boy, but I can't promise anything.'

Then, out of the blue, came an urgent phone call 'Two weeks in September,' whispered the Major. 'Liberace can't make it. Now don't forget, you promised the songs and lots of gorgeous jewellery . . . diamonds I think would be nice.'

Sullivan broke the news to Shirley. He would get two hundred pounds from the Café de Paris of which one hundred pounds had to go to Jack Hylton. There's no such thing as a free lunch. I've got to get you a new dress and a new song, but in the long run it will be worth it. Bit worried about the jewellery, though.'

'Diamonds!' said Shirley, looking into the future. 'I love diamonds.'

Bernard had written to Shirley telling her how much he missed her, Monte Carlo had become suddenly very flat and boring once the royal wedding was over and the weather hadn't been very good. At the Gala he'd read a sonnet to Princess Grace, but he was dressed in a medieval costume with tights and a long cloak and felt a real fool, but the French were always crazy about tights and cloaks. Things were livening up a little now, however, because Marlene Dietrich had turned up to make a film. They were both staying at the Hôtel de Paris and Marlene had invited him round for a glass of champagne.

Shirley sent Bernard a picture postcard, telling him she was going to appear at the Café de Paris for two weeks in September, wasn't it exciting? It would be nice if he could come over. She'd been to a new club in Finchley and met two old friends, Gloria and Pepe Davies. Didn't Bernard come from somewhere near Finchley?

P.S. Balls, I love you.

A chance meeting and Pepe Davies was back in Shirley's life. He had promised that this time he would not be jealous. Shirley was glad to have him back; she'd missed his friendship.

Sullivan was busy making preparations for the Café de Paris. This venue was far more sophisticated than the Astor. A new tight black dress was being made for Shirley with a band of mink around the bust, and he had found a new songwriter, and a pianist to play for her. The songwriter, Ian Grant, wrote two numbers for her, 'My Body's More Important Than My Mind', and another called simply, 'Sex'.

'My Body . . .' suited Shirley very well. Her fresh young voice hinting, in the nicest way, at the kind of wickedness beneath.

Shirley was growing quite confident, when the missing Liberace suddenly surfaced and said he was now ready to appear at the Café de Paris. Shirley's opening had to be put back until the end of September. Michael was philosophical: it would give Shirley a day or two's good publicity, and allow her more time to perfect her songs. The phrasing and the emphasis on certain words was all important.

She was working so hard that, on the day before her opening, she broke down at a rehearsal and began to weep. Michael called a halt, took her home in a taxi and told her to relax, rest, and try and get a good night's sleep. Shirley always worried because her voice needed sleep.

She did try to relax, she even went to the cinema with Barry, one of the boys who lived at Olivelli's. Watching a movie always relaxed her. When they got home Shirley said she would make some tea while Barry went back to his room to find her a book. As soon as he left, the door burst open and in charged Pepe Davies, who must have been lurking outside, full of anger and jealousy that Shirley had been out with another man.

Next morning Sullivan had a telephone call from Papa Olivelli. In a voice filled with emotion and doom, Papa said that Shirley could not stop crying and Sullivan should hurry round. 'Why?' asked Sullivan.

'Because last night that boy, Pepe, tried to kill himself here.'

Sullivan was out of the Mapleton Hotel and round to Olivelli's in record time. He found Shirley in bed weeping, her eyes swollen, and looking more like a bedraggled teenager than a glamorous singer. Between sobs she told her story. When Pepe started insulting her she told him she couldn't take any more and he must get out and stay out. He yelled back at her, 'All right, you won't be seeing me any more!' and stormed off.

She heard his car roar down the road, then turn and roar back. Suddenly there was a terrific crash, and she rushed downstairs into the street. Jammed between the heavy closed gates of a petrol station was a wrecked car. Lying next to it was Pepe, his face covered with blood. Someone called an ambulance and Shirley sat beside Pepe trying to comfort him but her friend Barry prevented her from going in the ambulance, reminding her of tomorrow's opening.

'And now he's on the danger list,' the distraught Shirley told Sullivan. 'I must go to him.' Sullivan talked to her about Pepe's unreasonable behaviour. It was not her fault, but he was going to ruin her life if she let him get away with it. She began to calm down and he sensed her relief that someone else was taking over. He told her that Pepe had loving parents to look after him; she had to try and carry on. He reminded her that her mother was coming up from Cardiff especially to see her opening. Shirley finally agreed and got up to wash her face. She did well through an afternoon's band rehearsal, got through two houses of *Such is Life* and was right on form all the time. Then they went by taxi to the Café de Paris.

Shirley gasped with amazement as she opened the door to her dressing room. The room was overflowing with baskets and bouquets of flowers. There was a pile of telegrams ready to open. She was overjoyed. Sullivan said afterwards, 'If I helped a bit with a few extra flowers and telegrams I knew it would please her'.

Juhni Sullivan and the dresser both helped Shirley get ready. The new dress showed off her beautiful shoulders. Then they opened the boxes of diamond jewellery that Michael had hired from a Bond Street jeweller just for the opening night. Shirley took a deep breath – her first diamonds! The dresser fitted the necklace, then the earrings and finally clasped the bracelet around Shirley's wrist. 'Aren't they fabulous,' Shirley whispered in awe. She looked spectacular. Her mother, sitting quietly in the room, was as overcome with delight and wonder as her daughter.

'They're worth ten thousand pounds,' Michael told them.

'Then I'm scared,' replied Shirley

The diners had finished eating, soft music was playing. At last it was cabaret time. Shirley glided down the opulent staircase as if to the manor born. The audience in their evening gowns and jewels and immaculate dinner suits applauded, the clapping reaching a crescendo by the time she stood in front of the microphone. 'Thank you, thank you,' she said in a small voice with a marked Welsh accent; her accent always returned when she was excited. 'Good evening, ladies and gentlemen.'

There were journalists and writers at the Café de Paris that night who still remember Shirley Bassey's debut. Some of them had once called her voice young and raw, but now, they said, her voice had matured and developed. Her songs were recorded at the Café de Paris and hearing the old recordings nowadays her voice is vibrant and electrifying.

Bernard did come over from Monte Carlo to hear her, and was astounded at how much she had changed in a few short months.

Her voice was like a trumpet, a trombone, he thought, and what was more she had real allure. He had been seeing quite a lot of Marlene Dietrich and he realised that these two women had something in common, they both invited fantasy.

That night at the Café de Paris Shirley could do no wrong. Those long tapering fingers really got to the audience; not only could the girl sing like an angel, she positively sizzled with sex. In the dressing room afterwards Sullivan couldn't stop hugging Shirley and while they danced around the room, he carolled, 'We've done it, Shirley, we've done it!' They'd hit the top rung of the ladder for the first time. Liberace, with his mother and his brother George, came round to congratulate and kiss Shirley and tell Sullivan that he was doing a great job.

Michael and Juhni were going on to Churchill's nightclub in Bond Street together to celebrate with their publicist, Philip Ridgeway, who had undertaken to return the diamonds to the jeweller.

As soon as they arrived at Churchill's, Ridgeway rushed up to them. 'Have you got them?' he asked anxiously. 'The boxes of diamonds?'

But Sullivan had rushed off, forgetting to take them. He hurried back to the Café de Paris and into Shirley's dressing room. It was empty. Shirley and her mother had gone, the jewellery boxes were there, but they were empty and not a diamond in sight. Sullivan gave up, he only hoped that Shirley had taken the diamonds home with her. If not, God help them all.

Shirley and Eliza, in the meantime, had wondered what had hit them. Michael had left without a word about what to do with the jewels. Shirley complained to her mother. 'He told me they are worth a fortune, he even told me he'd hired a detective to look after them. What a lie that was, where's the detective? And what does he do? Bugger off and leave us holding the baby.'

'Perhaps we'd better take them home with us and put them to bed then,' said her mother.

The two women walked gingerly up Shaftesbury Avenue, sure that out of some dark doorway would jump a mugger armed with a revolver or a knife. They got home to Olivelli's in one piece and locked the bedroom door and window. When they felt they were securely barricaded in they made themselves a cup of tea, and the new star and her mother tucked the gems under Shirley's pillow and went to sleep.

Sullivan as always woke them up too early. He came round armed with all the newspapers. The reviews for Shirley were sensational. 'Don't look at them now,' he croaked, his throat raw from anxious chain-smoking, 'just tell me where they are, please!'

Shirley, never at her best before twelve midday, pulled her pillow down and showed him the gleaming baubles. 'Never again,' she snapped. 'Look after your own bloody diamonds in future.'

Shirley's hard work in preparing for the Café de Paris was well rewarded. She was in demand now, the press clamouring for interviews and pictures. The *Sketch* and the *Tatler* ran full-page studio photographs of her and the daily and Sunday papers carried stories about this extraordinary girl from Tiger Bay.

The Major decided that Shirley was much too popular to let her go after two weeks and extended her contract for another seven. Shirley didn't bother to ask 'What next?' She knew that Sullivan would have something up his sleeve. She had to stay in *Such is Life* until December, and as long as she was under contract to Jack Hylton, he had a right to part of her earnings if she worked elsewhere. Financially, she hadn't done very well out of the Café de Paris.

An American called Sammy Lewis did see Shirley at the Café de Paris and made her an offer to appear at his hotel in Las Vegas but, not only wouldn't she be free until January 1957, but Lewis would not pay fares and travelling expenses to America.

Shirley visited Pepe Davies in hospital. He had serious injuries and was taking a long time to recover. One of the medical staff asked Shirley if it was true they were getting married.

'No,' said Shirley, 'he's got this on his mind. It isn't so.'

To Shirley's distress, Pepe's doctor suggested that it might be a good idea not to disillusion him too soon. 'Just go along with it a bit, it might help him to get well.'

To cheer Shirley up, Michael promised her a Christmas bonus of one hundred pounds. It was the fee she would get for a single broadcast from the stage of the famous Olympia Theatre in Paris, who had invited her to sing 'Stormy Weather' and another number. Shirley had never been out of the United Kingdom and was very excited about her trip to Paris.

The day after they arrived fog descended on London Airport and Les Paul, the composer and her pianist, who was bringing the band music with him, found there was no way he could get to Paris in time for the performance. The boys in the band at the Olympia Theatre, however, came up trumps at rehearsal. Shirley sang a few notes and gave them the right key, and the rhythm and brass did a kind of jam session, then someone gave the fiddles a helping hand and the magnificent orchestra of the Olympia really got it together.

That night Shirley sang 'Stormy Weather', and 'I Can't Give You Anything But Love', to rapturous applause. Next day, before they went home, Shirley did some shopping in Paris.

The next big thrill and major challenge was around the corner. America.

8

America on a Shoestring

Shirley would not budge, she was transfixed. She sat on the edge of her bed in the Waldorf Astoria, a look of childlike wonder on her face, as if she was living the story and loving every moment.

'How can she do it?' groaned Michael Sullivan. 'There's all of New York waiting outside this window.' To him, at that moment, it was the most exciting city in the world.

Lily Berde, who was Sullivan's new love, said. 'She's in the sweetie shop. She's never had it so good. She can sit on her bed and see every goddamn film she's ever missed in her life. She's got ten channels there, baby.' She gave Michael's arm a squeeze. 'Isn't it sweet? She told me that this is the first time she's ever seen a television in a bedroom. Where she comes from they nail the set down in the parlour. Honey, give her time, its a big jump from Olivelli's to the Waldorf Astoria.'

'But we're only here for five days,' whined the exasperated Sullivan.

Lily was on a goodwill tour sponsored by the the Greek government. She had been sent to London as an exponent of Greek dancing and while there had met Sullivan. Now she was on her way to Hollywood to meet a Greek tycoon and was doing the journey the slow way with Sullivan and Shirley, stopping off in Las Vegas en route. Sullivan and Lily were very fond of each other and Juhni and Sullivan's marriage was on the rocks.

Michael and Shirley were in New York because if Shirley was going to be successful on an international level she had to make an impact on America. Michael had organised a short-term ninety days contract with the powe ful William Morris agency, who had booked her an appearance at the El Rancho in Las Vegas.

'El Rancho is one of the best,' Sullivan told Shirley, 'Eartha Kitt and Sophie Tucker have appeared there. All these hotels are there for the gambling but the bigger they are the more important are the stars who appear in them. After Las Vegas, they've booked us into Ciro's in Hollywood. It's a restaurant and nightclub. Everybody goes there.'

For all his optimism, Sullivan knew that he was taking a big gamble. Berry, back in Reigate, had paid their fares and given them two hundred pounds spending money. In 1957 foreign exchange regulations were severe and obtaining dollars was very difficult. Until they reached Las Vegas and Shirley stood in front of a microphone and sang they had only Berry's money to keep them going.

It really was America on a shoestring budget and if anything went wrong they'd be in trouble. The William Morris office knew of their difficulties but they dealt in salaries and could only pay out what Shirley earned. Lily paid her own way and could help a little but she was also travelling on a restricted budget.

Sullivan didn't want Shirley to know exactly how bad his

finances were. She was riding high on her success at the Café de Paris, telling journalists that she was going to buy a mink stole and Jaguar. The Café de Paris had been a great publicity coup, and had brought several offers of work. Hiring the diamonds had also been a good stunt, but the nine-week run, far from making money, had cost money. After deducting half of Shirley's salary at the Café for Jack Hylton, the remaining one hundred pounds had to cover Shirley and the pianist's salary plus Sullivan's expenses. It was never enough. Sullivan did not expect Shirley to understand, but he knew that if his gamble succeeded Shirley would have New York, Las Vegas and Hollywood to add to her list of successes, and all of America would one day open up for her.

An invitation to make a record for the Columbia label had brought them to New York. Although the session, with producer Mitch Miller, had been difficult and dispiriting, Michael had taken advantage of the visit to capitalise on an interview Shirley had given in London. She had told *Ebony*, the Afro-American magazine who ran a six-page feature on her, of her huge admiration for Sammy Davis Jr.

When they arrived in New York, the magazine was on the newsstands and Sullivan hired a publicity man, Ed Gollin, to give Shirley a night on the town that included a visit to the theatre to see Sammy Davis starring in *Mr Wonderful*. If they went backstage and met Sammy, even better. Sammy, one of the nicest and most generous of performers, told Shirley he had read the feature, loved it, and promptly invited them both to supper because 'You've been saying such nice things about me.'

Sammy took them to a famous restaurant, Danny's Hideaway, and afterwards to see Frank Sinatra, who was appearing at the Copacabana. Davis and Sinatra were close pals; they had formed a little group along with Dean Martin and Peter Lawford which became known as 'The Rat Pack'.

After the show Frank Sinatra came to sit at the head of the table. Frankie didn't like being looked at, he didn't like being spoken to, in fact that night Frankie didn't care for human contact. Four gorillas in dinner jackets kept the unitiated away. Shirley bent forward to take a look at him, another of her idols, and a woman shoved her back. The women were just as bad as the men.

The owner of the Copacabana, Joe Padella, came and sat next to Shirley. He looked pretty tough, too. 'Whadda ya do?' he asked her. 'Sing,' she replied. 'Where?' he asked. 'I open in Las Vegas next week.'

'Okay, sing for me.'

Shirley told him that she was under contract to the El Rancho. She was sorry but she couldn't sing for him.

'You gotta sing for Joe Padella!' He got up, glaring at her, then he shouted, 'Hey, Frank, this dame won't sing for me.'

He started getting mad and walking up and down. Sinatra ignored him which made him even more angry. 'Frankie!' he yelled.

Frank Sinatra was busy talking to someone. 'Never mind, Joe,' he called back, waving a hand at him to sit down. 'Never mind.'

One of the gorillas came round to ask Joe to stop bothering Frankie. There was an argument. Somebody pushed somebody. The tension in the Copacabana suddenly increased.

Shirley whispered to Ed Gollin, 'Let's go. I'm frightened.' Sammy Davis noticed what was happening. Swiftly and discreetly he ushered Shirley and Ed Gollin out to his waiting car, and instructed his chauffeur to take them back to their hotel. The incident had rather taken the gloss off the evening, but it was nevertheless a special night for Shirley Bassey who before long, would join the ranks of the famous is whose company she had briefly found herself.

*

Las Vegas looks a magical place from the air, especially when seen for the first time. Night had fallen and the plane flew over miles of dark empty desert until, suddenly, a long strip of light appeared below. As the plane banked, the brilliant coloured neons of the 'We Never Close' hotels grew nearer and Shirley could even see the hotel where she was going to stay illuminated in a giant sign: El Rancho.

On the drive from the airport, Shirley and Lily ooh'd and aah'd at the neon signs announcing that Peggy Lee or Tony Martin was appearing at this hotel or that. There was no sign over El Rancho that Shirley Bassey was coming, just a big one for the Lili St. Cyr show. 'Isn't she a stripper?' asked Lily. Inside the hotel they were assaulted by the terrible clatter of dimes going into fruit machines. Gambling was what Las Vegas was all about, never mind Peggy Lee or Tony Martin or Shirley Bassey. Any singer and her manager were small fry, the entertainment was just to provide a pleasant background during dinner, and the quicker the punters got back to gambling, the better.

Shirley and Lily couldn't wait to get at the fruit machines, either, after Sullivan checked them all in. The management told him that Shirley would be expected to have three evening gowns, but she'd only got two. 'Then get her another from the store in the arcade and we'll take it off her pay check!' The El Rancho management behaved in the grand manner, but their clientele was mostly composed of little old ladies wearing brightly coloured crimplene trousers and white canvas plimsolls. However, Michael soon found out that it was these little old ladies who paid for a highball and dinner and demanded that the singer wear haute couture dresses.

Las Vegas brought one surprise after another. Shirley was installed in a beautifully appointed wooden chalet in the grounds, but Michael and Lily had to stay in a motel. It was Shirley's only free night – she would open the following evening – so Michael took the two girls on the town to visit some of the other hotels on the strip. Next morning he was called to the apartment of Beldon Katleman, manager of El Rancho. In spite of the luxury of the apartment there seemed to be a hint of Mafia about the meeting. The handsome Jewish gent who lounged back in a white towelling bathrobe was, on the face of it, quite friendly about Sullivan's lack of local know-how, but there was no mistaking the veiled threat as he took Michael to task about the previous evening's outing. 'No more nightclubbing with that girl of yours,' Katleman warned. Don't do it again, unless you want to be stoned or beaten up. They don't like it in this town. You'd better tell her.

But Michael never did tell her. He was shocked at this blatant racism, and couldn't bring himself to mention it to Shirley, even when she voiced her surprise that nobody was asking her out on a date after the show. He had once asked her if she had ever suffered any discrimination and she'd replied, 'It means nothing.' She'd told him how her mother being white had made a big difference to her and how, when kids at school called her 'Blackie', 'I didn't cry. I used to punch them. Let *them* cry.'

She had told him, too, about certain landladies on tour who would claim to be full. 'I just turned my back and never let it get the better of me. If people stare at me then I tell myself it's because I wear lovely clothes. Otherwise it would drive me mad.'

At the El Rancho, the guest singer was something served up with the dinner. Shirley was instructed to sing louder if the audience couldn't hear her – their was no question of their quieting down during her numbers. That was the attitude and she had to put up with it. It was a far cry from the attentive silence at the Astor or the Café de Paris, but at least the pay was good. After this experience, Shirley vowed that when she was really famous, she would never again allow herself to be thrown in with the dinner.

That, and the lack of male admirers, aside, Shirley enjoyed her first trip to Las Vegas. It was there that she bought a beautiful ranch mink, her first. It was dream come true, which Michael allowed her to have on condition that she undertook to pay it off at a hundred dollars a week. At her first press reception, she wore the mink draped on her shoulders.

Her first review came from a local columnist.

'Have you heard Shirley Bassey sing at El Rancho? This is news of the highest order. This twenty-year-old wonder from Cardiff, England [sic] opened in the feature spot at the Lili St. Cyr show. She is unbelievable, her voice is sensational, her delivery is strong and she is charm itself to look at. That quotient X that makes her a star, a full time star, is present in Shirley Bassey in full measure.'

The management of El Rancho booked Shirley to return for the next two years, but unfortunately the hotel caught fire and burned to the ground before the year was out. Shirley, Michael and Lily waved goodbye to Las Vegas with its Fort Knox hotels and mafiosi hoodlums with no regrets.

Shirley Bassey was on her way to Hollywood.

Sullivan rented a car and drove them across the desert to Los Angeles; 'I want a hotel with a swimming pool,' announced Shirley, as they drove down Sunset Boulevard. She'd been earning nearly two thousand dollars a week and deserved a swimming pool.

That evening the girls dolled themselves up for a night out at the famous Ciro's, Shirley had grown up in the postwar hey-day of cinema and loved to read all the fan magazines which peddled tales of stars such as Betty Grable or Rita Hayworth finding true love as they danced the night away at Ciro's. Anybody who was anybody had to be seen at Ciro's. When Michael and the girls walked in, however, it was obvious that ten years had passed since Tyrone Power danced with Lana Turner, and everyone knew Rita Hayworth had gone to live in Paris with her new husband, Prince Aly Khan.

It was very dark inside the club, but Michael nevertheless totted up the heads of the paying customers through the gloom and realised there were only thirty people listening to Frances Faye, the talented and famously risqué American entertainer. He wondered how the owner of this no longer very popular nightclub, who had brought them over from England, was going to dredge up two thousand dollars a week for Shirley. They sat down and ordered a drink as the band began to play. It was surprisingly good. Shirley smiled. If anyone could do it, she could.

Shirley's opening made a great impact on Sunset Boulevard. Some of the English colony attended, including Pamela Mason, wife of actor James Mason and daughter of the man who owned the Odeon cinema chain. She was one of the leaders of Hollywood society, and declared that Shirley had great talent, that she brought youth and freshness with her. Shirley was at her most electrifying at the opening and business at Ciro's improved. Unfortunately, even this didn't help the owner, Herman Hover. He offered Sullivan three hundred dollars and the rest next week. This went on throughout the six-week booking. It paid for Shirley's hotel but that was about all.

Then a bill arrived from Las Vegas; Shirley's gambling on the fruit machines had been put on to her El Rancho slate and this was one bill that had to be paid. Sullivan gave Shirley a stern lecture on the dangers of the little extras that mount up when put on your hotel bill. She must have taken this lecture to heart because for the rest of her life hotel bills were sacrosanct. One of the worst rows Bernard Hall ever had with Shirley was over the price of a cup of coffee he had drunk which found its way on to her hotel bill.

The William Morris agency came to the rescue and booked Shirley into the Riverside Room in Reno with their own guarantee of one thousand five hundred dollars a week. They would also attempt to recover some of Shirley's back pay from Herman Hover.

Shirley came into her own in Reno, a typical 'Wild West' town, where cowboys in stetsons still ambled around in search of rich divorcees, and there was probably still a stereotypical Sheriff in town. Shirley was a smash hit at the Riverside and she was happy and confident. She'd taken Las Vegas in her stride, and they wanted her back next year. She'd wowed them in Hollywood, so Reno was more like a holiday. She could do her act, then afterwards she could take her pick from the many invitations that flooded in and go out to have some fun.

There was no shortage of proposals in this town where divorce was so easy. Shirley was in a romantic mood when one of her suitors started talking about a wedding, and before she knew it she was engaged and being congratulated over the local radio. Fortunately, she quickly came to her senses, realising that she had fallen for a line, and broke the 'engagement'.

She had two more proposals which were fun – but she didn't take them too seriously. There was a convention of midgets taking place in Reno and most of them fell in love with Shirley. One of her songs was the 'Let's Do It', and one of the lines in the song was, *'even little men who have to reach do it.'* One of her admirers, a gentleman midget, sat right in front. Shirley asked one of the Moroccan acrobats on the same bill, what she should do. 'The last thing I want is to hurt him.'

'Don't change a word,' came the sensible advice. 'Just look him in the eye, give him one of your best smiles, and sing it.'

The week before they left Reno to return home, a letter came from Johnny Franz with the great news that, 'The Banana Boat Song' had gone into the charts. Johnny Franz's faith in Shirley had been justified and, in time, thousands of pounds of royalties would come rolling in. Michael Sullivan now had a top performer on his hands, and could bargain as never before. Back in England, Shirley's record would be playing everywhere, on BBC TV, on ATV, and on all the radio stations.

The name Shirley Bassey had real power now. Sullivan called Leslie Grade in London. Without hesitation, Leslie, a really great agent and booker, said he would like to present Shirley Bassey in variety, and would pay their airfares back to London.

Shirley really began to grasp the fact that fame had arrived when Johnny Franz met her at Heathrow with a battery of press photographers and a toy boat filled with bananas. She was driven from the airport to a suite at the Mayfair Hotel, where she would meet the press and the booking agents. She loved the luxury suite to which she was shown. 'It's going to cost you sixty pounds a day,' warned Sullivan, reminding her that she now paid her own bed and board; this was not Olivelli's. Shirley beguiled the press and delighted the bookers and, the following day, told Sullivan she had received an invitation she could not refuse. She was going to stay with the mother of an old friend, absolutely rent-free. 'Who?' asked Sullivan, determined to keep his eye on this valuable girl. 'Gloria Davies,' replied Shirley.

Gloria was the sister of Pepe Davies, the boy who gave her a backhander during the run of *Such is Life*, and who nearly ruined her first night at the Café de Paris when he wrapped his car around a steel gate. This boy was bad news for Shirley. 'I thought that was all over,' Michael said. 'Do you know what you're doing?'

Shirley told him that the accident had changed Pepe. He had been very ill for a long time but now he was all right, and she could handle the situation. She'd be sharing a room with Gloria. 'Where do they live?' Sullivan asked. He was fearful of the situation, but Shirley was no longer the naïve teenager, and she had a mind of her own. Of course, saving sixty pounds a day was a consideration, but he thought Shirley would be unwise to allow this troubled boy back into her life. Sullivan remembered him as a fair, rather average-looking boy. Shirley, deliberately vague, waved away all thoughts of problems.

Leslie Grade arranged another Hippodrome provincial tour for Shirley. This time, it was a number one tour and, for the first time, Shirley Bassey would have top billing. To her delight, the third week of her tour would be in her home town, Cardiff. Sullivan too, was delighted at this news; there was nothing he enjoyed more than a publicity campaign. He got in touch with Jack Thomas, a friendly Welsh journalist based in London. 'Tell me all about Cardiff,' he asked 'We must plan a great big homecoming.'

Shirley, of course, knew all about Cardiff. She was thrilled to be going home. The first thing she would do would be to see her mother and Sharon. And she had wonderful news. For the first time in her life she had earned big money in America, and now she had a hit record that would eventually bring in more money. At last she could find enough ready cash for a down-payment on a house for her mother, not just any house, but one in a nice location on the Newport Road, towards the soft green hills of Wales, and away from the docks and the sea and Splott.

This was the first of three houses that Shirley bought for her mother. It wasn't very big – just one bedroom – but her mother said it was big enough for her, and so light and airy. In the years to come Shirley would buy Eliza another larger house and then a bungalow.

'I've got everything I want,' declared Mrs Bassey Mendi. She'd been a widow for some time now. She had heard that her first husband, Henry Bassey, was dead, and that Mr Mendi had also died. She confessed to a journalist that she had never found problems with her mixed marriages. Living as she had done in Tiger Bay, where races intermixed freely, she had found no problems. She had never wanted to travel or leave her small corner of Cardiff. She did not think her marriages had affected Shirley. But her own life had been so enclosed, she could understand the problems that Shirley might encounter in the big world outside.

Eliza Mendi loved all her family but, houses aside, Shirley's visits always brought her special pleasure. She'd given Shirley a charm for her bracelet, a gold disc shaped like a gramophone record, which Shirley always wore. Her mother always said how generous her youngest daughter was; how she would pay to have the house painted when it needed it, how she always brought her mother the beautiful bouquets she'd been given. 'She was always like that,' Eliza recalled. 'Even as a little girl everyone had to have a present at Christmas. She even saved up and bought me a teaset once.' Shirley would talk about taking her mother abroad with her one day, but Eliza preferred to stay put, happy in her new home. She said, 'I've had hard times, but now they are all over. I do worry over Shirley, it's only natural isn't it? But God rewards, and I couldn't have anything better in the world than to know she thinks of me.'

There was something else Shirley could do while she was in Cardiff – talk to her sister Iris about Sharon. Shirley knew perfectly well that Iris and Bill wanted to adopt the child, whom they loved very much. Sullivan was always saying, 'Why don't you let your sister adopt Sharon? You're going to travel around the world and you can't drag a kid along with you.' Shirley did not agree, she would never let anyone adopt Sharon. She'd gone along with Sullivan's insistence that Sharon must be kept a secret for the time being, but some day, perhaps when she was well-known, people would be more understanding and it wouldn't destroy her career.

She had another worry. She was going back to the New Theatre in Cardiff with top billing. In 1954 she had appeared there in the cast of *Hot from Harlem* and the locals in Tiger Bay thought it was a sleazy revue. In 1956 she had gone there in variety with second billing, but now in 1957, like a dream come true, she was going home, top of the bill, and was worried sick that they wouldn't like her.

Sullivan said, 'What about that club you used to belong to? Wasn't it called the Rainbow Club? Now how about making them a presentation?' Shirley was immediately suspicious. Sullivan had a way of making her money disappear. 'It'll come out of publicity expenses,' he explained. 'I think two hundred and fifty pounds might be a good idea.' Shirley was impressed. This was a large sum, and the Rainbow Club had once been an important part of her young life.

The rousing song, 'There'll be a welcome in the hillsides when we come home again to Wales', could have been Sullivan's theme song. He was going to leave no stone unturned. There'd be bands, there'd be fanfares, trumpets, bugles, and maybe a ladies orchestra with the girls wearing those tall black Welsh hats. A big parade, of course, perhaps a Druid or two and a Welsh choir. And behind it all, would come the open limousine with Shirley Bassey enthroned on the back seat, brushing away a tear as she waved to the crowds lining the streets.

'Forget it, Mr Sullivan,' said the Cardiff police when Sullivan went round to show them his itinerary. 'This will be on a Sunday, you say. In this town people go to church on a Sunday.'

'But I'm bringing home one of your National treasures,' pleaded Sullivan.

'Not on a Sunday,' said the cops.

'But people in show business have to travel on Sundays. Last show Saturday night, open Monday matinee.'

'In Wales you will still be arrested, Mr Sullivan.'

Sullivan neglected to tell Shirley about the risk of arrest if they went ahead with his plan. In fact he didn't tell her anything at all about her welcome home. Much better to make it a surprise, especially if they arrested her. And if that did happen, it would certainly make the front pages, which would be no bad thing. However, he did abandon some of the wilder elements of his scheme.

British Railways were much easier to deal with than the Cardiff police. They agreed to a great banner being tied across the front of the train while it rested at a red light outside Cardiff Station. When the train arrived, the platform was five-deep with members past and present of the Rainbow Club, and as the train glided in, the band of the Boy Scouts struck up, closely followed by the big drums of the Boys' Brigade.

Shirley's surprise at her reception was so great that she began to cry. She was still weeping when a little dark girl, her hair arranged in plaits on top of her head, handed her a huge bouquet of lilies and irises as she was led outside to where the limousine awaited her. Perched high on cushions with her ranch mink stole draped behind her, surrounded by garlands of flowers, and the bouquet on her lap, Shirley brushed away her tears and smiled for the photographers. The big parade set off down the wide mile towards the Queen's Hotel. 'Start waving,' whispered Sullivan. More shining limousines followed, filled with newspaper staff and photographers, waving flags and dispensing balloons. Cars from *The Empire News*, *The People* and *Phillips' Records*.

Six hundred people lined the streets, and Shirley, who'd only seen this kind of thing in the movies, outdid them all, waving, throwing kisses and having fun. She was back where she grew up and she recognised faces in the crowd and exchanged greetings. 'Yes, it's great to be home,' she shouted.

Outside the Queen's Hotel, the family waited. Shirley's mother, of course, her sister Iris, with little Sharon, her other sisters and her brother Henry, and the sisters' husbands and children. Screams of joy from them all, then tears and laughter, and little Sharon clung to the skirts of her beautiful Auntie Shirley. Shirley Bassey was well and truly home again.

Inside the restaurant champagne was drunk until the luncheon that Sullivan had arranged was ready to be served. The family sat down at a large round table, talking animatedly and Sullivan suddenly felt like an intruder. He decided not to join them.

The formal handing over of the cheque for the Rainbow Club took place on the stage of the New Theatre at the end of the second house on Monday. Later that week Shirley went back to the Rainbow Club in Tiger Bay. 'I only left here about three years ago,' she told the children, 'but it seems such a long time ago now.' Perhaps she remembered that night when she stood outside the Freeman's house shouting up to a window 'Iris! Open up. We're going to London. We've been discovered.'

9

HOSTAGE IN ROOM 5XK

SHIRLEY CAME BACK from Wales ready for anything. The homecoming had been more wonderful than she had ever imagined. At the Rainbow Club where she used to dance and sing as a kid, she'd been fêted like a princess. Not only had the children loved her, but all of Tiger Bay seemed to be squashed in that small hall to hear her sing. She'd worn her stage dress, the oyster silk covered with pearls and a big puff of tulle round the bottom. They were so proud of her that she cried when she went on stage, but inside she felt as happy and excited as if she were at the London Palladium singing before the Queen. When it was over young Neil Sinclair from Frances Street had handed her a beautiful bouquet of flowers. Talk about a perfect homecoming. It had been magic.

Even Leslie Grade couldn't put a damper on her high spirits when he told Sullivan to ease up. 'Stop calling her a star,' Grade admonished, 'in my eyes she's still a beginner. Now if I can get her somewhere top-notch like the London Hippodrome and you can keep the house filled, then we'll see. Forget the Café de Paris. Just show me that she won't flop in bigtime London.'

That didn't bother Shirley, she knew she could fill the London Hippodrome. They had to wait for that two weeks Leslie Grade had promised to come along, but Sullivan had another tour worked out, this time in Europe. The only shadow on Shirley's horizon was Pepe Davies' attitude towards her. She enjoyed living with his family, but he always made such a fuss when she went away on tour. And he didn't seem to understand that she needed to be taken out at night after the show. Rehearsing all day then performing in cabaret was hard work, especially when one had to pack up every few days and move and on to the next city. She deserved some fun now and then. If only Pepe wasn't so jealous. She knew Sullivan would say 'Serve you right' if she asked his advice.

While she was in Cardiff her old friend Annis Abraham, who had a nightclub in Cardiff, told her about a special cure for acne his sister had discovered in Egypt. Shirley's skin had always worried her, so if Sullivan was arranging quick tours to Scandinavia, Belgium and Monte Carlo, why not one to Cairo as well? 'Cairo!' cried Sullivan when Shirley brought up the idea of a tour to Egypt. 'We've been kicked out of the Suez Canal. They don't even like us over there. We're going to Belgium anyway.'

Shirley enjoyed the European tour. Berry, Sullivan's partner, and his wife Sylvia went with Shirley to Belgium. Sylvia always remembered one particular nightclub owner's enthusiasm for Shirley's performance. 'I've never heard anyone like her,' he told Sylvia. 'As soon as she starts singing, the customers sit up. She's electric.'

The two girls had fun together, even giggling at the strange toilets where an old woman gave them each one sheet of toilet paper and where the men walked in too. Sylvia found Shirley as young and unspoilt as ever, but realised that Sullivan was still very tough with her. He demanded that Shirley give her best at every performance, which, indeed, she did, but he would blow up her ego one week, then deflate it the next. 'There is a difference between a star and Miss Shirley Bassey,' he would say. 'It is about one thousand pounds a week. Remember that, so no more tantrums until you're earning a lot more money.'

Shirley was a girl full of spirit and Sylvia was sure that one of these days she'd explode and tell Sullivan to go to hell for good.

One of Shirley's bookings was at the Sporting Club in Monte Carlo. It was always an honour to be asked to sing at a charity gala, but not always a pleasure to entertain the spoilt international set. A fortune was always spent on the flowers, the guests always wore their most exclusive couture gowns and finest diamonds, but their manners were appalling. They came to look at each other and gossip.

Sullivan had been warned that these events were often a case of 'take the money and run', because the audience didn't give a damn who was singing. But he knew that Shirley, young and inexperienced, would think that the rudeness of this particular audience meant that she had failed to please.

The manager of the club told Sullivan, 'You must warn your singer that her name, Shirley Bassey, is unknown here. She won't go down well. No-one does. Even Marlene Dietrich was ignored. Complete silence!'

'She'll be very hurt,' said Sullivan. 'It's her first time here.'

'Then tell her a little lie, that because the Sporting Club is open to the sea the applause floats away.

Back in her dressing room Shirley was on top of the world. She had met the son of a Greek millionaire who had a yacht in the harbour. He was in the audience and she was seeing him after the show.

The stage was built high and Shirley could not easily see what the audience were doing at their flower bedecked tables – ignoring her while they ate, drank and talked. At the end of Shirley's performance the applause was negligible. Afterwards she said to Sullivan, 'You were quite right, the applause does float out to the sea.'

It didn't matter because Shirley went on to sing at another nightclub for the next seven days where she was a great success. The Sea Club as it was called, was somewhat downmarket. It was partly in the open air and a big tree grew right in the middle of the club floor. At the Sea Club everyone was crazy about Shirley, and Shirley was crazy about her new Greek boyfriend.

Bernard Hall, 'Balls', came back from a tour with his twelve beautiful English girl dancers and someone said to him, 'Did you know that Shirley Bassey was here? She stayed at that little hotel on the hill.' He drove up to ask the owner of the hotel about Shirley. He felt sad that he had missed her, but that was how it was in show business. He was packing up to go back to Paris for the winter and disbanding his troupe of girls. At the end of the season he found them exhausting and he was glad to be going solo again in the Parisian boîtes.

Noël Coward, who came to Paris often, loved to hear about Bernard's experiences on tour. 'I have to act like their mother,' Bernard would tell him in exasperation. 'They even ask me to go out and buy their damned Tampax.' Noël wrote a novella about Bernard and his girls, and it was published under the title *Me and My Girls.*

In London autumn had arrived and Leslie Grade said he was not only booking Shirley into the London Hippodrome, he was backing the show. 'She had better be good,' he told Sullivan. He pointed out that even some of the world's biggest stars could come unstuck when they took a chance at London's theatreland.

Sullivan and Shirley quarrelled over the tight gold lamé dress he wanted her to wear. She wanted something lacy and full. Sullivan was right and he won. He also thought that the first half of Leslie Grade's show was tacky, the acts not good enough, but Leslie Grade naturally disagreed, and overruled him. Grade also thought that Sullivan's idea of a giant oyster shell from which Shirley would emerge was ostentatious. 'It will never work,' he said. But Sullivan had his way on that one, and it did work. As always, Shirley rose to the occasion and made a spectacular entrance through the clouds of pink chiffon that veiled the oyster shell. A reviewer next day wrote. 'The magic of her hands, her vibrant throbbing voice. She looked like a dream. A new star was born. I saw it happen.' At the end of two weeks Shirley Bassey had conquered London as top of the bill at the London Hippodrome. She was not yet twenty-one years old.

Shirley was going out to Australia to work at the Tivoli Theatre in Sydney as soon as her next engagement at a Mayfair nightclub was over. However, Michael Sullivan, who'd had a chest complaint, decided to leave earlier, not only for the beneficial sunshine but also to arrange advance publicity and get the giant oyster shell built. Her act would be exactly the same as the one they had presented at the London Hippodrome.

Michael's carefully laid plans were upset when he received a worrying telephone call from a lady in Bayswater. He'd been concerned about Shirley's private life for some time, ever since they'd returned from America in fact. Her living with the Davies family in Bayswater obviously had its advantages, and they were a nice family, but there was the young and lovesick Pepe. He did not accept the relationship was over and that Shirley had men lining up in droves to take her out.

Mrs Davies telephoned Sullivan to explain that she had asked

Shirley to leave, and as he was her manager would he please find her accommodation elsewhere. Her son found it hard to cope with Shirley going on dates with other men. From her tone, he understood that there had been some trouble.

Sullivan booked Shirley into the Cumberland Hotel at Marble Arch, just a short taxi ride away from the Bagatelle, the nightclub off Berkeley Square where she would be appearing. It was a good hotel, moderately priced, and Shirley was duly settled into room 5XK.

With Shirley organised, Michael prepared to leave for Australia as planned. Two days before his departure, he attended band call at the Bagatelle, to find Shirley far from happy. She complained that the music was all wrong, and she wanted the pianist changed. Michael calmed her down, but he felt very uneasy. As it happened, Shirley's stint at the Bagatelle did turn out to be successful and before he wished her goodbye to catch his plane to Sydney, Sullivan asked her to be sure to get in touch with Berry and Sylvia if she needed help of any kind. Shirley agreed that Berry would act as her manager in Michael's absence. He reminded her that 'the boys' (her dressmakers) had promised to deliver her new dress on time, and he told her to have a good rest on the Sunday before she took the plane. He'd be waiting for her at Sydney airport.

In the early hours of Monday, 10 November 1957, the strident ring of the bedside telephone woke Sylvia Clarke at her home in Reigate. She switched on the light and picked up the receiver. Who on earth could be calling at this time of night? A man's voice said, 'I've got some bad news for you. Shirley Bassey has been murdered.'

Sylvia came awake with a jolt. 'What are you talking about? Who are you? Where are you?'

'I'm there,' said the man. 'They're inside you see. I heard the gun-shot. But the music keeps playing. It's Frank Sinatra's "Swinging Affair."'

Berry, who had woken up and taken one look at his wife's stricken face, took the receiver from her. 'Who's there?' he cried, but the line went dead. The phone range again almost immediately. This time it was the police. They wanted to know if they were speaking to Mr Leonard Beresford Clarke, the partner of Mr Michael Sullivan?

'What's happened?' Berry was getting agitated. 'Has Shirley been hurt?'

The policeman hesitated. 'It's a difficult situation. The young man has barricaded the door. Do you know this boy? His name is Terence Clyde Davies?' Berry looked at Sylvia as he repeated the name.

'It's Pepe, the boy who crashed his car. Shirley's been living with his family. Is it true what that man said? Is Shirley dead?'

Berry continued his urgent questions to the police and finally put the receiver down.

'Pepe's got a gun. He's holding Shirley prisoner in a room at the Cumberland. They're trying to prevent him from killing her. His father's on the way over to try and get her out. And you say this Pepe is just a boy. My God!'

Sylvia never forgot that terrible night, waiting to know whether Shirley was dead or alive.

Sullivan was roused in Sydney. The British *Daily Telegraph* was ringing their Sydney Office. 'Get Sullivan. Tell him Shirley Bassey's in a shooting but we don't know how bad it is yet.' A shocked Sullivan hurried to the *Telegraph* office and spent a sleepless night there, waiting for the tape machines to flash out news. Nothing happened, the telephone lines were blocked.

Meanwhile, a terrified Shirley Bassey was suffering much more than either Berry or Sullivan. She was trapped in her room at the

Cumberland with a crazed boy who held a loaded gun to her stomach and said he was going to kill her. She knew the gun really was loaded because he had already blasted the telephone to pieces.

Shirley described it afterwards, 'It was Sunday night. I came back from the cinema with my friend Peter Quinton. We went up to my room because I had to wait for the delivery of the green dress I was taking on my tour. It was special, there was a lovely stole embroidered with emeralds, they weren't real but they shone marvellously.'

The phone rang while she and Peter were chatting. She knew who it was at once. Pepe! 'I've got some flowers for you, Ma'am,' he said in a fake American accent intended to confuse her. 'What's your room number please?'

'How come you deliver flowers at midnight? Shirley asked. 'Take them back to your mother in Bayswater.' She put the phone down.

Peter Quinton knew all about this ex-boyfriend. As far as Shirley was concerned it was a love affair that was over long ago. She was still friends with Pepe's sister, but he had to understand that she didn't want to see him any more. The year before when he was in hospital after the car crash he had asked her to marry him. She didn't take it seriously, but she said yes because the doctor told her not to upset him. Now the relationship was over once and for all, and she wished he'd leave her alone. And was leaving for Australia the next day. She asked Peter not to open the door to anyone unless he knew who was there.

While she was in the bathroom, Peter opened the door to the 'two boys' bringing the green gown. It was admired, and Shirley started packing it into her big blue travelling trunk. There was another knock and one of the boys innocently answered it.

That was when it all started. Shirley heard a shot. She jumped, and when she turned round the boys had gone. And Peter, with blood streaming from a wound on his forehead, was wrestling with Pepe. Shirley screamed, 'He's got a gun', Peter had obviously been hit over the head with it. Suddenly Pepe moved towards her and Shirley felt the gun pressed into her stomach. Pepe yelled, 'Tell him to get out or I'll pull the trigger. I'll kill you.'

Peter staggered out of the room to get help, and Pepe started barricading the door. He seemed to go mad. He pulled her heavy blue trunk across the room and pushed it against the door, then, suddenly gaining enormous strength, picked up a chest of drawers and heaved it on top of the trunk. He started shoving chairs and side tables, everything movable in the room, against the door. With that done, Pepe began shouting how much he loved her and why didn't she love him in return? How many men had she had before him? His mother had told him about these men. Did she know what his mother had said? He was ranting and raving, she'd never seen him as bad as this.

He ordered her to switch on her record player and the room was filled with the sound of Sinatra singing 'Night and Day'. Pepe demanded a drink. All she had was liqueur whisky. He poured some down his throat, didn't like it, and spat it out. Then he made Shirley telephone his mother and tell her he was going to kill her then himself.

Shirley got his mother on the phone and passed on the message. Mrs Davies laughed, she didn't believe her. So Pepe snatched the phone and repeated his threats. Then he fired into the instrument, which shattered into a hundred fragments. This noise made the police outside the door start shouting, 'Let the girl out!' The dog they had with them started to bark, and Shirley want to scream, but knew she must not do this. It did something to him. What was she going to do? She had to control herself because Pepe had these lightning changes of mood due to his injuries in the car accident. A sudden movement might make him pull the trigger.

In the meantime, police had moved the people out from a room that faced Shirley's across the courtyard. Shirley's curtains weren't drawn so they had a reasonably good view of what was going on. Pepe sat on the bed fiddling with the gun. He demanded that Shirley change the record every time it finished, and he demanded that Shirley kiss him. She refused. He said, 'Kiss me or I'll pull the trigger.' She shook her head. There was another explosion as he fired the gun again, and Shirley blacked out. The police watched from the room opposite. Shirley came to. 'Now will you kiss me,' Pepe demanded of Shirley, 'or shall I kill you.' This time she acquiesced. It was a nightmare.

Then Pepe's father arrived to try and persuade his son to see reason. From beyond the locked door, Mr Davies shouted, 'Come out, son. She's not worth the trouble. It's all her fault,' but his pleading only enraged Pepe further, and he fired two shots into the door. Then he noticed the window. He jerked the curtains partly closed, and told Shirley to take off her clothes.

As Shirley recounted to Sullivan on her arrival in Sydney, 'By now I was getting hysterical. I'd been in this room with him for over two hours. He kept jumping up and down, jerking the gun as if to shoot. Then he'd sit and listen to the music. "Take your clothes off," he kept saying. So I removed my sweater and skirt. I was now in bra and pants. But, like Pepe, I realised that the peep show might still be going on. People were watching us. "Take it all off," he said. I didn't want to do it, but by now I'd given up. When I took the rest off, he pushed me on to the bed and started kissing me. And it was all quiet and I thought he would go all the way. Suddenly a detective got worried about the quietness in the room and started banging on the door. This made Pepe suddenly jump and seemed to take him mind off everything. He pointed the gun and fired at the door again.'

Shirley was now crying uncontrollably and begging Pepe to let her go. She was on her hands and knees and pleaded with him. Suddenly, his mood switched 'Do you want to go?' he asked.

'Yes,' begged Shirley.

At this, he shouted at the police outside the door. 'Hey, you out there, are you still there? I'm going to let her go. I don't want to see any of you when I open the door. Keep out of my sight. If I see you I'll kill you. And I'll kill her too.'

The detectives shouted, 'All right, you won't see us. We'll go.'

'I was frantic in case he changed his mind again,' says Shirley. 'I stood there waiting. I asked him if I could get dressed, and he said yes.

'I didn't dare fiddle around with underwear, so I reached for my skirt and sweater.' She watched Pepe drag down the barricade and prayed that no-one outside would interfere. He then opened the door and pushed her out. Shirley said, 'I just collapsed. Somebody, I think it was a policeman picked me up and carried me to a bed. I remember seeing Peter with a towel around his head. I must have been conscious but inside there was this hysteria. I couldn't move. I just lay on this bed. I never did sleep the whole night. Someone kept coming in and looking at me then going out, but I never knew who this was. I heard them say that they had got the boy out and he had fired into his own leg. A detective from Scotland Yard came in and said he wanted a statement. A few minutes after that a doctor gave me an injection.'

Sylvia back in Reigate had the first positive news. 'She's out. She's alive!' She never did find out who the man was that had first telephoned her to say that Shirley had been murdered. Sullivan had to wait a few more hours for relief, when the tape machine flashed 'Shirley Bassey leaves London airport en route for Australia.

Next morning the police questioned Shirley. She told them her story and they informed her that Pepe was in hospital, because he had indeed shot himself in the leg – accidentally, they said. The press got their stories, and one reporter came in and told Shirley that he had seen everything through the window. That worried her more than anything. How many people had seen her in the nude?

'I've had a terrible time,' said Shirley, when she spoke to the journalists. 'I thought I was going to die. They were the most terrifying hours of my life.' The daily newspapers in London printed Shirley's story as she flew to Australia, but none of them could describe exactly what had happened, for Shirley was still in a state of shock at this point and the full details weren't known.

Peter Quinton, a piece of plaster over the wound on his forehead, escorted Shirley in a chauffeur-driven car to Heathrow, and saw her safely in to the terminal. Shirley said goodbye to him and climbed aboard a plane for the arduous thirty-six hour flight to Sydney, Australia.

Only yesterday, when her two-week booking at the Bagatelle ended, she'd been packing her trunk and looking forward to going to the cinema with Peter. Suddenly on their return, in the small hours mayhem had erupted and brought her close to death. Now she was on a plane to Sydney, still suffering shock from the ordeal. Only Shirley's strength of character and her fortitude had got her through the whole horrific experiences, and would carry her through the testing days ahead.

Australia Welcomes Shirley Bassey

A giant banner greeted the exhausted singer on her arrival at Sydney Airport, where Sullivan had laid on as much razzamatazz as he could muster. On the tarmac with her manager were three television cameras and crews, twenty journalists, bouquets of flowers and a big stuffed kangaroo. Inside the airport building was another TV crew where a special stage and microphone for Shirley had been set up beside a large table laden with drinks and an iced 'Welcome Shirley' cake.

Sydney airport in 1957 was comparable to the old Gatwick – a nice little country airport – but that day in November it was all geared up to receive the heroine of the hour. She came towards them looking drained and rather miserable, the result of her recent ordeal and a thirty-six hour flight. The journalists waved their notepads and shouted 'Coo-ee!' While the TV cameras took in the picture of Michael Sullivan with his arms wide getting ready to hug Shirley. She marched up to him, evaded the hug and hissed, 'You sent me tourist class! Do you know what I've been through? Then you put me through thirty-six hours of misery!' She stalked off, pent up with rage and fury, and in such a hurry that she collided with the mob of journalists.

Sullivan grabbed a bouquet and chased after her. Shirley pushed her way relentlessly past the journalists, giving them the old Tiger Bay heave-ho. One of them unwisely brought up the words 'gun' and, 'shooting'. Shirley snapped, 'Why don't you try it sometime?'

Another called, 'How about now, Miss Bassey? She hit him with her handbag. 'Get out of my way.'

Sullivan, still clutching the battered bouquet, worked his way through the crowd trying to soothe the offended journalists. 'Poor girl's exhausted, that's what it is. Too much happening. All this is such a novelty for her.'

A boy who'd had his ankle kicked by mistake, groaned, 'She's a novelty all right.'

Then a tall handsome man stood in Shirley's path with an outstretched hand. 'Tivoli Theatres, Miss Bassey. I'm Bruce Gordon. Come with me. You've had a terrible time. My car's waiting.'

'Don't forget the press,' yelled Sullivan panting up to him. 'Television's waiting.'

Bruce Gordon was every girl's dream come true: tall, dark, handsome and rich. He could tame any tough Australian Sheila and knew he'd have no trouble handling Shirley. 'Just say hello to my folks all over Australia.' Sydney radio was transmitted to the whole of the continent.

As good as gold, Shirley mounted the stage in front of the television cameras and told Australia how glad she was to be there. 'You've no idea how glad. I just love the sunshine and I think that Sydney is wonderful.' She looked as if she meant if and, indeed, she did. Shirley loved Australia from the word go.

When Shirley had had a week to settle down and talk to Sullivan about what had happened to her, she began giving interviews to the press. One of her most successful was headlined, 'The Trouble I've had with Men,' in which she was quoted as saying, 'Everyone knows the trouble I had when my ex-boyfriend burst into my hotel room the night before I left to come here. I felt sorry for him. I liked him at first and went out with him for quite a while until I went to the States.' Then, explained Shirley she had met so many interesting men during her American tour that by the time she came back to London she had outgrown him.

Finally, after detailing the many reasons why and how men had brought her trouble, the article concluded with Shirley's declaration that, 'When a girl's reached the top she has to be careful of all kinds of things, but especially men.'

Shirley was indeed very attractive to many men; she had about her that touch of 'forbidden fruit' that was exciting, she was famous and glamorous. To Pepe Davies, she was the girl he loved with all his heart. After he had released her at the Cumberland, he had written and signed a suicide note which he pushed under the door to the waiting police. In it he wrote, 'Shirley Bassey is not to blame for the killing.'

Fortunately Pepe did no more than wound himself in the leg.

He was taken to St Mary's Hospital, Paddington, where he lay in bed, beat his chest and said, 'I want to suffer. Don't you understand what I have done?'

Superintendent Marner, who was at his bedside, told him that when he was fit to leave hospital he would be charged with an offence. He cautioned Terence Davies, who said, 'I know that. Look, I could have shot Shirley if I wanted to. But why should I? I love her. I just went mad at the time and now I want to suffer.'

Sullivan had arranged that they would spend all the winter in the sunshine of Sydney and Melbourne. Shirley was having a great success with the same exciting performance she'd given at the London Hippodrome. A replica of the giant pink and grey oyster shell had been built and Shirley's nightly entrance through it delighted the Australian audiences. There were plenty of offers for her from around the country.

Bruce Gordon had become her steady boyfriend and, when he was busy, Gaby Rogers of Phillips Records took her out, on trips to the Blue Mountains, the zoo and the beach. She was having fun at last. Her hotel room was always filled with flowers, she had a television, a record player and all the new records. Phillips were pleased that her records were selling well in Australia.

On a 100° Christmas Eve in 1957, Shirley, Sullivan and Lily, who was back on the scene and appearing at Sydney's Tivoli Theatre, went to a champagne party that carried on till the early hours. At the party, Lily found Shirley sitting in a corner looking very miserable. She explained sadly that she was homesick and she wished she was in Wales with her family. 'Every Christmas I used to get a pillowcase filled with presents,' she began to cry. People crowded round to cheer her up, while Lily and Michael decided that Shirley should have her pillowcase filled with presents.

After Shirley was tucked up in bed, Lily and Sullivan went

shopping in King's Cross, where they found a funny old shop that sold knick-knacks. They bought enough to fill a pillowcase. They weren't expensive gifts but they all looked very pretty when wrapped in gift paper and tinsel. Just before dawn Lily got herself up to look as much like Father Christmas as she could and crept into Shirley's room with the pillowcase. Unfortunately, at that moment Shirley suddenly woke up and saw that someone wearing a hood and long coat had got into her room. Terrified she screamed blue murder until Lily switched the light on and gave her the pillowcase.

Next day it was still one hundred in the shade, but they were all so worn out that they spent most of Christmas Day in bed, getting up only to eat their dinner and have a drink to wish each other a 1958 that held no more problems for any of them.

Back in London, Pepe made a short appearance in court and was granted bail. Some months later, while Shirley was still in Australia, Pepe appeared before Mr Justice Cassels at the Old Bailey. Pepe's barrister pleaded that his client had sustained brain injuries during his car crash and that, because of his 'bangs on the head', he was a very sick boy when he held Shirley Bassey prisoner at the Cumberland Hotel. Prosecuting counsel, Mr Christopher Humphries, called him 'a stupid, silly, lovesick youth,' and the Judge said in his summing up. 'You were in a hair's breadth of almost having to stand trial for what would have been a charge of murder.' He sentenced the accused to three years in prison, but Pepe was still declaring his love for Shirley as he was led down to the cells.

It was thought that Pepe had received a prison sentence because he had fired two shots at the door knowing the police were outside and he might have killed one of them.

*

In January 1958, Shirley Bassey celebrated her twenty-first birthday. She was now legally in control of her career. Sullivan promised that her new white Jaguar would be waiting for her when she arrived back in England. For years she had been in a vulnerable position, needing someone to guide her and Sullivan had been the strong man behind her. However, she didn't fully trust him. Interested parties, with an eye to taking her over themselves, told her that he was ripping her off financially and, although that may not have been true, she often believed it.

The relationship between Shirley and Michael would have to change.

Whatever his faults, however, Sullivan was an experienced member of his profession. He knew what to do when there was trouble, and when and if the next disaster struck Shirley, as it probably would, he could look after her and find some way to soften the blow. As it happened, trouble blew up quite quickly in the new year.

He was in the cinema late one particular afternoon. Halfway through the film his name was flashed on the screen with a request that he go at once to the Tivoli Theatre. He hurried there and found Shirley in her dressing room in hysterics. She was crying wildly but no-one could get any sense out of her. She had broken down in the middle of a song and started to cry. As soon as Sullivan saw her he knew the show must be cancelled, she wasn't fit to perform and he had to get her back to the hotel. He didn't attempt to question her, but when they reached the hotel he learned that she had received a frightening telephone call from London earlier that day.

Up in her room Shirley began to calm down and, gradually, she told Sullivan what had happened at the theatre. 'I was in the middle of the song' – her voice broke – 'suddenly it hit me. I know you always warned me and now it was happening. My career was over and everything was finished.'

They had found out about her baby; they were going to publish her story and make her out to be worthless, bad. 'Oh, Mikey,' What shall I do? I wish I was dead.'

10

A Very Important Property

The gentleman's agreement between Shirley and Fleet Street had ruptured just as Sullivan had predicted. Half the newspaperman in London had known for some time that Shirley Bassey had a daughter but they had sat on the story. Good luck to the kid, why harm her. Then someone wanted to sell a story, make a quick buck, and to hell with promises. Sullivan was philosophical about it. This story was too good to be kept under wraps much longer anyway now that Shirley was doing so well but, as Shirley said, it hadn't happened to him, had it?

Shirley's phone call that morning was from the Sydney representative of the London *Daily Sketch*, asking if she would be available to talk to a reporter from their London office. She would? Then they would book a telephone call to her from London. Shirley thought it was just another routine publicity call to ask her how she was getting on in Australia.

That afternoon the call came through, but instead of the usual cheerful greeting a brisk male voice said, 'It's about your baby, we're going to publish on Monday!' Shirley was stunned, paralysed with shock, as she listened to this strange man's voice. 'You can't stop us, we've got the birth certificate, that's proof enough.' He was talking about Sharon, her baby, her little daughter, as if she was some kind of commodity he was putting up for sale.

Shirley's shock and devastation was not overdone. This was the Fifties, and if a girl of sixteen had a baby she got rid of it by adoption, fast. Never mind if she wanted to keep the baby; usually the family could not bear the social stigma or, as in Shirley's case this baby had to be supported, so she sent part of her salary home every week. Sullivan had told her three years ago that if the newspapers found out about Sharon it might go against her badly and damage her career. In the popular imagination she was the tigress, the firebrand who tempted men, not the girl who hurried home to put a baby to bed. Brave single mothers were not welcomed by the English, and Australia was even more prudish. The news of an illegitimate child would not go down well here in Sydney.

When Shirley had the call Sullivan was unavailable, he'd said he was going to the cinema. Shirley sat on her bed, overcome with shock. She hadn't fully recovered from her ordeal in London; she still had nightmares about that night at the Cumberland. Would it never end?

She told Sullivan that she had laid down and closed her eyes. She could only take so much. Her whole being slowed down, and she must have fallen asleep. When she opened her eyes again she felt strangely numb and she didn't know why. To her surprise it was time to go to the theatre. Shirley said later that the shock had completely eradicated the phone call from her mind. All she knew was that she must go to the theatre.

At the theatre she went on as usual and was into her first song when her memory came back 'The telephone call! . . . It really hit me like a blow,' she says. 'For three years I'd had this secret, now it had ben ripped away from me and there it was. My wickedness would be splashed across a newspaper for everyone to see. I loved my daughter, I was not ashamed at all. But it was the way this was being done to me, so cold, so calculated. Selling my dearest secret for money. I seemed to turn to stone. I could not sing. I don't know what happened to me. And then someone put an arm around my shoulders and led me away to my dressing room.'

Sullivan had heard enough. He took over, he knew exactly what to do, they'd still got time. If this little bastard wanted to hurt Shirley, he knew he could find another newspaperman who might be willing to spike the little swine.

Arthur Helliwell, Tony to his friends, had a Sunday column in the high-circulation tabloid, *The People*. Tony had been with Sullivan that night at Churchill's nightclub three years ago when they had seen Ben Johnson's Ballet for the first time and Louise Benjamin had said, 'I know a singer called Shirley Bassey.' If the British public read an article slanted in Shirley's favour – and God knows the kid needed some luck – if the article came out the day before the *Daily Sketch* exposé, it would help her.

Sullivan put in an urgent call to Tony Helliwell and explained what had happened. Shirley then talked to Tony for three quarters of an hour. She told him the truth about what had happened to her, how much she had wanted her baby, how she had never considered allowing Sharon to be adopted in spite of great pressures. Sharon lived with her sister because her mother worked. If she had her way Sharon would be here in Australia with her. Shirley poured out her worries and her hopes. Tony said he would do his best, and his column on Sunday would be mostly Shirley's story.

An Australian magazine interviewed Shirley at Sullivan's instigation and the article was headlined, 'Give the girl a break.' In London on Sunday *The People's* column scooped the *Sketch's* unkind article, but on Monday the Australian radio and local newspapers did make the most of what they considered a juicy scandal. Reading the papers, Shirley grew increasingly anxious about appearing at the Tivoli that evening.

When she burst through those pink and grey folds of the oyster shell what would she find? A half-empty house? Would she smell the hatred and distrust that can rise like a miasma from an audience. Would they boo her? Shirley was very vulnerable, alone on that stage and very frightened.

She emerged through the clouds of chiffon and everyone seemed to be holding their breath, even the orchestra. A brief silence, then someone shouted 'Keep your chin up, Shirley!' Another yelled, 'Good on ya, Shirl!' The Australian audience knew it took guts to stand there in front of them. Sympathy for the girl suddenly overflowed and the clapping started. The applause grew, there was cheering, and Shirley bowed low to her audience. Then she brushed away her tears and sang.

After the show Shirley went back to her dressing room which, empty at the beginning of the evening, was now filled with flowers. Sullivan had not been at all sure which way the pendulum would swing. An audience cannot be influenced by a newspaper article, even if they've bothered to read it; admiration for a performer comes from the heart. Sullivan had kept the flowers hidden. If things went wrong they might be used as a comfort, but this was what they were really meant for – a celebration.

Shirley felt some good had come of this latest ordeal, despite the agony and fear. Her daughter, Sharon, was now hers in front of the world. During the rest of her Australian tour, the people took Shirley to their hearts. When they were in Melbourne and the

Queen Mother arrived on a State visit, Sullivan and Shirley were invited to a garden party. Shirley was excited at the prospect; she adored the Royal Family.

By the time they'd been in Australia for six months Sullivan knew it was important to go back to England or they might risk losing the momentum of Shirley's career there. As an added inducement to leave Australia, he told Shirley that her belated birthday present now had a number plate 'SB 19'. 'Two years late,' declared Shirley, but no girl minds losing a couple of years off her age.

Before they left Shirley developed abdominal pains that would not go away. It was the old trouble of an inflamed appendix and the doctor who was called advised her to stop swimming, whether in hotel pools or the sea, until the pains went away. The three of them, Sullivan, Lily and Shirley were going home via Hawaii and San Francisco.

Unable to swim, Shirley went shopping instead. Honolulu was designed for ardent souvenir hunters like Shirley, and she spent every dollar she had, determined to give her family the best gifts ever – and there was a big Hawaiian doll for Sharon.

Sullivan had warned Shirley about the dollar shortage and overspending and refused to pay Shirley's hotel bill. How did she think he was going to find the money?

'I don't know, you're my manager. You find it.'

Sullivan lost his temper, Shirley lost her temper and there was a great row. This was not unusual, everyone knew that they quarrelled constantly, but this was a particularly nasty one. Shirley shouted that she didn't expect him to give her the money, she just wanted to borrow it. 'Find me the fare to Milwaukee,' she cried, 'and I'll go and stay with my sister Gracie and get out of your way.'

He snapped back that he wasn't in the States for fun, he'd come to find Shirley some lucrative bookings.

CERTIFIED COPY OF AN ENTRY OF BIRTH
PI DILYS O GOFNOD GENEDIGAETH

GIVEN AT THE GENERAL REGISTER OFFICE, LONDON
FE'I RHODDWYD YN Y GENERAL REGISTER OFFICE, LONDON

Application No. } Y 2934
Rhif y cais }

| REGISTRATION DISTRICT / DOSBARTH COFRESTRU | Cardiff |

| 1934 | BIRTH in the Sub-district of / GENEDIGAETH yn Is-ddosbarth | Cardiff Central | in the County Borough of Cardiff / yn |

Columns: / Golofnau:-	1	2	3	4	5	6	7	8	9	10*
No. / Rhif	When and where born / Pryd a lle y ganwyd	Name if any / Enw os oes un	Sex / Rhyw	Name and surname of father / Enw a chyfenw'r tad	Name, surname and maiden surname of mother / Inw, cyfenw a chyfenw morwynol y fam	Occupation of father / Gwaith y tad	Signature, description and residence of informant / Llofnod, disgrifiad a chyfeiriad yr hysbysydd	When registered / Pryd y cofrestrwyd	Signature of registrar / Llofnod y cofrestrydd	Name entered after registration / Enw a gofnodwyd wedi'r cofrestru
	Eighth January 1937 182, Bute Street UD	Shirley Veronica	Girl	Henry Bassey	Eliza Jane Bassey formerly Metcalfe	Ship's Fireman (Mercantile Marine)	E.J. Bassey Mother 182, Bute Street Cardiff	Twenty third February	F.W. Lock	
								PM 7	Registrar	

Shirley aged six at Moorland Road Primary School, Splott.

Loudon Square, Tiger Bay, where Shirley played with Iris Freeman.

The famous Ship & Pilot pub down by the docks in Tiger Bay.

Shirley aged fourteen on a Moorland Road School holiday at Porthcawl, 1951.

BEN JOHNSON

WITH HIS DANCE GROUP

present

Espainia

"CARIBBEAN HEATWAVE"

BRITAIN'S MOST EXOTIC FLOOR SHOW

The Ben Johnson ballet group
(*above*) where Shirley was
engaged to sing in 1955, and
of which Shirley's friend
Louise Benjamin (*right*) was
a member.

Shirley on stage in 1956 at the Adelphi with the Al Read show, *Such Is Life.*

Shirley wearing the dress made especially for her first performance in the Hippodrome tour at Keighley.

New Theatre flier from 1958; Shirley tops the bill above the man who had auditioned her for Welsh radio in 1952, Wyn Calvin.

Shirley returns to a rapturous homecoming in Tiger Bay, and sings to her old community (*right*) in 1957.

A 1958 publicity shot

Shirley before a performance in Antwerp with Sylvia (*far left*) and
Berry Beresford-Clarke (*left*).

Shirley with her mother and two sisters, Marina (*left*) and Iris.

Shirley with Pepe Davies (*top*) and next to him her mother holding Shirley's daughter Sharon, and Sharon's foster parents Bill and Iris Denning with two children, 1956.

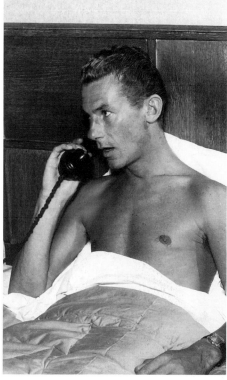

Shirley with American singer Johnny 'Cry' Ray on her Belgian tour.

Shirley's first manager, Michael Sullivan, recovering from TB before leaving for the Australian tour in 1957.

Shirley with her poodle Beaujolais in her Stanhope Place flat, 1958.

Shirley in Cannes, 1962.

Bernard Hall ('Balls') – friend, colleague and occasional lover, 1966.

Peter Finch

Shirley with first husband Kenneth Hume, Sharon and Samantha in 1964.

Shirley sings in cabaret, Melbourne, 1966.

Glittering and provocative: a trademark Bassey performance, Bournemouth, 1974.

(*Left*) Shirley in Las Vegas and her husband Sergio Novak, 1968.

Shirley's daughter, Samantha Novak with a baby (not her own) not long before her death in 1985.

Shirley with her family in Monte Carlo: Samantha (*left*), Mark, and Sergio (1977).

Shirley with her friend Baudouin Mills and her daughter Sharon, after receiving
the CBE at Buckingham Palace, 1994.

Shirley curtsies to the Queen, watched by Michael Caine and
actress Joan Collins (1998).

'You're supposed to be my manager,' she shouted at him, 'and you can't find me one hundred dollars.'

Shirley telephoned Berry and Sylvia in Reigate and asked them to wire money to her. She returned to London the next day and the Beresford Clarkes met her at the airport. Shirley had learned a lesson she never forgot. She had finally realised that she had to come to grips with her financial affairs and, in the years to come, she learnt as much about money matters as an accountant. Managements held their breath when she arrived. It wasn't easy to do Shirley Bassey down on a contract.

She had learned her lesson the hard way. Sullivan afterwards insisted he had left money for her at the hotel, that he had returned to the hotel later to make sure she was all right, and discovered she had not taken his money. Instead she had left him a note. In it she wrote, 'I hope you are happy with what you have done. May God forgive you because I never shall.'

It is quite likely that she meant those last few words, and probably the relationship between Shirley Bassey and Michael Sullivan began to deteriorate from that day. Berry was sure that Sullivan would never have abandoned her, but now he and Sylvia had a sick, unhappy girl on their hands and the first thing was get her well. The consultant who was called in to see Shirley agreed that her appendix needed watching and she must rest.

She was in an ideal place to recuperate, a large country house on the top of Reigate Hill that had thirty rooms and acres of land. Shirley fell in love with Sylvia's white Pekinese dog called Bumble. 'I wish I had a little dog like this to sit with me in my white Jaguar,' said Shirley and then mentioned Michael for the first time since her return. 'And where's the Jaguar that he promised me?' Which meant that she was now prepared to overlook the quarrel in San Francisco.

Michael arrived with the press and photographers and a white Jaguar with blue leather upholstery, and a big blue bow. Sylvia had arranged something else. In the driver's seat sat a little white poodle with a blue satin ribbon around his neck, straight from the Pilgrim's Rest Kennels on Reigate Hill. As Sylvia said, 'I'm not sure which Shirley liked best, the Jaguar or the dog.'

Leslie Grade was unimpressed with the press photographs of Shirley and her Jaguar. 'They'll be saying Shirley who?' he said scathingly. 'She's been away too long.' He agreed to send Shirley off on a provincial tour, but she had to climb back to the position she had held before she had gone to Australia.

Getting Shirley lost for a few days was Sullivan's first publicity ruse. SHIRLEY BASSEY MISSING! NATIONWIDE SEARCH FOR GIRL SINGER. IS SHE STILL ALIVE? Sullivan's ruse worked. Even the police believed him. The country was alerted to her face on the front page of every newspaper. Then a wily journalist found out that Sullivan had bought a return ticket to Bath, and the ruse turned sour. Sullivan had holed up a disgusted Shirley in a hotel in Bath. She was spending her time watching television while everyone was looking for the missing star. The police nearly locked up Sullivan, and Shirley was able to leave the hotel in time for her first night at the Chiswick Empire. Someone threw an egg at her from the gallery. It missed and Shirley thought it was some nice person throwing her a flower.

Sullivan's next plan focused on the biggest show business event of the year, one that would be televised and transmitted to every sitting room in the land. It was, 'The Night of a Hundred Stars', to be staged at the Palladium at midnight in late July. Shirley just *had* to be up there with Sir Laurence Olivier and all Britain's biggest stars.

He rang the organiser and gave him a message that could not be ignored. Miss Shirley Bassey is very anxious to help your deserving charity and is prepared to offer her services. But it seems that her name has been overlooked. Can it be that there is some colour prejudice in operation?

Certainly not, came the answer. Sullivan was promised a return telephone call and in a few minutes Shirley was in. Sullivan was jubilant, he knew that Shirley would walk away with the show. She simply gloried in illustrious surroundings, and the more stars that surrounded her, the more she could shine. They both worked very hard, rehearsing without let-up. Shirley would walk down a staircase. The impact of any performer coming down a staircase is always sure-fire. The dress would be beautiful and daring. She would astonish and excite as she sang 'The Birth of the Blues'.

And that is exactly what happened. There was a great roar of approval and sympathy for this girl, whose private life and reputation had been shredded so unfairly on the front pages of the newspapers. She sang what the papers next day called the most exciting rendition of 'Birth of the Blues' ever heard in London. The man with the golden trumpet, Eddie Calvert, joined her, and the two of them stole the show. Shirley brought youth, glamour and, above all, her voice and Eddie Calvert his virtuosity. The audience broke into tumultous applause. Shirley had proved she was inimitable, and unbeatable. After that night, she was in demand as never before.

Johnny Franz of Phillips Records had always believed in her. Now he asked her, and not Michael Sullivan, what she wanted to record, 'Choose a number for the other side of this record,' he told her. She knew exactly what she wanted. Les Paul, a musician who had often played for her in the past, had played a number for her on his piano, and she had fallen instantly in love with it. 'What's it called?' asked Johnny Franz.

'"As I Love You". It's wonderful, Johnny. You know it has this middle eight, which is me. I can change key and hit. Then attack! I love it.'

'You can't have it,' Johnny said flatly. 'It's against all the rules. You can't have two ballads on the same disc. You've got to give me a beat number.'

Shirley wouldn't give up. 'This is me. This is my song. Please Johnny. I've always done as you asked, now give me this song.' She won. Shirley recorded the song and gave it everything she had. Both Johnny Franz and Shirley knew it would be a hit. When it came out that year, 1958, it was top of the charts, then it was top again in March 1959. Shirley loved it. She knew this was a song that suited her voice. At the same time she recorded, 'Kiss Me, Honey Honey, Kiss Me.' It was jazzy and bright, but as far as she was concerned, 'As I Love You' was her favourite. The two songs climbed the charts together.

As Shirley had two records right at the top she was asked to sing which ever song she preferred on the most popular music television programme, *The Top Twenty Show* with Joe Loss and his orchestra. Naturally she chose her favourite, 'As I Love You'. This song had been her baby from the beginning, she had cosseted it, sung it on all kinds of spots, on radio and television, and accepted fees as low as five pounds just to plug it, just to get it where she knew it deserved to go, to the top of the Hit Parade.

Sullivan, however, wanted her to sing, 'Kiss Me, Honey Honey, Kiss Me,' on the TV show and, without telling her, deliberately sent the wrong music to Joe Loss. Expecting to sing, 'As I Love You,' Shirley went to the *Top Twenty* studio to give her favourite song its final accolade. She was astounded and disappointed when she discovered what Michael had done. She was also furious, and the crack in their relationship widened further. It was, after all, a stupid and arrogant action for Sullivan to have taken. And it was one that Shirley would not forget.

*

Shirley had now moved into a home of her own, a furnished flat in one of the apartment blocks in Dolphin Square, near the embankment between Chelsea and Victoria. Dolphin Square was quiet and attractive, a popular and fashionable place to live. None of the apartments were particularly large or grand but they were comfortable. It was very central, and the people who lived there often just needed a 'pied à terre' in London: members of parliament, businessmen and women, writers, actors. It was a safe place for a woman on her own.

Shirley's flat was in the same block where she and Bernard Hall had said goodbye the year before when he went off to Monte Carlo. One of Shirley's favourite features in the Dolphin Square complex was its large swimming pool. Shirley was a good swimmer and she loved the sport.

She was beginning to earn big money now, but both she and Michael knew that as soon as their current agreement expired, the next contract – if there was one – would be very different.

Shirley drove her white Jaguar down to Cardiff to see her mother and Sharon regularly so Annis Abraham was no longer needed to meet her train. However, she often called in at his nightclub before she returned to London, and it was there that she met his two partners, Clive Sharp and Maurice King. They were running a new discotheque-cum-drinking club in Soho, in which Annis had a share, and Shirley promised to call and see The Showbiz Club soon.

Michael had seen a show, *The Folies Bergère*, at the Winter Garden in Blackpool and realised that this was the perfect vehicle for Shirley. It had featured a beautiful dark girl who sang and danced. He discussed the idea of renting the sets and props and turning *The Folies Bergère* into a brand new show in London. It would be retitled *Blue Magic*, and open at the Prince of Wales Theatre.

All these arrangements were put on hold when Shirley, still doing her variety tour for Leslie Grade, appeared in Birmingham. Michael had stayed in London but Berry was with her and, of course, her little poodle, who she had named Beaujolais. In the middle of the night Shirley rang Berry to say she was in terrible pain. A doctor was called and gave the usual grumbling appendix diagnosis with assurances that she'd be all right tomorrow. Berry was not convinced, he remembered the sick girl he and Sylvia had met at London Airport. 'I think she ought to go into hospital, and we find out once and for all what's really wrong.' Berry may well have saved Shirley's life. If he hadn't intervened it might have been too late. The appendix had ruptured and she had peritonitis. She was found to be seriously ill and needed an emergency operation. After she recovered from the surgery, she needed a long convalescence, so Berry took Shirley and Beaujolais back to Margery Hall and Sylvia in Reigate.

The warmth and kindness of that household was exactly what Shirley needed to help recovery. 'She loved home cooking,' remembered Sylvia. 'Spotted Dick was one of her favourite puddings. She loved the family atmosphere of our home. My old mum and Shirley got on like a house on fire. My sister used to bring her baby and we'd tuck her into Shirley's bed. She was happier than I'd ever seen her. Sometimes I wondered whether what she was doing was worth all that stress and trouble. She had a great talent, no-one could do it like Shirley, it had brought her fame and money but there didn't seem time for happiness. In the end, I think I decided that she had this overwhelming need to be famous, she had a need to use her voice so she just had to get on with it.'

When she was better, Shirley and Sylvia dressed up to the nines, Sylvia wearing one of Shirley's mink stoles and went to watch a tennis match at Wimbledon. The reigning Wimbledon champion,

American Ashley Cooper, had sent Shirley tickets. 'I remember how very attractive Shirley looked,' says Sylvia. 'She just mowed the men down. That day we really felt we were the bee's knees. I was sorry when she drove off to Dolphin Square.'

Before Shirley started serious preparations for the new revue, *Blue Magic*, Sullivan got together a complete variety show to do a short tour for Moss Empires. Shirley would have the second half of the show to herself, and Sylvia and her partner, the dancing sister act, would be part of the first half. 'We opened the first half,' laughed Sylvia in recalling that time. 'And you can't get much lower than that, but we loved every moment. And the show did so well. Of course Shirley was our big star, so we had full houses in every town we visited.'

Sullivan realised that Shirley had a new boyfriend, Clive Sharp. He knew vaguely that Clive Sharp and his partner Maurice King were, as he said, 'two faces you would see around London.' He didn't consider them in the same league as he was professionally, but Shirley was over twenty-one and her choice of boyfriends were out of his control.

Annis Abraham found out that Shirley and Clive Sharp were more than just good friends when Clive and Shirley visited his nightclub in Cardiff. As usual Annis asked Shirley if she would sing a song. Shirley agreed quite happily but, when she got up, Clive put out a hand and held her back, he said, 'Shirley must not sing here', as if he had some control over her movements. His actions were noticed by a number of people and Annis was disturbed. He was a business associate of these men, he had introduced Shirley to them. 'Who are those men sitting with Shirley Bassey and telling her what to do?' a customer asked Annis. 'They're just advisers,' he said.

The next time Annis visited The Showbiz Club, the drinking club in Soho in which he had an interest with Sharp and King, he found Shirley sitting in the lobby, waiting for Clive. Inside the club, Clive was chatting up some girls sitting around the bar. He was shocked. Like most people in Tiger Bay he took great pride in Shirley's success, and Clive was letting her sit outside waiting for him while he joked with these women. For Annis, brought up with Tiger Bay's strict moral code, it showed a lack of respect.

Sullivan was the next one to wonder what it was all about. He was deep in preparation for what he thought would be Shirley's first musical. He'd met Clive Sharp, Shirley had brought him to dinner at his new house near Woking. Just another West End face who ran a drinking club in Soho he thought. Not what he'd have advised, because drinking clubs in Soho could get a bad name. But there again, if Shirley had fallen for the guy, it was not his affair.

Before rehearsals started for *Blue Magic*, Michael thought it would be a good idea to try out new songs from the show at a town not too far from London. Colchester in Essex was the chosen place and he went down there to see how Shirley was getting on. In her dressing room sat Clive Sharp and Maurice King. Sullivan went down a second time – to discuss business, and the same pair were once again in Shirley's dressing room. Shirley said to him. 'Anything you want to say, you can discuss, in front of these two gentlemen.'

Clive Sharp, who Michael had thought was just another boyfriend, was now, it seemed, taking a role in her business life as well as her romantic one. He was, said Sullivan, gradually and subtly taking Shirley away from him. When Shirley failed to turn up for two rehearsals, Michael went round to see her at Dolphin Square. Shirley told him that the contract he had with her, signed when she was a minor, would now have to be reviewed.

The day of reckoning had arrived and Sullivan felt he had no-one but himself to blame. He should not have been surprised either when, after two new contracts were drawn up, the first between the producer of *Blue Magic* and Shirley, and the second between himself and Shirley, she declined to sign the latter.

By 1959 Michael Sullivan's reign was over. Jock Jacobson, an agent with links to MCA, the giant American monopoly, was taking his place as agent and booker, with Clive Sharp and Maurice King as Shirley's managers. Her new managers banned Sullivan from going backstage at the Prince of Wales Theatre, but he went to the opening night of *Blue Magic*, and saw how well the girl he had discovered four years earlier now succeeded as the star of a big West End revue. It was a bitter pill to swallow.

February 1959 was not the happiest month for Sullivan. He was sueing Shirley for eight thousand pounds, because his contract with her was still valid, and he could not move on and manage anyone else until that action was heard in court.

Time went by, then less than a month before the court case in January 1960, Shirley rang him up and said that she wanted to see him. 'Are you doing this to get out of the court case? he asked.

'No, Mikey,' she answered in the sweetest way. 'Come round and let's talk.'

By then Shirley had left Dolphin Square. 'I'm fed up with furnished flats,' she declared, and bought a house in Stanhope Place, Mayfair. Every time Shirley moved in London from then on, it was to an ever more exclusive address. She had paid twelve thousand pounds for her narrow terraced house overlooking Hyde Park and a stone's throw from Marble Arch. It had four bedrooms, two reception rooms, dining room, two kitchens and two bathrooms (one of which had a pale pink sunken bath) and the little white poodle Beaujolais loved it. 'Now I've got roots. I've furnished a guest room,' said Shirley, 'and perhaps my mother will come and stay. I'm dying to see her face when she walks in.' Outside her house was a red Chevrolet convertible which had replaced her Jaguar.

When Sullivan rang the bell, her hit song, 'As I Love You,' chimed out. The door was opened by Gerda, Shirley's German housekeeper, and Shirley was really pleased to see him. As they talked she told Sullivan that the first year of freedom had been wonderful, then she started missing the man who had devoted himself completely to Shirley Bassey. She had a good agent but he was part of a big corporation. 'I need someone who thinks I am enough', Shirley told him, 'someone who will look after me and my career, like you.'

Instead of meeting in court, Michael and Shirley signed a new contract. Shirley would pay Sullivan the customary twenty per cent and she would pay her own expenses.

Three weeks later they were in Sydney at the start of a two-month Australian tour. Shirley was now used to making her own decisions and if she wanted something done she expected everyone to do it; she was no longer the girl who could be ordered about. Shirley had grown up and Sullivan found it hard to adjust. They still had one or two noisy battles, but now Shirley always won.

At one nightclub Shirley found the audience were very loud. They never stopped talking and didn't seem to care whether she sang or not. Finally, she had enough and decided to ask her pianist to play her off. Sullivan made a scene in her dressing room. 'The audience expect to have the whole programme . . .' Shirley cut him short. 'I had finished my act. As an encore I would have sung another song if they'd wanted it, but I decided that they didn't.' Sullivan knew finally that he was no longer in control.

On the way home from Australia they decided to spend a few days at the Americana Hotel in New York. It was always useful to renew old contacts and make fresh ones. Shirley seemed very happy to have met a friend from London in the hotel lift. Later she introduced him to Sullivan; his name was Kenneth Hume. Sullivan remembered having met Hume once in London. He was in television, and one of his many jobs was making advertisements for ATV (Associated Television). He was a bit of an all-rounder, a bit of a mystery.

Kenneth Hume was shorter than Shirley, about five-foot-four, and sandy haired. He was in his late thirties, and had a bit of a pixie look, with a turned-up nose and rather big ears. He was obviously a Londoner and there was just a touch of the cockney barrow boy about him now and then when he raised his voice. He was making a great fuss of Shirley and she loved every moment of it.

Once back in London Sullivan was negotiating a six-week season at the Opera House in Blackpool for Shirley when the owner of the exclusive Les Ambassadeurs club in Park Lane telephoned to say that Shirley and Kenneth Hume were in the club and had just announced their engagement. Sullivan could hardly believe it. 'Give them a bottle of champagne from me,' he said.

Shirley herself gave an interview in which she explained in greater detail what had happened. 'I liked Kenneth,' she told the interviewer, 'but I didn't fancy him. It was one of those things that crept up on me. Then suddenly over dinner it hit me, Boing! It was magic. Sexual chemistry is the key to a relationship. It's wonderful when it happens,' Shirley declared. It was obviously enough to make Shirley and Kenneth announce their engagement at Les Ambassadeurs.

Sullivan had made it his business to find out what he could about Shirley's fiancé. When he next saw Shirley alone he said to her, 'You can't marry Kenneth Hume.'

'Oh yes, I can.'

'Shirley, he's a known homosexual. Listen to me, it never works.'

'Oh yes it does. We love each other and he will change for me.'

'I don't believe it.'

'Mikey,' said Shirley. 'You don't know Kenneth Hume. I know much more about him than you do.' Shirley enjoyed a level of ease and familiarity with homosexuals that Sullivan could never share. Bernard Hall, one of her earlier lovers, had been bisexual. He'd been a good lover and a good friend.

Yet when Bernard Hall heard about Shirley's engagement to Kenneth Hume he, too, could hardly believe it. He was touring in Spain when one of his girls produced an English newspaper and showed him a picture of Shirley and Kenneth. 'Do you know him?' she asked. 'Yes,' said Bernard, 'I know him well.'

It had been a friendship that had started when Bernard was a drama student at the Italia Conti stage school in the mid-1940s. He had been seventeen and Kenneth must have been about twenty-one. 'I was buying an apple for my lunch and Kenneth was on the other side of the barrow. I thought that Kenneth was part of the market. "Wotcha cock," he said to me with his gap-toothed grin and bright eyes. He was soon calling me Bernie, which I hated.'

Bernard noticed that people were always stopping Kenneth in the streets of Soho, asking him if he could get them this or that. 'Okay, but it'll cost you.' I knew that one day Kenneth would be rich, even though he was killing himself with sixty cigarettes a day and junk food. And he never relaxed for a moment, he was always on the go. He hardly drank wine or spirits, it was cups of tea all the time.

It sounds odd,' continued Bernard, 'but we weren't at all jealous of each other. I was good-looking and ambitious but I also knew that I hadn't Kenneth's brains. I used to think he had a touch of genius. We were friends, Kenneth was kind to me when he didn't have to be, when I was a kid without a bean.'

There was nothing sexual in their friendship. Bernard hadn't homosexual tendencies in those days, and Kenneth's inclinations tended towards blonds who had a touch of choirboy innocence about them. 'Not that I even thought about things like that at the time,' said Bernard. 'I was young and broke and we just used to chat. I liked him. He had an East End accent in those days, and I used to think of him as "the little cockney sparrow", but he knew everything that was going on in London, and he was crazy about the stage and the screen although he was not well-liked in the film world. I guess you could say he was a typical '"wide boy" of the time.'

Even so, he found the idea that Kenneth and Shirley were in love hard to take. He could not accept that Kenneth had fallen in love with Shirley in the accepted sense. Kenneth was openly homosexual and even if he was having a bisexual fling with Shirley, he would probably revert quite quickly to the kind of encounters he preferred.

But Bernard eventually conceded that Shirley was very young, she was only twenty-two and she might believe she was in love with him. She certainly needed someone to look after her, and if Kenneth liked people he was honest with them so he might well be good to her.

The happy couple went off to Cannes for the 1961 Film Festival. They stayed for a few days at the Carlton Hotel in great style and pictures were taken of them with Shirley looking glamorous in diaphanous beachwear and Kenneth lounging in white pants and a smart towelling shirt. Kenneth played roulette at Juan les Pins, the next casino resort down the coast. Back home in Soho he was known as a gambler, a man who could always be relied on to make up the number in a game of cards. In the South of France, John Mills (not to be confused with the actor) who ran Les Ambassadeurs marvelled at the way Kenneth played three roulette tables at the same time – and actually won.

The couple drank aperitifs on the smart Carlton Terrace, and dined at the most expensive restaurant on the Côte d'Azur at La Napoule. Kenneth was in his element. A beautiful, exotic looking wife-to-be made him an object of envy for the first time in his life.

Shirley returned from France for her six-week season at the Opera House, Blackpool. There was an unhappy feeling of a *ménage à trois* in the air backstage. Shirley, the star of the show was driven backwards and forwards to the stage door by Kenneth Hume in his hired Rolls Royce while Sullivan, who was still Shirley's legal partner lurked unhappily in the wings.

Kenneth told Sullivan that he thought it might be a good idea, if, now that he was managing Shirley, Sullivan could make himself useful in other ways. For instance, he could stand in the wings for Shirley's performance holding a box of tissues and a glass of water, so that she could dab her face and take a sip of water now and then.

Sullivan knew perfectly well that Hume was trying to humiliate him, to insult and anger him so much that he would walk out of the theatre in a rage and perhaps lose his rights over the show completely. At last, he suggested that if Hume was so anxious to get rid of him he should meet his lawyer and buy him out.

Michael Sullivan received a cheque for ten thousand pounds and this time his relationship with Shirley Bassey was finally over. Kenneth Hume was now in charge.

11

MARRIAGE AND MEN

Thursday, 8 June 1961, The *South Wales Echo*

SHIRLEY BASSEY WEDS

Shirley Bassey, the singer from Cardiff, wearing a pink costume with toque hat and veil to match arrived at the Paddington, London, Register Office just before 9.30 a.m. in Mr. Hume's light coffee coloured Bentley – registered number KH 14. About two minutes after the bride had entered the building Mr. Hume arrived wearing a dark blue suit with a rose in his lapel. About fourteen minutes later bride and groom appeared arm in arm. A group of housewives with prams shopping in the busy street wished her 'Good luck, Shirley.'

It was Shirley's first marriage. She was twenty-four. Shirley had several times refused marriage proposals from film producer, Kenneth Hume. But now she had married him. Shirley herself offered one reason why she gave in at last. She said, 'Kenneth was eleven years older than me. My father left my mother when I was about two and for a long time I was looking for a father figure in all my men.'

The news of Shirley's marriage was not well received by all. Someone said, 'All he does is strut down Wardour Street and pretend to be a film producer. He'll spend all her money on gambling.' Even actress Diana Dors, who was well known for her good sense of humour as well as her bad taste in men, wasn't too keen on Kenneth Hume. 'I haven't always picked the right men, but I certainly was lucky when I missed that one.'

But with Shirley, Kenneth seemed to show another side. He was a better manager for her than Michael Sullivan. Apart from being her legal husband there was always an element of protectiveness in Kenneth's attitude to Shirley. From the beginning of their marriage they would have slanging matches with each other and the air would turn blue with expletives, but Shirley was used to such scenes; her noisy quarrels with Sullivan had been well known throughout show business. If you wanted a quiet life with Shirley you let her make the decisions, but the men in her life often enjoyed the drama of an argument.

Kenneth Hume had an office of his own in Wardour Street when he married Shirley. He had staff, and connections in the profession whom he could call on. Sullivan had started his management of Shirley on a shoestring, and apart from Sylvia and Berry, never delegated anyone else to look after her. But Kenneth Hume made sure there was always someone with her on tour who would take care of her. He did not tour with her himself, although he'd sometimes make a quick visit to wherever she was, but he never put himself in the position of being at her beck and call. She could telephone him wherever she was in the world and complain and he'd listen, but he didn't always act.

Hume was very lucky to have an exceptional office manager in Leslie Simmons, who would arrange timetables, hotels and planes to perfection. All Shirley's tours were well planned and if the boss didn't interfere nothing would go wrong. Kenneth Hume would negotiate her fee and make sure she was paid both well and on time. He took good advice on the best way to invest and increase Shirley's money.

It seemed obvious why Shirley had left Sullivan for Hume. Apart from her husband's superior business acumen, he had a more sensitive and gentle nature. Bernard Hall has said, 'In spite of the fact that Kenneth could be a number one bastard, mean and cruel and secretive, with his eye always on the main chance, I thought that this toughness of his didn't go all that deep. I sensed at the time that this was true and found out later that he was vulnerable in many ways. He looked after his interests and decided which company was most profitable for her.'

On Kenneth's advice Shirley had left Phillips, and was now with EMI Records. In 1961 she made six recordings, produced by Norman Newell. They included, 'You'll Never Know', 'So in Love,' and 'As Long as He Needs Me' from Lionel Bart's *Oliver!* This record proved to be one of Shirley's biggest bestsellers. With Hume's help, she was on her way to becoming a major recording star. Like Sullivan before him, he knew what enormous returns there were in the recording side of the business.

Hume negotiated contracts for Shirley in America. She sang in Las Vegas and New York, then toured the East Coast of America and Canada. For Shirley it was solid work, just as it had been with Sullivan but her life had always been that way. There really was no let-up. Apart from the big international tours there were the European appearances; she went to the Tivoli Gardens in Stockholm, to nightclubs in Brussels and Antwerp and to the South of France where she played nightclubs, cabarets and casinos all along the Côte d'Azur. Most British entertainers enjoyed doing the South of France. For Shirley it sometimes meant a one-night stand at a gala at the Monte Carlo Sporting Club or at a summer casino, like Juan les Pins or Cannes. The fee always included two days or more in a first class hotel and the sunshine always helped.

A year after her marriage, Shirley went back to Cannes. Bernard Hall was driving along the Corniche when he saw a poster outside the Cannes Summer Casino, a large picture of a honey-coloured girl wearing an outrageous evening dress: a skimpy jewelled bra attached by two jewelled straps to a fragile skirt that ended just above the navel. There was rather more of her supple body on view than of the exotic dress. 'Miss Shirley Bassey,' said the poster, 'will arrive for next week's Gala.'

Bernard Hall was still based in France and worked the winter in Paris and the summer in Monte Carlo. He toured with four of his girls, dancing and singing in the casinos along the Côte d'Azur, as The Bernard Hall Quintet. Since they had first met in 1956, he had followed Shirley's career and marriage through the newspapers. They had occasionally communicated, but he longed to meet her in the flesh again.

Riches, the man from the Eddie Marouani Paris Agency who looked after all the English performers, met Shirley's plane at Nice airport as a matter of course. Bernard had telephoned him for the time of arrival and he was there too. Down the aircraft steps came Shirley, holding the hand of a little seven-year-old girl. She was Sharon, Shirley's daughter, who had come with her for a short seaside holiday.

The affection between Shirley and Bernard was unchanged and they were delighted to see each other. Vic Lewis, from Kenneth Hume's London Office, had come with Shirley to look after her, but seeing the attentive Bernard he realised this an opportunity to have a little holiday himself. Bernard drove them all to the Majestic Hotel where Shirley was staying. Up in Shirley's room they all gossiped for a while then Riches left; soon after, Vic Lewis followed suit, leaving the old friends to catch up, and saying, 'See you at band call tomorrow Shirley.'

Sharon solemnly unpacked her little bag. She was a thin child but quite tall for her age. She had brought two books with her to read and someone had obviously told her never to interfere while grown-ups chattered. Bernard thought he had never seen such a delightfully well behaved little girl. She did all she could to please her mother, asked for nothing and smiled shyly when anyone looked her way. Iris and Bill had brought her up really well.

Bernard also noticed that Shirley was a very caring mother. When Sharon was young and Shirley had to pretend to be her aunt, she had guarded against showing too much affection, but now it was all out in the open. Shirley was a married woman and everything had changed. Bernard remembered Shirley once telling him 'Kenneth gave my daughter Samantha a name.' Apart from that Shirley didn't discuss her husband at all. Bernard and Shirley were delighted to see each other again and the three of them had tea on the hotel terrace, then went across the road to play on the sands with Sharon.

Bernard took Shirley for a drink at the Carlton that evening then, before going out to dinner, they went up to see Sharon. She had had her supper and was sitting up in bed reading one of her books. She said she'd be perfectly all right; she knew where all the bells were, and the maid who brought her supper said she'd look in again. She said she'd try to stay awake until her mother came home.

Bernard loved playing Uncle to Sharon and had a rare glimpse of Shirley as a mother. But somehow he couldn't see Kenneth Hume in the role of father, anymore than he had seen him in the role of Shirley's husband.

For Shirley, coming over to sing at one of the Casino galas was a good way to have a little holiday and earn money at the same time. All expenses were paid: airfares for the star and her manager, two or three nights at a top hotel and a fee of around seven hundred pounds for each appearance. But what Shirley hadn't realised was that at the Summer Casino there were no dressing rooms for the stars, no entrance and no stage door.

The stars would, if possible, dress at the Majestic, then walk in the dark across a busy road filled with speeding traffic. They would then walk past the dustbins to the back of the Casino, descending right underneath the building past concrete pillars and steel girders, and clambering over the rubble of what was once the building site to reach the iron steps clinging to the side of the Casino. On arrival, the star in question would look as if he or she had miraculously stepped straight out of the sea into the Casino.

The Summer Casino faced the sea and there was no wall behind the stage so it was open to the elements. The audience faced a wonderful floodlit panorama of the Côte d'Azur – the famous 'String of Pearls' comprising the Monte Carlo Casino and the Nice Casino, with all the yachts lit up in the harbour.

Bernard picked up Shirley at the Hotel Majestic as he was going to act as her dresser in the rubble underneath the Casino. The beautiful and delicate dress and stilt-heeled shoes were too delicate to risk darting through the heavy traffic of the Corniche. Jeans, heavy boots and a pick axe would have been more suitable attire than the dress, which was made of diaphanous white material decorated with little bouquets of handmade glistening flowers. Bernard carried the dress over his arm and the matching shoes, plus everything else she needed, in a bag. Shirley had her make-up on and her wig in place as she clung to Bernard's arm while he steered her very carefully towards the high steps that led to the stage.

When the diaphanous dress was safely fitted, the delicate shoes in place, the wig flicked up and the make-up checked, Bernard got her over the uneven surface of the concrete to the bottom step. He watched her climb the perilous steps rung by rung. When she was safely there he snatched up the bag and hurried round to the auditorium in time for the roll of drums and the voice that announced: 'Mesdames et Messieurs, Ladies and Gentlemen . . . Miss Shirley Bassey.'

Then it all happened. The brass serenaded the orchestra and then the orchestra exploded with the sound of every instrument. The music poured forth and then she stood there, the goddess who had walked out of the sea. She opened her arms wide to the people who had come to listen to her.

The applause flows over the goddess. She looks so beautiful. The music is fantastic. She belts out the first number, the one designed to make everyone happy. 'On a Wonderful Day Like Today' . . . She progresses through her repertoire, song by song, all timed and chosen to draw her audience closer to her. A touch of *tristesse* with 'As Long as He Needs Me,' but strength, too, and power. Now here comes *her* song, and she gives it everything she has.

Bernard a performer himself, knew she was now experiencing one of the greatest feelings in the world, one you would do anything on earth to have. It wells up like a torrent inside and takes everything you are with it, and then it flows from you to consume those people out there.

After the show Shirley and Bernard were both on such a high that it was going to take a long time to come down. They laughed, they clung to each other, they drank champagne, they tried to eat but couldn't. Who can eat when you're as high as a kite? Finally, when Shirley thought she might be able to sleep, he escorted her up to her room. Sharon was fast asleep in her bed, her book lying open next to her.

Bernard said he'd better go but he'd be back tomorrow to take her to the airport. They stood whispering outside the bathroom door and he put his arms around her and kissed her. He felt exactly as he had six years ago when he held the nineteen-year-old Shirley in his arms, Shirley must have felt the same because her foot went up and her heel pushed open the bathroom door, and she drew him through it . . .

The married life of Shirley Bassey and Kenneth Hume was unusual, to say the least. To begin with they did not live together. Kenneth had a flat in Westbourne Terrace, Bayswater, and remained there after his marriage; Shirley bought a house in Chester Square, Belgravia, and moved in with Sharon, a nanny and a butler. It was one of those tall storeyed town houses with numerous stairs and a room for the hired help to sleep in right at the top. The kitchen is in the basement, the study and dining room on the ground floor, drawing-room on the first floor, bedrooms and bathrooms on the second, nurseries on the third.

As neither husband nor wife were the kind who wanted anyone to cook them three square meals a day, and they were not really into entertaining, the dining room was practically unfurnished.

Kenneth, who lived mainly in his own flat, had bad eating habits, preferring fast food that wouldn't tie him down to sitting at a table. Shirley's favourite room was always the bedroom and every morning at 12.00 she had breakfast brought up to her there by the butler. On the tray there was always a plate of scrambled eggs.

After two years of marriage, Shirley had come to terms with the fact that she and Kenneth could not be happy as husband and wife. She later said that they were very content together at first but Kenneth could not cope with their marriage. He told her that when he married her he wasn't that much in love with her. Shirley had believed completely in his love and later admitted that this was a devastatingly hurtful revelation. From the moment he told her, she began falling out of love with him. Conversely, and perversely, when he realised what was happening he wanted to try again.

Each did love the other in their own way, but 'in love' was over for good. It became an open marriage and Shirley felt she was free to act as she wished. Kenneth was her manager and he master-minded her career; and whenever she needed advice, anywhere in the world, she always called Kenneth to ask for help.

He knew she saw other men and would ask, 'Did you enjoy your date with so and so?' Shirley would then ask how he had found out and he always said, 'a little bird told me.'

And Shirley was always away on tour. Every year after Christmas, in January or February, Shirley went out to Australia. She had remained enormously popular there and would tour for two or three months. She had friends – Bruce Gordon in Sydney and the Irishman John McAuliffe in Melbourne. A few months later John's name would unexpectedly be linked in London with hers.

Shirley returned home from Australia in the Spring of 1963, and to publicise her next concert Mr and Mrs Kenneth Hume called a press conference at the Dorchester Hotel. Not only was Shirley going to appear at the Talk of The Town, but Kenneth had other, more startling news for the journalists: Shirley was pregnant. He was going to become a father.

'What do you make of it Mr Hume?' asked a journalist.

'I'm pleased,' said Kenneth, 'although a little baffled.' He had every reason to be a little baffled. His wife had been away for months and now she was having a baby in November.

'Didn't you and Shirley split up before she left for Australia?' enquired the same nosy journalist. They all enjoyed needling Kenneth who most of them either knew or suspected was gay. 'Didn't you tell us it was because of irreconcilable differences. What were they, Mr Hume?'

'We're together now,' said Kenneth sharply, 'that's all that matters.' The happy couple explained that it had been difficult for Shirley to conceive, they had tried so many hotel bedrooms all over the south of England without success.

'But now,' said Shirley, displaying the sense of humour which had become a valuable weapon, both on stage and off, 'I'm pregnant and I'm knitting socks and I don't know how to turn the heel.'

Samantha Hume was born on 7 November 1963, in the London Clinic in Harley Street, weighing six pounds, ten ounces.

Shirley took the tiny baby, Samantha, and a nanny, with her on her January 1964 tour of Australia.

This was the year of *Goldfinger* and on her return to England she reigned supreme thanks to the James Bond blockbuster. It had happened this way. On one of her tours, Shirley's musical director was budding composer John Barry, a fine musician and a young man destined for fame. During the tour, John said to Shirley, 'I know your policy is never to listen to music without lyrics, but please listen to this.'

'Because it was John Barry who asked me and I liked and respected him and loved his talent,' explained Shirley, 'I broke my policy and listened. As I heard the first few bars, I knew, and I said, "I don't care about the words, I love the music."' The title song for *Goldfinger*, for that's what it became, was a world hit. Shirley's voice, displaying all its incredible pitch and range, opened the film and set its tone. It was a dynamic performance, although Shirley had found the recording of the song against the rolling background of the changing credits one of the hardest things she ever had to do.

Shirley became known internationally as 'The Goldfinger Girl'. Crowds of her fans gathered at airports all over the world, serenading her with the song. Noël Coward and Bernard Hall went to the première of the film together. Afterwards Noël enthused to Shirley, 'My darling girl, what a wonderful voice you have.' It was a huge compliment from the man known in his profession as The Master and a harsh critic.

Noël Coward was always sure that he had a great deal to do with the success of *Goldfinger*. It was he who brought the original James Bond to the screen. He telephoned Ian Fleming, the author who created 007, and said, 'I've just the boy for you, next to me, right here in my house. He's your James Bond,' and then he took Sean Connery, an ambitious young actor round to meet him.

With the success of 'Goldfinger' and with Kenneth behind her, Shirley's career flourished. She liked the routine of coming back from Australia with the knowledge that the right kind of bookings had been fixed up. One of them was the popular theatre restaurant, the Talk of The Town, off Leicester Square, which had once been the London Hippodrome. Before Samantha was born Shirley had appeared there and now in 1964, she had a return engagement at the venue which played host to the best: Eartha Kitt, Lena Horne, Judy Garland, to name but three.

Bernard Hall met Kenneth some time before this and saw how much he had changed. Traits that he had noticed when they were both young were now more exaggerated. He was still the same mixture of bravado and insecurity, but now he was like quicksilver. There'd be charm, but if you said the wrong thing you'd get an icy blast of his foul temper. Kenneth could be insufferable and demanding, and an almighty great crack was appearing in the House of Hume which would soon split wide open.

Shirley's new musical director, Kenny Clayton, newly engaged by Vic Lewis at Kenneth Hume's office, walked right into a family drama and wondered what had hit him. A musical director plays for the star, he sits at the piano at the side of the stage, playing but watching the star all the time. He tours with the star and is very important, because he is there to support and help. If the star has little musical background, he will advise. He is the rock if the performance starts going wrong. Kenny Clayton is now there for Shirley Bassey, paid by her and her husband. Shirley could quarrel with her husband, her stage manager and her road manager, but any star with sense does not quarrel with her musical director, for without him she does not sing.

Musicians are usually gentle creative people, not destructive influences, and Kenny Clayton was hoping that he and Shirley Bassey would get on well. This particular morning in a Belgravia Mews studio Kenny Clayton was feeling happy, it was his first appointment as musical director. He had played in orchestras, as accompanist, and was known for his musical ability. He was a good tempered man, and enjoyed the company of women.

This morning they were going to rehearse the songs for Shirley's opening at the Talk of The Town. She arrived and walked straight over to the piano where Kenny was sorting through the music. They chatted and Shirley said she would open the show as usual 'On a Wonderful Day Like Today'. It took time, but they were just getting to the right key for Shirley and he was playing the song through again when a door slammed. In marched a short man who stared at them and banged the door shut behind him. He was in a very bad temper as he yelled, 'That's all wrong.'

Shirley took one look at the intruder and rapidly exited into a side room. The man came to the piano, his face creased with anger. 'You do not play it that way,' he shouted at Kenny. 'You've got it all wrong.' Over the man's head Kenny saw Vic Lewis frantically signalling him to play it cool – this was the star's husband. Kenny understood; husbands could be difficult, and this one paid the piper. He smiled at him pleasantly. 'That's what rehearsals are for, Mr Hume, to get it right. Now how would you . . .' He never finished the sentence. Hume struck the top of the piano with the flat of his hand, and shouted, 'Don't you tell me what rehearsals are for. I tell you!' With that he stormed off to give Vic Lewis hell at the other side of the room.

Shirley reappeared, ignored her husband, snatched up her handbag and made to leave. Shirley was going and thy hadn't even started the rehearsal. 'What about the opening number?' Kenny asked desperately.

Shirley rapped out instructions. 'Play it like Johnny Mathis, 45. That's how I want it.' Then she was gone.

As Kenny described it, 'My mouth just dropped open. This was the first time in my career. I'd been asked to listen to Johnny Mathis singing his song and arranged my piano accompaniment to match. However, if Shirley wanted it this way, it was her right.'

The bad-tempered husband had now backed off and Vic Lewis hurried over to tell Kenny not to worry about 'this bit of trouble'.

'But Vic,' said Kenny, now feeling very insecure about his new job, 'He is the husband, and it is not going well.'

'I'll support you all the way,' said Vic staunchly. 'You just get through the music. He'll leave you alone now.'

Kenny wondered if they were always like this. Two people who had everything in the world to make them happy and yet they seemed as miserable as sin . . . Kenneth Hume was now acting in a bizarre fashion, walking up and down the rehearsal room chain-smoking and muttering to himself.

If Kenny had known that Shirley had gone off to meet her lover and that her husband was apocalyptic with rage it might have helped him understand the situation. Kenneth Hume, once such a complaisant husband who used to ask Shirley how she'd enjoyed her dates with other men, was now becoming a raging inferno of jealousy.

The reason was that this lover wasn't just a business tycoon or a bronzed Adonis, he was a famous international film star and he and Shirley were so much in love that Kenneth Hume could see all his work, his energy, and his ambitions going straight down the drain. He was going to fight tooth and nail to keep Shirley and her latest recording, 'Goldfinger,' as his own.

In March 1964 Peter Finch was to return to the West End theatre after years in films. He had just finished making two pictures in England, *The Girl with Green Eyes*, with Rita Tushingham and Lynn Redgrave, and *The Pumpkin Eater*, with Anne Bancroft. But the theatre had become more important to Peter Finch, it was a kind of renaissance after, as he saw it, wasting time as a well-paid film star. He was now picking up the sceptre that Laurence Olivier had once promised him.

Chekhov's *The Seagull*, was the play directed by Tony Richardson at The Queen's Theatre, with an all-star cast: Peggy Ashcroft, Vanessa Redgrave, Peter McEnery, George Devine and, as Trigorin, Peter Finch. On opening night the critics considered that Peter Finch gave one of the finest Chekhovian performances ever, he was absolutely riveting. Audiences could now look forward to his seasons at Stratford and the Old Vic. 'A great actor, of whom England can be justly proud, is back from films and playing on the stage.'

The Seagull was Peter Finch's best, and last, performance on stage. During its run he met and fell in love with Shirley Bassey.

When Shirley hurried out of the rehearsal with Kenny Clayton to get away from her husband, Kenneth Hume, the love affair between her and Peter Finch had been going strong for three months, since March. They were both ready for a big love affair and they got it; the classic *coup de foudre*, the thunderbolt that welds two people together through hell and high water. By the time it was over, two divorces were taking place and there had been heartbreak on both sides.

Shirley met Peter Finch in a West End restaurant, when some

people he was with stopped at her table to say hello. Peter went out of his way to ask Shirley to come and see his play at the Queens. In fact, they had met briefly before, and Shirley had been impressed. Finch was a man who captivated women. He was forty-eight at the time, tall, with a fine head and thick greying hair. He had the kind of mature good looks that seemed to improve with age.

Peter had come to London in 1949 from Sydney, Australia. On their first Australian tour after the war, Laurence Olivier and Vivien Leigh had singled Peter out in a local play. He had risen to the top in Sydney with his work in radio plays, and Olivier told him that, if he decided to come to London, he should look him up. Almost at once, Peter took up the offer and, with his young Russian ballerina wife, Tamara, arrived in London. With Olivier's help, he was given a major role in *Daphne Laureola*, starring Dame Edith Evans at Wyndham's Theatre. Critics raved about the magic of his voice, and the yearning way he looked at Edith Evans.

Vivien Leigh always fascinated Peter. She was a breathtaking beauty; volatile, unstable, and unable to resist men despite being Olivier's wife. Vivien and Peter began an affair in Australia – it was an item of hot gossip in theatrical Sydney – and continued it in London.

Many successful plays followed for Peter, and then came films. He was in demand as a leading romantic lead, and was cast opposite Vivien Leigh in *Elephant Walk*, filmed mainly on location in Ceylon. Then came the two month Hollywood shoot, and Vivien suddenly lapsed into the manic depression from which she had suffered for years and was replaced by Elizabeth Taylor. Tamara, back in England, was sent out to Hollywood to look after Peter.

When she arrived, Peter told her that she had to look after Vivien as there was no-one else to do it. Tamara voiced her suspicions about her husband's relationship with Vivien, but he brushed them aside, explaining that, 'In the English theatre we're civilised and sophisticated. People have light affairs. That's how it's been with me and Vivien.' Tamara and Peter's marriage never really recovered. She was tired of being neglected, financially as well as emotionally, and they separated in 1956. Tamara, with their daughter Anita, returned to Australia.

Peter Finch who made over a hundred films in his career, achieved star status and equivalent salary. He made *The Nun's Story* with Audrey Hepburn in Hollywood, *The Trials of Oscar Wilde* in England and *A Town Like Alice* in Australia.

When Peter Finch met Shirley Bassey, he had divorced Tamara and was married to Yolande Turner, an attractive young actress from South Africa. They had two small children, Samantha born in 1960 and Charles in 1962. They lived in a country mansion called Boundary House in Mill Hill just outside north London. It had ten rooms, five acres, a vegetable garden and a swimming pool.

The Finches seemed to have everything to make them happy but psychologically they were very different people. Central London was now too far for Yolande to socialise there much, so she joined the social set gave elegant dinner parties in Mill Hill which Peter did not often attend. Before *The Seagull* opened in London, Peter had been known to get up in the middle of a dinner party and walk out. He was fond of telling his guests that he'd been a roustabout, a jackaroo, and that he was really an Australian bum. This wasn't true, Peter was a kind and decent man although he sometimes drank too much. He couldn't spell too well and wrote phonetically, using an Australian accent, and wrote 'good-day' as 'good dye.'

Peter and Yolande had married in 1959 but, within five years, it had begun to disintegrate, largely because of Peter. If he was unhappy he drank heavily and brooded about the past, but, with the success of *The Seagull* and the beginning of his love affair with Shirley, he began to dream of a new and happier life.

He told his wife that, because of the exigencies of the play, he thought it better to stay in London rather than make the long journey home to Mill Hill each night, and he would stay at the Carlton Towers Hotel in Sloane Street. As Shirley's house in Chester Square was just round the corner, they would be almost neighbours.

Peter and Shirley were rarely apart. He called her 'Cheetah' because of the way she walked, and he adored her golden skin; she called him 'Finchy'. As their love affair blossomed, Peter read poetry to Shirley in bed. Shirley, like many women before her, was spellbound. She recalled, 'My love affair with Finchy was a thing of great passion. He was so handsome and knowledgeable, I could curl up and listen to him for hours.'

He told her about his childhood and she was fascinated. Born in London to cold-hearted upper-class parents, he was an unwanted child who was sent to Paris to live with his eccentric grandmother. She had taken him to India to live in an ashram. Only when the little boy wandered off and was found with his head shaven, wearing a yellow robe and living with a Buddhist monk, did the old lady decide to send him to relatives in Australia.

He met his father – who had married again and had three daughters – in London in 1949. He came to tea with Peter and Tamara at the Regent Palace Hotel. The conversation was understandably forced, and after half an hour, Peter's father wished him good luck and walked out of his life. Tamara and Peter looked at each other and she said, 'How very English.'

Shirley was thrilled to meet a man whose childhood had been as traumatic as her own, albeit rather more privileged. Peter enjoyed reading plays to Shirley and discussing them with her. She said at one time, 'I thought, here is my knight in shining armour. The fairy story I never had. Here is the man who will give me all I have missed in life.'

Peter was quite serious about them acting together, as rivals to Laurence Olivier and Vivien Leigh. He went so far as to ask his agent, Laurie Evans, to see if he could find them something to do together. It was two in the morning and the agent had been woken up by the lovers. 'And what was Miss Bassey's last play?' enquired Evans acidly.

Shirley opened in her six-week engagement at the Talk of The Town, and Peter came round every night straight from the theatre. He was totally entranced by the performance of the woman he loved, enticed by her sexy voice, her fabulous hands and the sinuous movements of her body.

She was well aware of Finch's reputation as one of the great Australian drinkers. She noticed that he did drink a lot, but he told her that when he was happy he could control his drinking. Others who knew him well told a different story. Hermione Baddeley, who acted with him in Hollywood, thought he was a great actor and said, 'His was a gift from the Gods, but he drowned it in alcohol.'

Kenneth Hume knew that Shirley and Peter Finch were not only in love but were also discussing plans for a life together – plans that did not include his wife's manager and soon to be ex-husband. He could probably bear losing Shirley Bassey the wife, but he could not bear to lose Shirley Bassey the star. He had poured his guts into the furthering of her career. He would fight for her, gamble everything. He would shame her, divorce her, but in the end she would come back to him.

Shirley said later, 'It was all Kenneth's fault. Our beautiful love affair began to change. He put detectives on to us. They watched every move we made. I became afraid to open the door. I could not trust anyone.'

So Peter and Shirley would go away to another hotel where they were sure no-one could possibly find them. But was the knock on the door, a waiter with the breakfast trolley or a detective dressed up to look like a waiter? 'I used to throw a sheet over my head if anyone came into the bedroom. Friends, employees, whom could I trust?' said Shirley, 'Kenneth was turning my life into a kind of hell.'

Kenneth Hume was going to pull out all the stops. He thought he knew Shirley. He would frighten her with his army of spies, but if that didn't work, he still had another trick up his sleeve. He thought that when this was all over she would forgive him, she'd understand it was for her own good, he was only looking after her interests.

For years Shirley's professional tours had been planned for her, the schedules, the bookings, the travel and accommodation arranged. Australia would begin the year; then it was home for the season at the Talk of The Town, followed by some of the smaller tours, not too far away – two weeks in Beirut, for example, some time in London, then appearances in Majorca, Monte Carlo and Belgium. Kenneth Hume's office manager had always done a splendid job. Although her personal life was in turmoil and she had all kinds of problems with Kenneth Hume, Shirley was too much of a professional to cancel any dates.

Her 1964 season at the Talk of The Town over and her children in the excellent care of their nanny, Shirley left her house in Chester Square and Peter Finch in the Carlton Towers Hotel for an engagement in Beirut. Soon after she arrived she agreed to talk to the journalists. They wanted to know if the rumours of an impending break up of her marriage were true.

Shirley decided to let them have the truth, yes, she told them, she and her husband had separated, and no, there was no possibility of a reconciliation.

'Are you disillusioned with marriage?' one of them asked.

'You bet I am,' replied Shirley, 'it's my first and I don't think I will want to try again. It's not one of those show business bust-ups, Ken and I just didn't get on. I am only sorry about my two children.'

Shirley stayed in Beirut for a fortnight, then returned to London, to Peter Finch, and to a stunning appearance at the Night of a Hundred Stars at the Palladium on 23 July. For the two lovers it was an ecstatic reunion. They had both hated every day apart. Now they were back together and could start making real plans for the future. Nothing must part them ever again.

12

THE END OF THE FAIRYTALE

IT WAS AUGUST and holiday time. Peter Finch's wife and children were in Italy waiting for his play to close in August so that he could join them in their rented villa at Puerto Ecole, a fashionable seaside resort down the coast road from Rome.

Peter and Shirley were as much in love as ever and optimistic about their future together. When his play closed, he was contracted to make a film with Sophia Loren in Israel. He wanted Shirley to go with him, but first he must go to Italy and ask Yolande for a divorce. Until now Peter had neglected to tell Shirley that although, as he said, married life between him and Yolande had long been as good as over, he had not told his wife about Shirley or of their plans.

And it was at this moment that everything started going wrong. The newspapers got hold of the story and decided to print in the *Evening Standard*. Peter, who knew nothing of this, arrived in Puerto

Ecole to a very icy reception. Journalists had been to see Yolande and discovered that she knew nothing. So they had told her.

Is it true, a distraught Yolande demanded to know? Peter tried to calm her down. Then a telegram arrived and Yolande opened it. 'Who is this woman who signs herself "Cheetah" and sends you her undying love?' She asked.

Yolande took too many sleeping pills and woke up next morning in hospital. Peter Finch was at her bedside. She looked at the man who'd done this to her, came to her senses and said, 'You're not worth dying for. I'm going to divorce you.'

When Finch eventually flew back to London he telephoned Shirley and asked her to meet him at the Pickwick Club. She must come at once. He greeted her with the news that he was at the end of his tether, and then ordered another drink. He always needed a drink when he was upset. His plan was that they escape together to Israel where he was to make the film. Shirley was not a great drinker, she had too much concern for her voice, but she realised that the man she loved drank too much. He had a problem.

Before Peter left for Israel he had an appointment to have dinner with Laurence Gilliam, head of BBC Features to discuss a programme he would make. Laurence Gilliam was a good friend because it was he who had given the actor his first job in London. They arranged to meet at a pub. When Gilliam arrived, with his producer, Finch was already there, sitting in a corner knocking back the whiskies. By the time they got to Wheelers for dinner he was too drunk to eat and had to be taken home to The Carlton Towers where a porter agreed to put him to bed.

'What a tragedy,' said Gilliam to his producer. '*The Seagull* will be the last time we shall have seen him on the West End stage. And he was so good, he was superb. But now it's all over. He can't remember his lines any more. It will be films and the idiot board from now on.'

*

Peter Finch went to Israel before the end of August. Shirley stayed in London, promising to follow him later but she was seriously worried. Apart from the fact that Peter was drinking more than he should he wanted her to put her career on hold and join him in Israel for the duration of the film; if she was with him, he believed, he would be happy and able to control his drinking. He was a possessive man and there was a part of him that liked the idea of being in control of the woman at his side. Shirley loved Finch but refused to jeopardise her career for him. Kenneth Hume, who was also starting divorce proceedings, was citing Peter as co-respondent, and Yolande was citing Shirley. Shirley and Peter had troubles enough without getting into financial difficulties.

In the past Shirley had always asked Kenneth Hume for advice, no matter what the problem. They were still co-directors of the company he had set up for her, and they still had to discuss finance and her future plans. When Kenneth heard what Finch had asked her to do he told her that she was crazy if she went along with it. He was emphatic that she must not sacrifice her career for Finch. 'How can you rely on such a man?' he asked her. 'You earn your own money. With me you were always in charge of your own money. Be careful! You've worked your guts out to get where you are.'

In spite of Hume's warning, Shirley decided to go to Israel. It was hot when she got to the northern coastal town of Nahariya. At once she sensed that all was not well; it wasn't just the location – the crew and the company were deeply distressed. The two stars were miscast, and the script didn't hold together.

Very loosely based on Lawrence Durrell's novel *Justine*, the heroine was now called, Judith and Sophia Loren was to play her as an international spy in very short, very tight hot-pants. Judith, hidden in a packing case unloaded from a cargo boat, arrives at a kibbutz, looking as fresh as a daisy after her long journey, to be greeted by a gloomy Aaron Stein, the leader of the kibbutz, played by Peter Finch.

Peter was drinking steadily, just enough to get through the filming, but too much to give a good performance. No script could dampen Sophia Loren's smouldering sex appeal, but the original high motives of Durrell's story had been lost somewhere in the desert. Originally set just before World War II, it had been updated to the present day, and it just didn't work.

Just six months after their idyllic love affair had begun, problems were arising for the lovers. Peter still wanted to marry Shirley, but he seemed to expect her to play the devoted wife – to the exclusion of her own career. Shirley was not prepared to give up everything she had fought so long and hard to achieve. This man could easily turn their love affair into a nightmare because of his drinking. After a few days in Israel and some hard thinking, she told Peter Finch that she could not marry him and had decided to return to London. 'I think it had been a dream for him,' Shirley said, 'a dream that could never have worked.'

Peter poured his heart out to whoever would listen. He told his audience that he was devastated. 'She only came out here to tell me that it is all off,' he wept. 'She's gone back to her husband.' He sank into bouts of drunken self-pity and blamed everyone but himself. At a dinner with the company he said that his affair with Shirley was the reason for the box-office disaster of his last film in South Africa and the Southern States of America 'Just because I fell in love with a coloured girl,' he moaned.

Most of the company found his attitude unbearable. 'You're just a reverse racist, Peter,' someone said. 'With you black's good, white's bad. Shirley isn't either, she's Welsh.'

Peter Finch finally decided that he and Shirley were still the best of soul mates. In fact he hoped that one day she would come back to him. He even thought that this would happen when he made his next film in America. He knew that Shirley's yearly trip to Australia would take place after the 1965 New Year, and after that she would be going to Las Vegas and Hollywood.

After the disaster of *Judith*, Finch was slated to make *The Flight of the Phoenix* on location in Yuma, Arizona, a serious story of a plane crash in the Libyan desert with a cast that included James Stewart and Richard Attenborough. After completing work in the Arizona desert the film would be finished in the Hollywood studios, and this was how Peter saw his chance of meeting up with Shirley again.

Peter and Shirley were, indeed, still friends, interested in each other's professional lives. He telephoned her before she left on tour. Would she come and see him in Hollywood when she started the Hollywood part of her tour? Taken by surprise, Shirley laughed and said maybe, but by the time she reached America plans had changed and she wired him in Yuma to say no.

A publicity woman working with the film company in Yuma was a close friend of Peter's and related how, when he received the wire, he wept and drank for two days. Finally he said to her, 'Shirley's a fabulous person and I'm mad about her but she's not really the sort of person I could marry. She's too ambitious.'

The two divorce cases were down to be heard in February 1965. Yolande Finch *v* Peter Finch, and Kenneth Hume *v* Shirley Hume. Kenneth Hume's evidence against Shirley was sensational. He alleged that Samantha, the little girl who was just over one year old, was not his child. She was the child of one of two co-respondents with whom his wife had committed adultery. One was Peter Finch, the other was an Australian called John McAuliffe. He demanded that these two men have blood tests to decide who was the father. He had proved from his own blood test that he was not.

What he hoped to gain from this revelation is questionable. It might have been the trick he kept up his sleeve as a last desperate gesture, but Shirley had moved on.

Peter Finch spent the day after his divorce at Tickerage, the country home of Vivien Leigh. She was now divorced from Laurence Olivier and living with Jack Merivale. Vivien and Peter had retained a very high regard for each other.

There always remained a feeling of what might have been for Shirley and Peter. They met by chance in Switzerland three years later. Peter was with a girl called Aretha, from Jamaica. A few days later, Finchy telephoned her, 'I can't stand it any more. I'm going back to Jamaica.' Shirley said, 'It was the last I ever saw of him.'

Peter Finch's career didn't really take off in a big way again until when he made *Network*, with William Holden and Faye Dunaway, for which he won a posthumous Oscar. He had been living in Jamaica and had finally married Aretha. They moved to Hollywood, where Peter Finch died aged fifty-eight in 1977. He had walked down to the Beverly Hills Hotel for a meeting with a producer when he collapsed with a fatal heart attack in the hotel lobby.

While the divorces were going through Shirley embarked on her annual Australian–American tour, with Kenny Clayton as her musical director and Vic West as her tour manager. Kenneth Hume said he would call in to see them in Las Vegas when they began the American leg of the tour.

Kenneth Hume was fully in charge of Shirley's career again. Their marriage was legally over but few who worked with them saw any difference. Bernard Hall, who knew them both well, said that Shirley's conversations with Kenneth were never typical of that of husband and wife, but then they never talked like manager and star either. There was still an intimacy between them, an emotion based on familiarity, affection and forgiveness.

Shirley, Kenny and Vic got along well and enjoyed themselves together. The stopover on their way to Sydney was Singapore. They stayed at the Goodwood Park Hotel where the owner, Freddie Euwe, introduced them to Matt Monroe, the well-known English singer who was having a stopover after finishing an Australian tour. 'Two top-notch singers in my hotel,' said Freddie, 'I'd love to have you sing in my cabaret.' Then he had a better idea. 'Let's have a concert. Let's all make money!'

Posters went up all over the town, and every ticket for the National Theatre was sold. Ex-pats still talk about the wonderful Shirley Bassey concert way back in 1965. No-one knew how it happened but there she was, singing in Singapore.

When the Australian tour was over the trio flew to Las Vegas where Shirley was always a big hit. To Kenny Clayton's dismay Kenneth Hume turned up as promised. Kenny had disliked Hume since their first disastrous meeting when Hume had behaved so badly. In his view, 'Kenneth Hume was a gambler. Not the roulette kind, more the fruit machine type. I knew he'd be more at home betting on the dogs or playing cards in Soho.' His big losses on cards were gossiped about in Denmark Street, and it was rumoured that while Shirley was singing her butt off all over the world, a lot of her money was being paid out in gambling debts to the Soho Mafia.

Kenny had his own feelings about the strange marital relationship between Shirley and Kenneth Hume. He blamed it on the common mistake women stars make when they marry a man in show business. They think the man will put them and their career first, but they don't. 'And Shirley's well out of that one too,' said Kenny, when she broke up with Peter Finch.

Long experience with female performers had made Kenny wise. It was never wise to mix business with pleasure. It was not that Shirley encouraged familiarity, but in Las Vegas Kenny was worried about the effect Kenneth Hume was having on her. 'She changed when he came,' Kenny recalled. 'She'd been a pussycat all through the tour. It was strange, but now I could hear him in her voice. Hume had this nasty habit of shouting and yelling and sometimes I could hear his rage in her voice. As I, and nearly everyone else in London couldn't stand him, I didn't like what I heard.'

From Las Vegas they went to Hollywood where Leslie Simmons at the office in London had rented a house for them in Coldwater Canyon. Shirley's Scandinavian nanny, Dagmar, flew out with the two children who were going to have a great holiday with their mother. Fortunately, Kenneth Hume had little taste for lounging around swimming pools and soon left. The others, who'd been working hard in Vegas, were delighted to use this pool built out on a ledge over the canyon. Way down below they could see the yellow blanket of smog hanging over Los Angeles. 'Shoot an arrow down there,' Kenny told the children, 'and it'll get stuck in the smog.' In Coldwater Canyon the gardens were lush and the air was clean. At night they'd hear the coyotes who came to drink at the swimming pool, and Shirley, said Kenny, 'was just like she'd been at the beginning of the tour – lovely to be with.'

They were in Hollywood to film two television shows. Kenneth Hume had sold an idea to NBC. 'Get the two Basseys together and let them sing.' He was talking about Count Basie, the famous American jazz musician and Shirley Bassey. NBC, were willing to take it up if Count Basie was free. The other TV spot was a song with Dean Martin on his show.

For a girl who usually stayed home and watched television, Shirley was enjoying going out and about in Hollywood. She even accepted an invitation to a barbecue and met Sidney Poitier, and the saw Leslie Bricusse and Tony Newley again. They had written the lyrics for Shirley's big success, 'Goldfinger'.

Televising the Dean Martin Show went well. Martin had it in his contract that he did not have to come to rehearsals so Shirley rehearsed with a stand-in. When the big day came, Dean charmed Shirley. He put his arm around her and asked, 'How do you like my socks?' They were pink and thick and awful. She told him so. His wife had knitted them. Dean was such a clever and experienced performer and so expert that Shirley loved the show. She said afterwards, 'He is the best.'

The Count Basie telecast was very different. Count Basie was an American icon, venerated by all musicians. Kenny Clayton says, 'At that time Shirley was not into jazz and swing. I doubt if she even realised what a great artist Count Basie was. He was one of the greatest exponents of jazz and swing in the world. To musicians his name was magic.'

But Kenny Clayton had his reservations about the idea because the two artists were so very different. Count Basie was away on tour so NBC, who knew all about his status, arranged a lightning visit for him. He would be flown in by the afternoon, televise three numbers with Shirley, and fly off again immediately afterwards. They knew just how lucky they were to have him at all.

All went well on the day. Shirley recorded four numbers in the morning and broke for lunch. Count Basie arrived as arranged, the director introduced everyone to 'Bill Basie', then said to Kenny, 'Will you show Bill how the song goes?' Kenny said he felt like the village tailor teaching Christian Dior how to sew. 'This is how I usually play,' he said nervously, and tried a bar or two. Bill Basie's creased old face split into a grin. He sat down next to Kenny on the piano stool. 'Enough of that shit,' he laughed. 'Let's try it this way.'

The atmosphere immediately became relaxed and everything went perfectly. Shirley's song was fine and the crew applauded her. Every number went exactly as it should, with an added touch of elegance and class because Basie sat at the piano.

When it was over Shirley went upstairs to change her costume for the last number that would close the telecast. While she was up there Bill Basie left to catch his plane and everyone, including the crew, suddenly vanished.

'Union break,' explained the assistant. 'They'll be back in twenty minutes.' Kenny, who had worked in America before, remember that these union breaks were absolutely sacrosanct to the crew. Woe betide anyone who tried to interfere with them. At that moment, Shirley came down the stairs from her dressing room and surveyed the empty studio. 'Where the fuck is everyone?' she demanded to know.

The director's assistant explained.

'What!' bellowed Shirley, 'Twenty minutes! Am I expected to sit in this crummy studio for twenty minutes?' Her voice rose with each word. Why hadn't he the common courtesy to let her know? She'd hurried through a change of costume and make-up so as not to keep anyone waiting. 'And what do they do?'

Kenny blushed with shame. That was not Shirley talking. It was Kenneth Hume. He had heard him saying to Shirley, in front of him, 'Every morning you go to the mirror and you say to yourself, I am a star and you bloody well make them treat you like a star.' There was even a trace of his husky cockney in Shirley's voice as she belted out the insults. 'I'd rather be sitting down on my backside like you,' Shirley blasted at the unfortunate assistant, 'Doing nothing.'

The director's assistant was on his feet. Would Miss Bassey like something to drink, some tea perhaps?

Shirley told him what he could do with his tea. Kenny sat and listened to this echo of Hume's voice ringing around the studio. Kenneth Hume, you evil queen, he thought. What had he done to her? If the crew could hear her they'd give her a bad time with her next number.

Shirley, perhaps, realised this, and suddenly shut up and sat down. She had gone too far. The director's assistant could pass on every insult to his superiors. Hume had told her not to let herself be treated like dirt but he hadn't taught her how to extricate herself gracefully from a difficult position.

But she did learn. In a television biography she made in Monte Carlo over thirty years later (1994), Shirley said, 'I used to make terrible scenes because I thought that was the way I had to act. Now I know better. I've learned how to say, "Sorry."'

Bernard Hall took a British European Airways flight from Paris to London on 12 September 1965, and by doing so, happened to become Shirley Bassey's next tour manager. Just before take-off a man hurried up the aircraft steps. He slid into the nearest available seat. Once they were airborne the man lit a cigarette, drew the smoke down into his lungs and exhaled with a sign of pleasure. He glanced across at the man in the next seat and his thin face split into a wide grin. 'Wotcha cock' he said. Bernard Hall turned to see Kenneth Hume.

They had met now and then over the years, and Kenneth looked much the same to Bernard, the yellow hair, the gap-toothed grin. He might be thinner under his expensive suit but he was as hyperactive as ever, the same wide-boy from Soho, chain-smoking, and tea-drinking while Bernard enjoyed a Scotch. He'd been over in Paris seeing about French television for Shirley. Had Bernie done much? And Marlene Dietrich, did she do much?

Bernard brought him up to date, and told him that he, himself, had done a lot of television in France and Switzerland. He gave Kenneth some useful names and added that he had never worked in British TV, which was considered the best.

'Think I can help you there, Bernie. How would you like a few days in November? Shirley's got a show.'

A few days' television would fit in nicely because the Bernard

Hall Quintet was appearing during the month of October at the Edmundo Ross Club in Regent Street. It was to be the Quintet's last appearance before they disbanded. Bernard had had enough of being manager, choreographer, lead dancer and sometimes nanny to four girls. He would probably tour with Dietrich in the new year and there was plenty of work for him at La Nouvelle Eve in Paris once the real season started on 15 September.

Before their plane landed, Kenneth told Bernard that Shirley was opening at the Pigalle that night and suggested he call round and say hello to her before her show. Bernard said that calling round before a show wasn't always a good idea. 'Tonight it is,' said Kenneth 'because I've got plans. See ya.'

Bernard did see Shirley before her opening. She let him into her dressing room then locked the door so that no-one else could bother her. He said he'd only stay a moment but she told him to sit down. The air was heavy with the fragrance of French perfume. An expensive bottle of Guerlain's 'Mitsouko' stood on the dressing table. He watched her use it. First she dabbed the scent on to a white face cloth, then she smoothed the cloth along her arms and legs. She wore only a flimsy kimono and was nude underneath except for a G-string. Nudity never bothered Shirley. Finally she stood up, lifted her wig from the base of her neck and gently touched her hair and neck with the flannel. The scent would waft out to the audience as Shirley made her sinuous body movements on stage.

'Zip me up, Balls, will you?' Shirley asked pointing to a black dress embroidered with sequins round the hem and layered with organza that hung on the dress rail. It was a glamorous number with a long split up the thigh. As he settled her into the dress she mentioned that Kenneth had told her that Balls would be doing some TV with them after her show closed in November. 'Go and stay with Kenneth,' she told Bernard. 'He's got this flat in Westbourne Terrace, save you money.'

She was made up and ready for the show, so he couldn't kiss her. Instead he touched her shoulder. Her muscles felt taut. She wanted him out of the way so she could be alone before the show. *Merde* he said, the word that, in the best theatrical tradition, he had often used to wish her luck in the old days.

Outside in the corridor flowers were arriving, basket after basket of red roses. The dresser waiting outside Shirley's door smiled at him as he looked at the profusion of blooms in amazement. 'From Mr Hume,' she said. 'I bet there's a thousand roses there.'

The Pigalle Theatre Restaurant was jam-packed. Every table was full. The wiry little figure of Sammy Davis Jr surrounded by his entourage filled one table, while other famous faces from the stage and screen could be seen elsewhere in the room. Dinner was over, there was noise and clatter as the waiters cleared away the remains of the dessert. They worked swiftly, they had to finish before Shirley came on. Every trolley must be wheeled out and the kitchen doors firmly closed. There must be no waiter service when Miss Bassey was on. Shirley had kept her vow that she would never be 'thrown in with the dinner'.

A small stage complete with microphone was silently moved out on to the dance floor in front of Kenny Clayton and his orchestra. Kenny, directing the orchestra, was at his place at the piano. There was a feeling of expectancy as the audience sat back in their chairs and waited for Shirley's entrance. Through the haze of cigar smoke Bernard Hall saw Kenneth Hume waiting for him at the back of the restaurant. Just as he'd said, he was there in Tray Alley, the strip of carpet where the waiters plodded back and forth in and out of the now closed kitchen doors. Kenneth was combing his yellow hair ready for action. He needed an audience and here it came.

There was a roll of drums and a voice announced, 'Miss Shirley Bassey.' The applause grew, a woman yelled, 'Shirley I love you.' Two women fans jumped up and clapped furiously. Screams of joy, waves of applause and Shirley was into her 'On a Wonderful Day Like Today' routine.

'She looks great,' said Bernard.

Kenneth nodded towards the spotlights. 'Rose pink crossed with ice blue.' The ice blue touched her skin with a frosty glow and made it look lighter, and the pink gave her radiance. Kenneth, however, wasn't going to waste time with words or listening to Shirley, he was already striding off at high speed to the furthest periphery of the room, Bernard hurrying beside him. As they moved, Kenneth kept up a constant flow of information about the song that Shirley would sing on TV, the one that Bernard was going to fit into a dance routine.

'Does Shirley like it?' Bernard asked.

'I like it,' said Kenneth.

Bernard would much rather have sat down and listened to Shirley singing than march back and forth with this human dynamo. Kenneth suddenly stopped dead and held up his hand. 'Shush! Just listen to this!' Shirley announced her next song. 'It's called, "The Second Time Around,"' she said, 'And it's for the man I'm going to marry.'

There was a brief hum of surprised expectancy from the audience, who then fell silent as Shirley spoke again. 'The man I'm going to marry is my ex-husband, Kenneth Hume.'

The fans leapt into action, screaming with joy. Those who knew Kenneth were less entranced at the news, but applause nevertheless swelled through the restaurant. Everyone clapped and chirruped with delight. An Engagement! Kenny Clayton played the first bars of 'The Second Time Around', and Shirley sang.

'What an actress,' said Kenneth with pride. 'She's good, Bernie, ain't she?'

Bernard was thoroughly bemused; living in France and out of touch with Shirley in recent months, he hadn't heard about their divorce. 'But you're already married' he said.

'Nah,' said Kenneth. 'We got divorced last February, didn't we. Now we're getting engaged. Wait till you see the ring. The press are coming backstage. We got champagne and roses'. He grinned at Bernard.

'You're joking,' said Bernard.

Kenneth winked at him. 'Keep it under your hat, Bernie boy.'

Bernard remembers that he gazed at Kenneth in disbelief. Was he insinuating that this was a publicity stunt to get Shirley's face on the front page? To promote some recording or other? Then he told himself to get real, this was showbiz after all.

Next morning there were pictures on the front page of the newspapers showing Shirley with her arms round Kenneth's neck, her cheek pressed to his, saying to the press, 'We are very much in love.' She was wearing an enormous square-cut diamond engagement ring.

The *South Wales Echo* took the event very seriously; after all, Shirley was their national treasure. 'There were so many flowers at the Pigalle finale that it looked like Covent Garden,' ran the write-up, 'and Shirley's dressing room was banked with one thousand red roses from Mr Hume. Said Mr Hume to the *South Wales Echo*, 'I didn't propose to Shirley – I didn't need to. We are both so much in love and I think we always have been.'

The quote continued, 'We haven't set a date for the marriage but I am leaving for America on Wednesday and won't be back for about a month. Shirley will be appearing at the Pigalle at a record-breaking salary of three thousand pounds a week'.

It was all wonderful publicity for Shirley's eight weeks at the Pigalle and any other career moves Kenneth might have been planning. Michael Sullivan, on reading about it in the press, wondered if Kenneth had bought the one thousand roses on a sale or return basis.

Shirley came to Bernard's opening at the Edmundo Ross Club in Oxford Street, after her own performance at the Pigalle was over. With her were two men from the Pigalle; Kenneth was still in America. Before she left, Shirley invited Bernard to go dancing with her the following night after both their shows were over.

Five extraordinary night followed. Each began in the same way: Shirley and Bernard were picked up at the Pigalle and driven by limousine to a penthouse flat at The Dorchester Hotel. Their hosts, three gentlemen from one of the Gulf States, awaited them. They were enormously rich and wanted to enjoy London night life in ideal company Shirley and Bernard would be offered a glass of champagne, then it was dinner at the private restaurant in the Dorchester. It was a very social meal where everyone laughed and made jokes. The hosts drank nothing but orange juice and mineral water. After dinner, the party would drive to the Colony Club to dance, Bernard always partnering Shirley. He said of those days, 'There was no better ballroom dancer than Shirley. She could follow like a dream. She was a natural.' They both loved dancing and relished being taken around in great style and luxury just to enjoy themselves.

'To cool off,' recalled Bernard, 'we would return to the table and drink whatever we wanted, champagne or mineral water or even lemonade. Shirley would crack jokes, pull the legs of the gentlemen from the Gulf, throw in a bit of sexy talk, and we'd all laugh uproariously. She was once again like the girl I'd first met years ago. Young, after all she was still in her twenties, happy and laughing. The serious woman always in control vanished, and the real sweet Shirley was back again, enjoying herself.'

Every night after the dancing was over and their hosts had departed, Bernard would see Shirley home to Chester Square. He was never invited in; it was always about four o'clock in the morning and they were both exhausted. Bernard had no idea how this invitation from the 'three wise men' had been initiated. It wouldn't have occurred to Shirley to tell him, but clearly, she was the real star of their evenings, the centrepiece admired by their hosts.

On the last night, when he dropped her off, Shirley said, 'Why don't you come round and see my house about twelve tomorrow, Balls?'

As Bernard stood on the doorstep ringing the doorbell of Shirley's home he reflected that whenever he met her, months, even years, might have passed, but she always acted as if he'd never been away and was just pleased to see him again.

The butler who let him in was black, tall and elegant and wore a starched white jacket with gilt buttons and black trousers. He said, 'Please follow me. Madame is upstairs.' Bernard saw at least twenty of Shirley's gold and silver discs decorating a wall on the way upstairs. Shirley was sitting up in bed with her breakfast tray in front of her, and he remembered the nineteen-year-old girl who had said to him, 'Balls, when I'm rich I shall always have breakfast in bed.' She'd made it; she was rich. Her bedroom was white and spotless, very feminine and very expensive. There was white lace on the bedcover, white lace edging the lawn pillows. The carpet was so white one was almost afraid to walk on it.

Shirley noticed his pleasure as he looked around and asked him to open the walk-in cupboards that lined the room. Each one was a small room in itself, meticulously tidy. There was one for evening gowns, another for performance costumes, one for suits, others for day dresses, sports clothes, shoes and furs. No wonder he had always called Shirley, 'Norah Neat'. She had always been fanatically tidy.

When he finally sat down Shirley told him that she'd talked on the phone to Kenneth Hume in New York and he'd suggested that as Bernard had 'looked after' Marlene Dietrich on tour, he might be the ideal person to look after Shirley on her forthcoming tour in January. He'd talk to him about it when he got back from America. 'What's Marlene like on tour, Balls?' she asked.

'She's just as tidy and neat as you are. She likes men just as you do, and she loves gossip.' It crossed his mind how alike these two women were in several ways, though dancing with Marlene was never as much fun as dancing with Shirley.

Their chatting was interrupted by a sudden commotion on the stairs outside. In raced a small noisy girl followed by a plump and breathless nanny. They were Samantha, aged three, and Thelma, her nanny, who had difficulty grabbing the naughty three-year-old. Samantha was quite a handful. She was quite different in looks to her older sister, Sharon, who was at day school. Samantha had light brown curly hair and dark blue eyes. She didn't look like her mother either.

When they gone, Shirley told him that both girls and their nanny would be coming along on the first part of the Australian tour: 'I always promised myself that one day my children would travel with me.' They talked about the tour, and about America, where it would finish.

Shirley had been among the entertainers who took part in the 1963 Second Anniversary party for President Kennedy. She was one of the most applauded stars, singing 'Everything's Coming Up Roses' and 'The Nearness of You'.

President Kennedy was probably Shirley's favourite, but she had an autographed picture of herself with President Nixon in a place of honour in the hall of her home.

'Did you know?' asked Shirley 'that I sang at the White House for President Kennedy? It was a big party. Funny how it came about. His wife, Jackie, had heard me sing in the Persian Room in New York. She raved about me, imagine! Go on,' she laughed, 'now match that, Balls.'

'I can't,' said Bernard, 'the best I've done is Grace Kelly.'

'The best I've done,' said Shirley, 'is having my two children. They were the two happiest times of my life.'

'Better than the Inauguration party?'

'Much better.'

13

THE STAR TATTOO

KENNETH HUME RETURNED from America in a good mood. Shirley was signed up for Las Vegas and the Royal Box nightclub in the Americana Hotel in New York. Bernard was going to choreograph the 'La Bamba' number for Shirley's television show and he was going to 'look after' her on her Australian–American tour. They'd leave in January, but meanwhile, Bernard would stay in Kenneth's flat in Westbourne Terrace.

The night of a thousand roses, the proposal of a second marriage and the diamond engagement ring were never mentioned. Shirley wore the ring and if a journalist asked when the wedding would be, she smiled sweetly and said nothing. Then, just before her tour of the Philippines, Shirley revealed to the press that she had cancelled her plans to re-marry her ex-husband, Kenneth Hume.

'We've decided against remarrying, we're much better friends as we are,' said Shirley. Bernard found that Kenneth Hume was quite easy to live with. Just as Shirley's house in Chester Square, Belgravia, was exactly the right address, Kenneth's flat in Westbourne Terrace was slightly suspect. It was too near Paddington Station and the area was nicknamed 'Hooker Heaven' due to the prostitutes regularly plying their trade right down to the Bayswater Road and Hyde Park. As soon as Bernard closed the front door behind him to go out, Daphne and Ruby, two of the regulars, always made a beeline for him. 'Evening, Ruby. How's tricks?' 'Hello, dear,' Ruby would reply. 'Bit slow. Anything for you?'

'No thank you.'

They got even shorter shrift from Kenneth who wasn't interested in girls.

Bernard found the flat rather spartan but scrupulously clean. It smelt of cigarette smoke – which would never have been welcomed by Shirley, had they lived together as man and wife.

Kenneth's private life was always kept that way. When Bernard once walked into Kenneth's bedroom he saw a short bamboo cane leaning against one wall 'What are you doing?' he asked. 'Growing tomatoes?' Kenneth knew what Bernard was inferring.

Living in Kenneth's flat Bernard was sometimes awakened by voices in the middle of the night. He wished Kenneth would be more careful because one of these lads could seriously damage Kenneth's career and his way of life with a newspaper headline.

One day Kenneth was so ill that he had to take to his bed for a time but tried to hide that he was sick. This was one of the keys to Kenneth Hume – his secrecy, the pretences, his desperation, contributed to the cruelty with which he ruined relationships. He was a manic depressive but he did everything he could to keep in control and not allow depression to interfere with his life until, as now, it suddenly attacked him. Bernard saw him lying in bed, curled up in misery. 'Go away, Bernie, leave me alone. You can't help, no-one can. Go away.'

Kenneth wanted no-one to see him like that, so vulnerable and pitiful. 'He looked like a frightened little boy,' Bernard recalled. His doctor came and saw him and, when he was better, Kenneth once more became his difficult, unpredictable, sometimes maniacal self, and the last thing he wanted was to be reminded of this terrible weakness.

Between rehearsals for a BBC TV show, Shirley was auditioned for a leading role in Lionel Bart's new musical, *Twang*. Bernard went with Kenneth to watch her go through the paces and realised that he knew rather more about staging a musical than Kenneth Hume did. It needed a man like Jack Hylton to get a musical off the ground, somebody who gave the kind of blood, sweat and tears that Kenneth Hume did not possess. Shirley did not read well for *Twang* and Bernard realised that she needed speech and acting lessons for which she didn't have time. However, none of it mattered on this occasion for *Twang* didn't survive as a show.

Kenneth was now determined to find a musical for Shirley, but there were others who saw great film possibilities for her. The distinguished director Sir Carol Reed, world renowned for films such as *The Third Man*, was to make the film version of *Oliver!* Reed wanted Shirley to play the role of Nancy, the tragic heroine, whose ballad 'As Long as He Needs Me', from the original stage show, had generated a chart-topping hit for Shirley. It was a wonderful choice. Shirley's voice and personality would have lit up the screen every time she appeared but, alas, Columbia Pictures finally turned down the idea on the grounds that audiences in America, especially in the south, might be offended when Nancy, if played by a dark-skinned woman, was murdered by Bill Sykes.

It was a real lost opportunity for Shirley. *Oliver!* would have been her entrée into the film world, and one can only speculate what that might have led on to.

*

The Sunday finally arrived in November 1965 when Shirley Basey's 'Show of the Week', was to be recorded for the BBC. Bernard had choreographed 'La Bamba' with his four male dancers, and the show was to be performed before a live studio audience. It would not, however, be shown to television audiences until nearly a year later, on 8 August, 1966.

Everyone turned up for rehearsal on Sunday morning: Shirley, Kenneth Hume as her manager, Bernard Hall with his four dancers and Kenny Clayton with his orchestra. Kenny had assembled a group of musicians especially for this recording – a common practice then and now.

By the time they got round to the final rehearsal before recording, the daylight had died and the audience queuing outside the theatre was getting very cold. Shirley had got through half of her numbers and 'La Bamba' was next on the list. Kenny Clayton was enjoying himself; the music was very good and Shirley looked great in her white tasselled dress. Everyone was happy.

Bernard, standing in the wings, was less happy as he watched the number begin. Getting through a long programme is always like walking a tightrope. Fall and you've blown it. And this number, 'La Bamba' involved dancing as well as singing. He was worried that Shirley might miss a step. Of course, the boys would cover up for her, but she'd get angry. Angry with herself, angry with the dancers, and angry with the song.

'La Bamba' began well enough. Shirley moved gently back and forth as she sang, and the four dancers stepped up the tempo of the dance as Shirley's song took on increased power and vigour. Then she missed a step. She stopped dead. 'Ken—neth . . .' when she was angry she always drew his name out, syllable by syllable, painfully, through her teeth. Her voice rose above the music. 'I can't do it. Stop!'

Kenny Clayton brought the orchestra to halt. Everyone froze. In the fifth row of the stalls, the best position for music and sound, Kenneth Hume jumped to his feet. He grabbed the back of the seat in front of him and shook it as if he wanted to wrench it apart. 'Madam!' he yelled, 'What the hell are you up to?'

'This song,' Shirley shouted back, each word loud and clear. This bamba crap. Take it out. I hate it.'

'You didn't hate it yesterday.'

'I hate it now. Take it out.'

Kenneth removed his cigarette from its holder. He stubbed it out carefully, inserted another, lit it, took a deep painful drag, then raised his head and shouted 'It's in and it stays in.'

This was Kenneth's song. The one he had engaged Bernard to choreograph, the number that *must* be shown on television with Shirley singing and dancing. The first step towards Shirley's musical produced by Kenneth Hume. He had to keep it in.

Shirley clasped her hands to together and began to rock back and forth. 'Bastard,' she screamed. 'Bastard! Bastard! Bastard!'

'Miss Bassey,' Kenneth yelled. 'Go to your dressing room.' Then he turned to the orchestra. 'Gentlemen, take fifteen minutes break.'

Shirley swayed and two of the boys who had danced behind her caught her before she fell. Bernard and the boys helped her to her dressing room where they laid her on a couch. Everyone started looking for a blanket, or something to cover her with, because she was trembling.

Kenneth Hume, still smoking his cigarette and looking tight with anger marched in. 'You've got a full orchestra waiting for you out there,' he snarled.

Shirley closed her eyes. 'So what? I'm the star.'

He surveyed her. 'Twinkle twinkle,' he said sarcastically.

She opened her eyes and looked up at him. 'I'm in pain,' she whispered. Bernard, looking over Kenneth's shoulder thought that

Shirley did look very frail, and Kenneth realised she was ill. He made the right decisions at once. The show was cancelled and the disappointed people queueing outside were sent away. Shirley's dressing room became a hive of alarmed activity.

An ambulance arrived. Kenneth and Bernard got in and sat opposite Shirley, prone and wrapped in blankets, and the ambulance took them to the London Clinic. Dr Ratner, Kenneth's physician and a well-known figure in London society, awaited them. Finally Shirley was wheeled away to her room. Bernard bent over her to wish her well. He could have sworn that she winked at him.

A few days later it was reported in the *Evening Standard* that Miss Shirley Bassey had left the London Clinic after a few days rest. On Christmas Day 1965 at Chester Square, Thelma, the children's nanny, cooked a splendid Christmas dinner for Shirley, Kenneth, Bernard and the two girls. There was a Christmas tree, and presents for the children and as Bernard left, everyone said, 'Another few days and we'll all be in the sunshine.'

In January 1966 Shirley and her two daughters, Samantha and Sharon, accompanied by the new tour manager, Bernard Hall, musical director Kenny Clayton, and the children's nanny, Thelma, arrived at London airport en route for Sydney, Australia. The press photographers were waiting for the happy little family. They looked a picture: Shirley in a black and white checked coat with a white lamb collar and little cap to match, Sharon in a flowered coat and hat, and the baby, Samantha, dressed up with little boots and mittens against the January cold.

Shirley, smiling and maternal, said, 'It's wonderful to take my children all over the world with me.' Reminiscing in later years, Shirley said that her tours were always mixed with sadness for, as her children grew older, they had to stay at school and that is when trouble started. 'The hardest thing of all,' says Shirley, 'was saying goodbye to my girls.'

By the time the plane came down in Delhi, a stopover for refuelling, Bernard wondered just what he had let himself in for. Managing Marlene Dietrich on tour had sometimes been difficult, but never like this. Thelma felt ill. Sharon and Samantha whined that they were too hot and wanted a drink, and Shirley had just told Bernard if he didn't like it he knew what to do. There was no air conditioning and a few tired punka fans whirred listlessly. Kenny Clayton had mysteriously vanished the moment the aircraft steps were in place. Canny guy, thought Bernard enviously.

Bernard and his female entourage stood abandoned in the middle of a noisy Indian bazaar which was the Reception area. 'I feel ill,' groaned Thelma. She'd been a bad aircraft passenger, feeling ill as soon as they crossed the English Channel.

Happy Indian families sat on the floor of the vast hall and tucked into picnics of curry and rice and chappaties as they waited for relatives to arrive from the Punjab, Patna or Calcutta. The smell of garlic, spices and frying koftas made Thelma feel even worse, and she had to be taken outside into the fresh air. Bernard sat the little group on an empty bench outside where they huddled together as flies dive-bombed them and the little yellow scooter-vans ran circles around them.

An old man with a glass barrel of lemonade on his back passed by and the children immediately cried that they were dying of thirst. Shirley let out a shrill warning about deadly germs and asked Bernard to find some nice clean sealed Coca-Cola. When he returned Thelma, who still looked green, asked pathetically when they were leaving. The children said it was too hot and Shirley sighed. Bernard said he'd try and find them a better place to sit. As he left he said to Shirley, perhaps unwisely, 'This isn't really for us, is it?'

Shirley stared at him as if he'd said something completely incomprehensible. 'Not for us?' she repeated as if she'd lost her senses. 'I'm going to Sydney. I've signed the contracts. I am going there, Sharon is going there, we're all going, and if you don't like the way we're getting there, then piss off.'

Bernard found a benign airport official who took pity on them and gave them a cool office. There was a punka fan overhead but the smell was now of sandalwood and a flit spray. The children fell asleep and the two ladies closed their eyes. Bernard sat staring into space and his thoughts wandered. He reflected on Shirley's determination to perform, come hell or high water, and suddenly came to a realisation. Shirley and Marlene Dietrich – how alike these two women were. They were unstoppable. Both seemed to have a dynamo inside themselves that drove them on, and if they began to flag, they'd always have something in reserve to fuel them right to the top; that special ingredient that kept their faces on billboards all over the world: the star tattoo.

As soon as they arrived in Sydney, they changed planes and left at once for Melbourne for a rest. The office manager back in London had got this one absolutely right: The Fairfax was a luxury hotel out of town and had a swimming pool. The children would be happy being looked after by Thelma while the three adults went to work. Kenny Clayton introduced Bernard to John McAuliffe, Shirley's Melbourne agent and the man cited by Kenneth Hume in his divorce case. There existed a happy relationship between them all until they discovered where Kenneth Hume decided they should work.

Kenny Clayton was the first to take a look at the Roaring Twenties nightclub. He came back with a strange story. 'The taxi driver told me that until last week the club was a chocolate factory, and you can still smell the chocolate.' Furthermore, in spite of Kenneth promising otherwise, they were going to have to work two shows a night. Kenny produced a handbill which read, 'Roaring Twenties Restaurant, for a limited season of 9 days February 3rd to February 12th [Two floor shows nightly] Miss Shirley Bassey. Book now. Entrance price £20 with a bottle of champagne on the table.'

That wasn't the only unpleasant surprise. The drink laws in Australia had recently been changed and it was no longer an offence to buy liquor after six p.m. So it was no longer necessary to go to a nightclub to get an after-hours drink – the pubs were cheaper. This would surely have hit the nightclub trade. They had to rely on Shirley's name to fill the place.

After a week of resting by the pool they all felt better, and Bernard and Shirley were back in their old friendly relationship, though not lovers as they had been in Cannes. Things were very different. She was a much more important star than he had ever been then.

As soon as he saw the Roaring Twenties Bernard knew Shirley wouldn't like it. Something very odd had been happening. The chocolate factory turned out to be a kind of village hall with a corrugated iron roof. It was now empty, with a hastily built wooden stage for the performers and room for the orchestra. The place designated as Shirley's dressing room was a disgrace, a couple of cane chairs and a table, a mirror, an electric light bulb or two. The story was that someone had chosen a cheap setting, pulled in a big star and was going to make a killing before the place was pulled down in a week or two. Shirley was expected to sit in this place for six or seven hours in the intense heat every afternoon and evening, with no air conditioning or fans. The Roaring Twenties was half an hour's drive from the hotel and there was a long wait between shows. Shirley's performances were very hard work, not the kind she could conclude and then walk away from. She had to be left alone for a time, to come down to earth again. This was no way to treat her and Bernard was appalled: Kenneth Hume must surely have known the kind of place they were coming to.

Shirley, Bernard and Kenny began the routine that would last for the next nine days. The car would call for them while everyone else was having an afternoon siesta. She'd go into the children's room and call, 'Bye now, Balls and I are off to work.' She'd pick up little Samantha and bury her face in the baby's round tummy, making buzzing noises, and the child would shriek with pleasure. Young Sharon would quietly watch them before they left, finally getting a kiss herself.

They'd drive through the suburb of Windsor which was filled with migrants building their houses, invariably witness a fight or two en route, and finally arrive at Chapel Street and the chocolate factory. Kenny Clayton would disappear until he came back later with the orchestra for the first performance. Bernard was acting throughout the tour as Shirley's dresser so he would remain with her. She was fortunate to have Bernard around who would sensitively blend into the background if required. If Shirley wanted to talk, he could be funny and witty, if not he kept quiet. He was the perfect dresser for a volatile star like Shirley.

The village hall looked a bit better now with curtains, jazzy cloths on the tables, and shaded electric lights, but it was still a dump. Shirley would apply her make-up, put on her wig and Bernard would help her into her dress. A final spray of perfume and she'd be ready for the first show. It was like the attack was about to begin. She reminded him of a little boxer going into the ring, arm muscles moving, the whole chest rising, the fighter going in to win.

The words came ringing into the dressing room 'Miss Shirley Bassey' . . . and then she'd take a deep deep breath and out she'd go, ready for anything. Cheers and shouts always greeted her, 'Australia loves ya, baby!' The noise level reached a crescendo. The adrenalin was flowing now and she was into her first number. Every number would be just as good and she'd be just as good in the second show, and the day after. She was the consummate professional.

Bernard would be waiting for her when she finished the early show, and, soaked with perspiration, Shirley would rip off her wig and throw it across the room. Bernard then took off her dress very carefully and covered her with large white fleecy towels. Finally he eased her into a white bathrobe. He'd hang up her expensive dress to dry and observe her sitting silent and exhausted and fetch her some tea. He knew she needed to be alone, for this was what he had felt in the past. Later she'd want to talk, but not yet. He looked after her by instinct and experience as well as with the skills learned from Marlene Dietrich, who had been his tutor. He admired Shirley's gutsiness and talent tremendously and he was falling in love with her all over again.

Shirley and Bernard both blamed Kenneth Hume for letting her sign a contract that meant two shows a night and hours spent in an unventilated box without even a lavatory. Shirley said she had put a call through to Kenneth in London, but had had to leave a message.

Bernard was having problems with Kenneth's money. Kenneth had arranged that Bernard should pick up Shirley's share of the club's takings at the end of each show, and bank it the next day. John McAuliffe seemed to be running the nightclub and it was to him that Bernard was expected to go. At the end of the first night John asked him to wait until tomorrow, because he had not yet counted the champagne bottles. Shirley was not pleased. Bernard must make John understand that it was a case of no money, no Shirley. If the money was not handed over every night she would not sing. Neither Kenny Clayton nor Bernard liked doing Kenneth Hume's job for him, but they did it for Shirley.

It was always part of Bernard's job to wake Shirley up every morning at twelve. He'd stroke her forehead gently until she opened her eyes. When her breakfast tray was brought up he'd sit with her and chat while she ate her breakfast. They were chatting when Kenneth Hume returned Shirley's call to him. Shirley told him how upset she was about having to do two shows a night in such a terrible dump. He heard Hume cut in and tell her that it wouldn't hurt her to do two shows a night.

Shirley told him what she thought of that. There was no bathroom, no toilet, no ventilation, in fact there was damn all. Kenneth's breezy comment came over loud and clear. 'You gettin' old? What's a marrer?'

That did it. The flood gates opened and Shirley unleashed a torrent of abuse. First, she was doing eighteen shows, shows in tropical heat, and that was the best he could say? She told him what she thought of him, how she hoped he would live to regret his words. He was this, he was that, she spelt it all out. When she'd finished she slammed down the receiver. Shirley then picked up the heavy breakfast tray. She raised it as high as she could and, in a great show of strength, hurled it right across the room.

Bernard wisely kept his mouth shut. He knew exactly how she felt. The night before she had told him that he reminded her of Finchy, the absent Peter Finch, and she'd asked why didn't he give up dancing and take up acting seriously, as that was where the money was. She showed that she cared about him and he loved her for it, and he loathed Kenneth Hume for treating her so badly.

Bernard knew that Shirley wasn't in love with him any more, but she was fond of him in her own special way. They had a loyalty to each other and the tenderness still remained. He was young and good-looking and a professional entertainer like herself. He knew all about the trauma of being alone on an empty stage, the dangers if something goes wrong, and how long it takes to get down from that high after a performance. His way to relax after a performance was to have a meal with friends, drink wine and talk until he was tired enough to sleep. Shirley's way was different, she could only eat very light meals, she hardly drank and she liked to return to her hotel, take off her make-up and go straight to bed. She would take two Tuinols to help her sleep, but they didn't always work.

Shirley worried that lack of sleep affected her voice, so they started a nightly routine to try and help her sleep. He would sit on the edge of her bed; they'd chat about the show, gossip, flirt, and after a time she thought she might doze off so he'd kiss her good-night, but that didn't always work either. Perhaps his goodnight kiss did get a little warmer every night and one night he didn't leave at all.

Bernard was happy that they became lovers again. There was nothing cold blooded about their nightly routine. He was excited by her touch and there was strong sexual chemistry. Bernard found Shirley incredibly desirable, full of fire and yet also vulnerable. They both enjoyed lovemaking and Shirley no longer had any problem sleeping.

Melbourne came to an end and only the fact that the children and Thelma would soon have to fly home was a slight dampener to their high spirits. By the time they left the children would have had six weeks of holiday. It was not a good idea to take them on the rest of the tour for some of it could be pretty rough, and anyway Sharon had to go back to school.

Of the two children Bernard found Sharon much the easiest. Little Samantha was always on the go and one of her favourite early morning pranks was going into Bernard's bedroom and stuffing cornflakes down his pyjama trousers. There was certainly some of Shirley's talent in her and Bernard taught her little songs and dances. A couple of years later Samantha sang and danced in a charity show at the Adelphi Theatre. The song, 'I'll Be Your Sweetheart', was one Bernard had taught Samantha in Melbourne.

Bernard with Shirley applauded enthusiastically, and afterwards her mother wept with emotion.

Sharon was very different, quiet and more of a loner. She would wrap the curtains in Shirley's Melbourne hotel bedroom around herself and while Bernard and Shirley chatted they forgot that she was there. She seemed to need to listen to grown-ups talking together. Her life had changed abruptly when she left her foster mother and father in Wales to live with her real mother. Shirley has admitted that she knew Sharon had problems adjusting and it took time, as well as a family tragedy, before she felt that at last they were close and had a loving and happy mother and daughter relationship.

In Sydney everything was good. The hotel was luxurious and the nightclub, the Chequers, was well run. Their agent, Charlie Baxter, looked after all the big stars who came to Australia, and he was full of laughs; a *bon viveur* who loved wine, good food and parties. After a month in Sydney Charlie would be travelling with them to New Zealand. He asked Bernard if he could be called upon to perform song and dance in Shirley's programme should other performers be unable to get to the various theatres. Bernard asked why, and Charlie told him it was the deluges of rain that characterised New Zealand and made transport impossible.

Two Chinese brothers called Wong owned the Chequers in Sydney and they advertised that they were getting the very best international talent in their shows. On Shirley's opening night she could do no wrong. Her audiences loved her. She was '*sinuous, tempestuous, with a voice that raises the roof*' said *The Sydney Sunday Telegraph*. Shirley wowed them with her performance. The papers were full of praise, they declared:

'*The return of Shirley the Tigress.*'

'*Shirley in a peep-holed dress shimmers and simmers.*'

'*Every man in the audience applauds to the last, lustful echo*'.

Before they left for New Zealand Shirley told Bernard that Charlie Baxter was after her. 'What shall I do?' she asked. Bernard realised that must mean she was at least partly interested. Charlie had already asked Shirley why she wasted her time with Bernard. 'I think Bernard's gay,' he told her.

'Not with me, he's not,' said Shirley.

But soon after they arrived in New Zealand Charlie, free of his Australian ties, was getting on with Shirley like a house on fire. Bernard realised this was the moment to bow out and their affair ended. Their relationship resumed to one of warm friendship. Bernard knew he would miss their nightly routines but it mattered far more that they remained good friends. As their plane landed in New Zealand, there, waiting for him, was his old friend Don from Paris.

Don was an American of mixed race. In Paris he had been a dancer with the Katherine Dunham company. When the company disbanded, Don decided that he liked English ways and would emigrate to Australia. His application was turned down because of Australia's 'all white' policy. Don hated being called black. Happily, the more liberal-minded New Zealanders welcomed him. He loved his new country and while they were in Auckland, Shirley and Charlie and Bernard and Don made a foursome. Shirley was interested to meet Don because of her old ties with the Ben Johnson Ballet, which had used some of Katherine Dunham's routines.

Shirley's liberal attitude towards homosexuals was unusual for 1966. Don was homosexual, Bernard was bisexual and Shirley told Bernard that she liked the fact that friendship with a homosexual man could have the warmth and love of an affair without the sex.

Australia's 'all white' policy offended Shirley. At this time there were posters everywhere encouraging people to, 'Keep Australia white.' As Shirley and her little entourage of three men left for New

Zealand, one of the Immigration officers at the airport had asked her whether she had enjoyed her stay.

Shirley pointed to one of the 'Keep Australia white' posters. 'Yes,' she replied, 'but I'm leaving now to keep Australia white.'

After the first week in New Zealand, the heavens opened and the rain came down in buckets. Their next booking was way out in the sticks and the Civic Centre looked like a sinking ship, there was water everywhere. The electricity was down, and there were no lights for the show.

'So we don't play,' said Bernard unhappily.

'Of course we do,' said the manager. 'The performers in the first half won't turn up, they'll never get over the swollen river, so you'll have to fill the first half yourself, Bernard. Can you manage it?'

One of Bernard's first jobs when he was seventeen had been with a concert party at the end of Whitby pier. He even remembered all the jokes. If they had made the tough Yorkshire people laugh they ought to go down well in this hellhole.

A crew of hardy men and local well-wishers moved in to save the situation. They mopped up all the water and more or less dried the place down. Then they hung up hurricane lanterns everywhere, and someone produced a wartime searchlight. The manager was delighted, he called Shirley to come and have a look. 'You just stand there in this great light and everyone will see you just fine.' The manager had never heard about the benefits of lighting a woman with a combination of rose pink and ice blue spots. Shirley shuddered.

Charlie had a fatherly talk to Bernard. 'You've got thirty minutes to fill. But listen, this is not Sydney so keep it clean, they're all rural here, no smut, keep it tidy.' Kenny got a local orchestra band, they rehearsed hard and got the sounds right.

Only Shirley was a bit tight-lipped. They need not expect her to appear in beads and a peep-hole dress. She'd catch pneumonia. She would be well covered in a long white dress and a long white cape coat. Bernard thought she looked like a gospel singer.

That evening the audience poured in, filling the hall and shaking giant umbrellas, pulling off yellow storm coats, sou-westers and rubber boots as they took their seats. The women emerged from their covers looking pretty in their summer dresses. And still they came, although every seat was taken. Where would they go wondered Bernard? Then he saw. Into one wall was built a giant organ that hadn't been played for years; it had more pipes and bits sticking out here and there than any organ he'd ever seen. Up they climbed, the bravest going to the top, others squeezed on to the pipes, and soon the organ was a solid mass of humanity which spilled out to every empty area on the floor.

Kenny and his musicians struck up 'There's no Business like Show Business', and the show and the audience were away. Bernard made his entrance and he could have been Fred Astaire from the applause. They laughed at every joke and when he sang 'Hello Dolly' they all joined in. The New Zealanders wanted to enjoy themselves, they wanted to sing and dance. This was a party.

Bernard's next song had them all on their feet, dancing in the aisles. Kenny and his orchestra could have come straight from the Hammersmith Palais de Danse the way they swung. One after another, the strong and the brave slid down the organ pipes to join in. They were all great dancers. Shirley, peeping from behind the curtain, was absolutely convulsed.

In the interval tea and coffee and sandwiches and cakes were served. When the crumbs were dusted away and the cups stacked up and everyone who had one was back in their seats, Kenny and the boys struck up 'On a Wonderful Day Like Today' and Shirley made her entrance.

She strode on looking for all the world as if she had come straight from the local Mormon Church. No thigh-high split dress, no bare midriff. She stood beneath the ghastly brazen glare of the wartime searchlight in a long white coat, hands clasped together as if she was about to begin a sermon. The audience went wild with delight, but first she had to sing.

The audience cheered her opening number to the rafters and Shirley bowed and approached the microphone again. Her voice was very strong and unusually serious. 'Last year,' she intoned. 'Men walked on the moon.' Shirley liked the sound of this phrase so she repeated it again. 'Last year men walked on the moon.' She was really going to drive that message home. 'Okay duckie, we know,' shouted some wit. Everybody clapped.

'Then why, oh why,' demanded Shirley, 'can you only find me this lousy searchlight?' This one horse town should take a hint from Cape Canavarel.

The audience thought this was the funniest thing they'd heard that night. 'Come on Shirl. Tell us another.' They clapped and cheered. Someone zonked an organ pipe and someone fell off. Screams of joy. Shirley knew when she was beaten. She threw off the terrible Mormon white coat, gave her dress a hitch, and revealed the slit to the navel; that length of thigh. 'Shirley, Shirley,' the hundreds of voices chorused and Shirley gave it her all. It was Shirley in the searchlight that night – at her very best; a night none of them would ever forget.

14

SHIRLEY CONQUERS NEW YORK

THERE WAS USUALLY a major disaster in every tour, and the Nile Club in Manila in the Philippines supplied as good a disaster as most. Manila was very hot and humid, and the Nile Club a stuffy smelly, pick-up joint. It was a long, narrow strip of a room with a bar and girls and a few tables. There was a small orchestra and an apology for a stage. Shirley was not the first singer ever to have appeared there, but she must have been the first one who wasn't a hoochie-coochie dancer too. The band had never seen a sheet of European music before, being able only to play their local bar room music on their native wind instruments, lutes and Filipino balalaikas. If the Roaring Twenties club in Melbourne had been a dump, the Nile belonged up a back alley in a Cairo bazaar.

Before Kenny Clayton grasped what he'd dropped into he handed out sheet music for Shirley's opening number. He sat down at the piano and happily started to play and sing 'Climb Every Mountain' to encourage the musicians. They smiled politely, picked up their instruments and joined in. The noise was ear-splitting, a jangled unmelodious din. Then he saw that all the players had their music upside down on their stands.

This looked like another Kenneth Hume balls-up. Hume had booked the Nile Club sight unseen, presuming they'd make the best of it; it was, after all, only a three-day stopover on the way to Los Angeles . . .

But Kenny Clayton was a man who never lost his temper. He remembered that Manila was used as an American base – somewhere in this city must be one man who could play, 'Climb Every Mountain' on the drums or the saxophone or something. In one of the local bars he found a half-American, half-Filipino boy who said he could play the drums. Shirley was boiling with rage, but she had signed the contract and, ever the professional, she'd do the job. She appeared at the appointed time, well-dressed, beautifully coiffed and perfectly made up.

The Nile Club's bartenders, the girls, and the trickle of clients who came in to drink were the only audience they had, but all the same every note rang out loud and clear in true Bassey form. Kenny and the drummer did their best, and at the end there was a little scattered applause. She sang two more songs, then said to Kenny. 'Now you can play me off.'

That night at the Manila Hotel there was an invasion of spiders as big as golf balls. In the middle of the night Bernard was aroused from his sleep. 'Balls! Balls! They're huge. Come and catch them.' Shirley cowered in the corridor while Bernard removed two monsters from her bed and threw them into the garden outside. When he tried to go back to his room Shirley grabbed his arm. 'You're staying in my room. I'm terrified of spiders.' There was no re-awakening of love's young dream, nor, fortunately, more spiders. Since the advent of Australian Charlie Baxter, both of them had moved on to pastures new.

Four days later Shirley and Bernard arrived in Las Vegas. Kenny Clayton had gone back to London to fulfil a contract touring with Matt Monroe. He was very surprised when Kenneth Hume gave him a thank-you present of a Rolex watch, with an engraving on the back, 'For services rendered.' Shirley missed Kenny. He was a top class musician, very supportive, and such an easy person to travel with. However, by then she had performed in Vegas and New York five or six times, knew the ropes, and got on well with the other musical directors of the various orchestras.

After a day's rest Shirley opened her 1966 six-weeks' season at the Sahara Hotel. She was, as always, a great success in Las Vegas and this year was no different. Las Vegas audiences appreciated her style of singing and not only did 'Goldfinger' bring gales of applause, but they loved the way she teased the concealed eroticism from typical showbiz songs such as 'Hey, Big Spender' from *Sweet Charity*. And of course the strident trumpet-like blast she injected into songs such as, 'I, Who Have Nothing,' and 'No Regrets'.

After her opening show, Shirley uncharacteristically allowed herself to sit in the Sahara lounge and enjoy a couple of glasses of champagne. In the dry desert atmosphere of Las Vegas, Shirley's first concern was her voice. She had two humidifiers installed in her suite, and told Bernard she would not stay long downstairs. A number of entertainers who were performing in other hotels congregated afterwards at the Sahara for a post-show drink and a chat. Bernard recognised some of the showgirls who has worked with him in London and Copenhagen, mostly English and American girls, and he was delighted to see Rudolph, an old friend from Paris, who had been a dancer at the Paris Lido.

Rudolph was tall and slim with blond hair and blue eyes and, was now earning two thousand dollars a night in Las Vegas for dancing in nothing but a rather large G-string. Rudolph couldn't take his eyes off Shirley, and she found him very personable. When she stood up to say goodnight, Rudolph was dashed.

When it happened again the next night, Rudolph demanded to know why 'anyone so beautiful as you always goes up to her suite after her performance. Why do you not stay below talking and having a drink like the rest of us?'

'Because,' said Shirley honestly, 'I love to watch television.'

'So do I,' exclaimed Rudolph, 'but I hate to watch it alone.'

From then on, after their shows were over, for the rest of Shirley's season at the Sahara, no-one saw much of her or Rudolph again.

Security at the Sahara Hotel was overpowering. Rather than use the lift all the time Bernard would run up stairs to see Shirley. On every floor he was stopped by armed guards. He became quite accustomed to a gun being pointed in his direction, but in the end had to accept that Las Vegas was run by the Mafia. The Sahara Hotel had everything to offer but freedom and nothing would tempt Shirley down at night. She and Rudolph preferred to watch TV, she told Bernard. It was the easiest way to pass the time and the safest. She'd seen how rough 'The Mob' could be on her first visit to New York years ago. Not even the fact that Sammy Davis Jr was often around, made her change her mind and come down from her room.

Bernard was now unexpectedly engaged to an American showgirl called Jillian from the Flamingo Hotel. If he married an American citizen he could get the much sought-after Green Card that would enable him to work in the States, and Jillian would become a British subject, able to work in London.

Bernard thought he'd better ask Shirley what she thought of the idea. 'She's a very nice girl, probably make me a very good wife,' he told her.

'You must be out of your mind,' she said. 'You need a wife like you need a hole in the head. Forget it.' He thought about it and realised she was right; he could only live with bad-tempered, power crazy, strong women like Shirley Bassey or Marlene Dietrich.

At the end of six weeks Shirley and Bernard boarded a plane for New York without further entanglements. Shirley had a full schedule waiting for her, including photo sessions and an appointment with a throat specialist before she opening at the Royal Box nightclub in the Americana Hotel.

In the meantime Bernard took Shirley to spend a day with Milton Greene, the man who was once close to Marilyn Monroe and who had taken many photographs of her. Shirley was going to be photographed for some of the covers of her new recordings, and Bernard's job was to get her in and out of her costumes, look after her make-up and ensure that the pictures were flattering.

Shirley held Bernard's arm as they walked back along Madison Avenue that afternoon when a taxi suddenly swerved to a halt by the kerb.

'Bernarr!' a voice called. To Bernard's delight, his old friend Gilbert Becaud, one of France's premier singing stars, young, good-looking and charming, hurried towards them. Apart from being pleased to see Bernard, whom he had known in Paris, Becaud had recognised Shirley, whom he had much admired, and was eager to meet her. He lifted her hand to his lips. 'Madame, mes homages. You are a great artiste.' There was something else Gilbert wanted to thank her for. He had written a song called, 'Et maintenant' which roughly translated means, 'And now'. Shirley had recorded it in English as 'What now, my love,' and it had gone to the top of the British charts. To his compliments, Gilbert added, 'And every time you sing that song, Madame, I get a commission from the music publishers. You are my beautiful benefactrice.'

*

There was one particular scene in the lift at the Americana Hotel that Bernard remembered about their stay in America. He and Shirley were going up in the elevator together. She was beautifully turned out with a mink wrap over an elegant dress. A group of men and women from a Southern state, perhaps Texas, got in. They were more flamboyantly and roughly dressed in checks and bright colours, not a bit New York style, and the men were certainly rednecks. They seemed to have been drinking, and one of them looked Shirley up and down and said in a loud voice, 'How come we get nigras riding with us folk in the same elevator?' Shirley's fingers dug deep into Bernard's upper arm as if to hold him back and stop herself, or him, saying anything. A brawl in the lift didn't solve anything and would reach to front pages of tomorrow's tabloids. It wouldn't do her any good.

Kenneth Hume arrived in New York very early in time for Shirley's first rehearsal at the Royal Box. He took a taxi straight to the Americana. On the way he read the careful itinerary arranged by his London office manager. By the time Bernard got there half an hour late at ten o'clock, Kenneth was exploding with rage.

When he calmed down he was eager to wake Shirley. He told Bernard he'd brought a new recording contract with him for her to sign. These days Kenneth was becoming a first-rate recording producer. 'Big Spender', Shirley's latest disc was going to race to the top of the charts. Bernard, who didn't really understand these things shuddered. How could Kenneth think of waking Shirley up early? Managers had been fired, partnerships ruined and agents kicked out for disturbing her before the magic hour of twelve mid-day. It was Shirley's opening night so he really had to keep Kenneth out of her room.

Breakfast arrived. 'Leave the trolley here,' Bernard told the waiter, 'I've got to wake her up first. Have a cup of tea Kenneth, it's nice and hot.' He looked at his wristwatch. Eleven-thirty. It might work if she didn't see the clock but he daren't go in yet. He looked at Kenneth drinking his tea and wondered how, having been married to Shirley he still didn't understand.

At eleven-forty-five there was no holding Kenneth back any longer. Bernard went in first and woke her gently as he could. Her dark eyes looked up at him then at the clock. They clouded. After she'd had a cup of tea, Kenneth marched in, waving his recording contract for her to sign.

It was a cool reunion at first. Kenneth could have waved a bunch of flowers or brought a gift, a little piece of jewellery, perhaps. Once he had sent her a full box of Mars Bars because he knew that she liked them. This time however, his gift was a recording contract – one with a difference. It was signing her to United Artists. He paced back and forth excitedly, telling her about it, he read out; 'that her American sales would rise dramatically, she was going to become a world-class recording artist who would compete favourably with the best of the American stars.'

'I don't know,' said Shirley. They understand me better in London and my voice is better there.' Kenneth brandished the contract again. 'It's all down here, you will record your future albums and singles in the UK.'

Shirley smiled and Bernard, watching realised he was mistaken. Kenneth Hume knew Shirley much better than he did. He was in charge of her career and she trusted him. It was irrelevant that he hadn't praised her success in the tour, and that after a five-month break there were no preliminaries. He was planning her future.

That night Shirley opened at the Royal Box and it was an important occasion. She really needed to conquer New York. The city was the jewel in the crown of her tour. When Bernard went into Shirley's dressing room he thought she looked a bit glum. She sat in front of her mirror concentrating on her make-up, dabbing her face with a powder puff.

He crept up behind her, leaned over her shoulder and whispered, 'Mirror, mirror on the wall . . .'

Shirley saw him in her mirror now. Suddenly her face lit up like a little girl who listens to a well-loved nursery rhyme and always knows the happy ending. In a deep, gruff voice he whispered again, 'Mirror, mirror on the wall who is the fairest of them all?' Shirley giggled and laughed, then he hissed in her ear, 'You! You, you black bitch. You!!' She was still laughing when Bernard kissed her cheek before he left and whispered '*Merde*!' for luck.

When it was all over and Shirley came off the stage amid tumultuous applause, a jubilant Kenneth was waiting for her in the wings. He put his arms around her and hugged her. 'You've made it,' he told her. Shirley looked radiant. These two had an unusual and unpredictable relationship, but there was a strong bond between them.

Next morning this bond seemed to have evaporated a little and Kenneth Hume was in a hurry to catch his plane back to London. 'Shirley's decided to have a holiday in Jamaica,' he told Bernard, 'going to look up her ancestors I should think, so she won't be flying back with you when the show closes.'

His racial jibe was ridiculous, and showed how glibly he talked of Shirley's parentage. Shirley's mother said, 'I could never get on with Kenneth Hume. I couldn't even talk to him.' She would have no doubt told him to mind his own business.

The American tour had been an unqualified success. As one Las Vegas reviewer had enthused, 'Shirley Bassey has the ferocity of Lena Horne, the trickery of Ella Fitzgerald and the dramatic appeal of Streisand. And when she sang torch songs about the men in her life, she gave off the same magical sparks as Judy Garland and the melancholy of Helen Morgan.'

But, more than that, Shirley Bassey had conquered New York.

*

No longer a rising star, but an established international name with guaranteed marquee value, Shirley Bassey arrived home in London in the Summer of 1966 to a fanfare of publicity. Kenneth Hume, meanwhile, had got well into his stride as one of Britain's most energetic recording producers, despite the fact that he made disgraceful scenes and many enemies.

At the studios of Associated Television (ATV) he caused one memorable scene at a recording of *The Eammon Andrews Show* that reached the front pages of all the newspapers. Eammon, with his easy Irish charm, was one of the leading lights of British television in the Sixties and Seventies, and an appearance on his show was always a plus, especially if you had a song to plug. Shirley had a new record called, 'Don't Take the Lovers from the World,' for which she and Kenneth had high hopes. She had recorded the number in the United States and it was released in England in August 1966, but so far it hadn't made any impression in the charts. Kenneth hoped the sight and sound of Shirley singing it on TV would make it move.

Associated Television were keen to please Shirley; she was a big star after all. They brought in an eighteen-piece orchestra especially for her and agreed to engaging Kenny Clayton as her musical director. But Kenneth Hume started making trouble at rehearsals before the live programme went out, declaring that the sound of Shirley's voice was not coming over well. He announced that he was not happy. Shirley's song was tried again. Kenneth was still not pleased. He barged into the control room and announced that, to ensure TV listeners would get the full Shirley Bassey impact, he himself would take personal control of the sound balance mechanism. This was an unprecedented demand. Producer Malcomn Morris and the TV technicians were incensed and told Kenneth this was out of the question; he was asked to leave the control room.

'I am not an enthusiastic amateur,' spat Kenneth through gritted teeth. 'I am a technician talking to other technicians on equal terms.'

Malcomn Morris again asked him to leave; again. Kenneth refused. The arguments grew heated, Kenneth's language became unpleasant, and security guards were called to remove him.

While all this mayhem was going on off camera, the first two thirds of *The Eammon Andrews Show*, which had been pre-recorded was being transmitted to the nation. When it finished, Eammon Andrews, live, appeared before the cameras to say that, unfortunately, Shirley Bassey was losing her voice and might not be able to appear. He omitted to mention that everyone had been running around frantically looking for a substitute who could go out live in Shirley's place.

The commercial break came and went, and it was back to the show. Music! Applause! And who is this lovely scantily clad lady making her way to the microphone Miss Shirley Bassey, whose voice has miraculously returned. She opens her mouth, filling the air-waves and a million living-rooms with 'Don't Take the Lovers From the World'.

ATV were incensed over the incident, but Kenneth told the press they had been fortunate to get Shirley Bassey's services for a mere two hundred pounds, considering what she was paid elsewhere. 'Miss Bassey,' he announced 'has just landed a one hundred and seventy five thousand pounds contract for the next three years at Las Vegas.'

Kenny Clayton was thoroughly ashamed of Kenneth Hume's behaviour, his scorn at the low fee while all the time it was just an extra bonus he was picking up. To get 'Don't Take the Lovers From the World' on to *The Eammon Andrews Show* was a great stroke of good fortune which stood to give a huge boost to the sluggish record sales. Kenny recalled, 'The bad language he used was deplorable. I know you get much more done by speaking quietly and being nice to people.'

After this debacle, Kenny Clayton said he would rather not work for Kenneth Hume again. With Shirley it was different, she had her tantrums, but there was no nastiness in her nature. He would work for Shirley, tour with Shirley, but never again work with Kenneth Hume, who was his own worst enemy.

There was one piece of good news in all this. Although, 'Don't Take the Lovers from the World,' failed to top the charts, it was an unusual song which demonstrated that Shirley was moving into more adventurous material than previously, and the release of her first United Artists album, 'I've Got a Song for You,' did very well.

Shirley has said, 'In the very early years of recording I had sung whatever was given to me, but deep down inside I said to myself that if ever I made it, nobody would ever again tell me what to sing.

'When I signed with United Artists in 1966, my voice was changing just like the new material. I didn't consciously attempt to change the way I sang, it was more of a natural development. I recorded the early United Artists albums in the USA, but I didn't particularly enjoy the experience of doing them there. I was much happier recording in the UK.'

Kenneth was full of all the clever bookings he had made for her. Apart from Las Vegas there were many worldwide contracts, a film to be made in Paris, and other American engagements. Kenneth told Shirley that she wouldn't have much time available to spend in London.

Shirley very much wanted to spend time in England in order to be with her children, which was why Kenneth's idea of a long-running musical in London had appealed to her. He talked about it again when, unusually, he accompanied Shirley to Venice for a gala appearance at the Hotel Excelsior on the Lido. There, they became friendly with one of the managers of the hotel, a tall handsome man called Sergio Novak, who looked more like a Serb than an Italian. He was charming and made sure they were well looked after. Kenneth like him, and so did Shirley.

Shirley talked to her old friend Tony Helliwell, the journalist from *The People*, about life and love. 'It seems that I had to get married then go through a divorce to really become mates with Kenneth, my manager,' she told him. 'He's helped me a great deal about money. I've learned to save and invest.' She went on to say that by the time autumn of 1967 came around she should be starring in a musical play, *Josephine*.

Kenneth and Shirley's friendship with Lionel Bart had been the inspiration for *Josephine*. Lionel's East End origins and cockney talent appealed very much to Kenneth. If Lionel could do it, so could he. Shirley's recording of 'As Long as He Needs Me' had sent Lionel's hit song to the top of the charts, and Carol Reed's interest in her for the film of *Oliver!* augured well for a musical with Shirley Bassey.

Shirley discussed the play in Hollywood with Anthony Newley, the new boy wonder, who was then married to Joan Collins, and at one time it was thought he might co-star as Napoleon to Shirley's Josephine. Kenneth fancied the idea of Napoleon as the hero of the show. He and Napoleon were both short (and, as many might have noted, both dictators!), and Shirley, like the Empress Josephine, who was a creole from Martinique, was a mixed-race beauty.

After various stops and starts, Kenneth Hume approached two young men to write the music and lyrics for his wife's musical play. The pair had written a musical called *Barnado Boy*, which they hoped would shortly be presented in the West End. Someone was commissioned to write the book, with its historical background. Then came a typical Kenneth Hume proviso to, their show

Barnado Boy, was not to be staged in London until *Josephine* had opened. The two young men agreed and set to work at once. By the beginning of 1967 everyone was talking rehearsal schedules and Shirley said she would cancel all her bookings whenever it became necessary. There were great plans about the musical going to Broadway after London, and then, possibly, becoming a Hollywood film.

At last it seemed that Kenneth was going to make all of Shirley's dreams come true.

15

THE ITALIAN LOVER

SHIRLEY BOUGHT HER mother a new house at 2 Glastonbury Terrace, Llanrumney. It was on the outskirts of Cardiff, further from the city than the previous one. 'It's so big,' exclaimed her mother, 'three bedrooms upstairs, and Shirley says I can have an even bigger one if I want.' At her age, however, getting on for seventy, she certainly didn't want a bigger house but she'd now got a garden, the first one in her life, and already she'd planted daffodils and tulips and crocuses that would come up in the Spring. 'I've got everything I want,' she said, as she always did. She was so happy when her daughter came down on one of her visits. There was a shiny sports car parked outside and the house was filled with flowers.

Kenneth Hume had never visited Eliza, even when he was married to Shirley. They had met just once and that was enough for both of them. 'I couldn't stand the man,' said Shirley's mother.

Kenneth was spiteful about Shirley's family, claiming she was 'just a meal ticket the them.' Marina, Shirley's sister refuted this accusation. 'I clean other people's houses so that I can be a meal ticket for my children.'

Shirley could never do enough for her mother, but the rest of the family were less important to her now. Iris and Bill, who had been Sharon's foster parents, were still a part of Sharon's life. Ella, who had once lived in Islington, and Shirley's other sisters who lived in Cardiff, saw her now and then when she came to visit their mother, but their biggest thrill always came when Shirley left them tickets at the box office for her latest show.

Her sister Eileen remarked that, 'Shirley gets a bit confused at times when the whole family with all our children pile into her dressing room after the show. But they don't stay long, and then we sisters and Henry, our brother, get an hour with her. And the champagne flows. There's lots of gossip and cross-questioning and hugs and kisses. She tells us about her trips abroad and her cabaret shows.'

Of the five sisters and one brother with their families living around Cardiff, only two of them, apart from Shirley, could sing – Marina, who is two years older than Shirley, and brother Henry, four years older. Henry always had an excellent voice, but he was too shy to go for auditions and never sang professionally. Marina looks like Shirley and has told how, when getting on a bus in Cardiff, if any pals of hers where sitting inside, they would always tease her by singing 'Kiss Me, Honey Honey, Kiss Me.'

In June 1967 Shirley was getting ready for her annual six-week season at the Talk of The Town. The title of the show that year was to be 'Farewell to Cabaret'. Perhaps the title was a good omen, she thought; with her new musical play she might really be able to say goodbye to cabaret, and the grind of continual touring would be over. While she was rehearsing she heard that Kenneth was ill. She accepted that he always smoked to much and never took care of himself. Shirley rarely asked questions. and she didn't know of the awful illness that had plagued Kenneth for a long time. Now it seemed that the depression had a grip on him and kept coming back relentlessly.

She know that he always worried about getting cancer, but he was only forty and, despite his constant moan that, 'my machine is cracking up,' she didn't take him seriously. She knew he took sleeping pills, she took them herself. In showbiz it was almost compulsory.

Kenneth recovered and felt able to face life again. His energy returned and he became over confident. When he saw Shirley to discuss the opening at the Talk of The Town he poured out his grandiose plans for *Josephine*, but told her it was taking a little longer than he thought to get it all together. However, he said, the advance publicity would soon begin and rehearsals would start shortly afterwards.

But this time his recovery didn't last very long. He had pneumonia, and became depressed again and couldn't sleep. He woke up one morning to find his doctor at his bedside. 'How many pills did you take?' the doctor asked.

'One, two, maybe three. I had to sleep.'

'You were deeply unconscious. We were all worried.'

His doctor brought in help so that Kenneth would not be alone. He brought in a psychiatrist for consultations. The main problem seemed to be the sleeping pills. Depression, even manic depression, is treatable, but no-one knew exactly how many containers of sleeping pills were hidden all over the house.

Kenneth promised he would be more careful in future. His doctor was not sure how capable he was of remembering, and worried that his patient wasn't eating. He was very emaciated. Eight days later, on 26 June, 1967, Kenneth Hume died. He finally took one pill too many, but it seemed unlikely it was suicide, as many people thought. Kenneth Hume had wanted to be well; he had wanted to live.

The front pages of the London papers carried pictures of Kenneth Hume taken when he was young and good-looking. 'Former husband of singer Shirley Bassey, Mr Kenneth Hume, aged 40, was found dead in his London home yesterday. A Scotland Yard spokesman said there is no suspicion of foul play, it is being treated as sudden death. Mr Hume had been ill for some time.'

As is common practice with sudden death, an inquest was held on 8 July, Professor Keith Simpson, the well-known pathologist said that the cause of Kenneth Hume's death was an overdose of barbiturates. He thought that Mr Hume had taken three or four sleeping capsules before his death. This was slightly excessive to the normal maximum dose but it is in no sense a massive overdose.

The Coroner asked, 'If this dose were given to one hundred healthy men of forty, how many would survive without treatment?'

'I would expect them all to survive if they were healthy,' replied the Professor.

The press reported that 'Mr Leslie Simmons, a business partner of Mr Hume said that although Mr Hume was divorced from Miss Bassey he had become friendly with her again and had established a harmonious business relationship with her. He was busily engaged in the preliminary stages for a new musical, *Josephine*, for which everyone entertained the highest hopes. It was the largest venture he had been engaged in.'

The Coroner said the outstanding thing in the case was that although Kenneth was depressed and suicide is a well-known risk during depression, he had never stated that he intended taking his own life.

A verdict of accidental death was recorded.

The former Mrs Hume was not present at the inquest and so she did not hear the result of the post-mortem or the verdict. She did not learn that the pathologist found out that Kenneth had quite serious coronary heart disease.

Kenneth's death came as a great blow to Shirley. It was completely unexpected. The truth about Kenneth's death had been kept from her and she had been fed various stories. London buzzed with gossip and rumour. Kenneth, it was said by some, had committed suicide by taking an overdose; others that he had killed himself because he had cancer. None of this was true. He had become so weak and emaciated and he so desperately craved sleep and one or two pills over the normal dose had killed him.

To this day the general belief is that Kenneth Hume committed suicide. A group of fans at one of Shirley's concerts only last year were heard arguing between themselves, still speculating as to the reasons for Hume's death.

Bernard Hall in New York had it right. When he read the news of Kenneth's death, he said. 'That chirpy little cockney wanted to keep his life. He had a lot of faults, but lack of courage was not one of them.'

'Kenneth would have wanted me to carry on.' Shirley told the press soon after Kenneth's death. She would open at the Talk of The Town, where she was booked for a month, as arranged. Nothing would bring Kenneth back, he'd have wanted her to sing at the Talk of The Town, he always insisted that she fulfil her contracts. He was the only man she had ever been able to rely on. So many men had let her down and now he had gone.

When she married him Shirley may have really believed that Kenneth would change his sexuality for her. There was an innocence about Shirley when she started her career and homosexuality was shrouded in mystery at the time. Bernard Hall was muscular and exciting and if he could make passionate love to her, why couldn't Kenneth Hume? She fell in love with Kenneth and always remained sympathetic and drawn to him. He'd always been there at the end of a telephone to give advice.

In spite of all her brave words to the press, Shirley did not get over Kenneth's death easily. For the past seven years he had occupied a central position in her life. First as a friend, then as a husband and always as the rock she could lean on when trouble came. She wanted him back again, in spite of the earth shaking rows they used to have, when they called each other every name under the sun. He never really upset her deeply, or put her down. She could even forgive the money he gambled away.

He'd always been there, telling her she was strong, helping her to believe in herself, but now she was on her own. At night she was filled with morbid fears that if she did not sleep it would affect her voice, that her career would be over. She was used to sleeping pills, she'd taken two each night for years, but nowadays to took much longer to fall asleep. On one particular night she was desperate for sleep. She took another pill and waited for sleep to come, an hour passed, she took another pill, more hours seemed to go by, and seemed as though the night would never end. She was obsessed with the thought that in the morning she would find herself with a harsh dry throat and she wouldn't be able to do her show. She found another pill. She *had* to sleep . . .

Shirley recalled later what happened next. She had a flash of awareness and it made her very frightened. What was the matter with her? Had she take too many pills? She tried to get up but it was difficult. Now she was floating, and it felt warm and good. Now if she closed her eyes she would sleep, but some sixth sense warned her – this was not sleep, this was death.

Fear made her stagger to the door. She couldn't call out, all she could do was mumble. Through her haze she dimly knew her secretary, Jean, was in a room down the landing. She managed to get there, she fell against the door, it opened, and then she remembered no more.

Shirley said that Jean undoubtedly saved her life. Jean realised there was no time to waste, not even time to ring for an ambulance. Shirley was only half-conscious and mumbling about pills, Jean somehow got her down two flights of stairs and into the car, and drove her straight to hospital.

The experience taught Shirley that sleeping pills can lull the desperate and the frightened into forgetfulness. After three pills, few people can remember how many they have taken. Kenneth had gone that way, and Shirley had almost followed him.

There was another tragic postscript. Shirley says that Jean Lincoln, the secretary who saved her life, was her best friend, that they were like identical twins. She was the only female best friend she had. Subsequently Jean, too, took an accidental overdose of sleeping pills, but she wasn't found in time. 'When she died I was so upset,' said Shirley. 'She didn't mean to kill herself, I don't think I have ever allowed any woman to get that close to me again. I loved her.'

Leslie Simmons, Kenneth's office manager, was looking after Shirley's affairs now. In July, a month after Kenneth's death, he gave out a press release that *Josephine* had been postponed. Without Kenneth Hume's ruthless drive and financial manoeuvring, the chances that the show would materialise were growing increasingly remote.

Two months later in September, the *Western Mail* announced, 'Cardiff singer's musical is off until next year.' This was another press release, and it meant that there was no money at the moment to finance the production. This was the mortal blow for *Josephine* from which it looked unlikely to recover.

In his last will and testament, Kenneth Edwin Harold Hume left his property to Leslie Simmons, his business partner, and Shirley Veronica Bassey and his relatives. Kenneth's estate was eleven thousand two hundred and eighty six pounds. Hardly the kind of money one would have expected a man like Kenneth Hume to leave; a man who used to drive around in a Rolls Royce and manage an international singing star. Eleven thousand pounds wasn't enough to back a West End musical.

Shirley said that Kenneth's affairs were in a mess, and it was confirmed that he had left gambling debts, but Shirley must have learnt some business lessons from Kenneth for, after his death her finances started to improve.

One of the good friends who now helped Shirley was Bo Mills, who had also been a friend of Kenneth's. Bo, whose real name was Baudouin Mills, was half-Canadian and half-Belgian and had an antique business off the Portobello Road. He was tall and good looking, and was to remain a fixture in Shirley's life for some time to come, even appearing with her on *This is Your Life,* in the Eighties, when Shirley gave him a hug and said enigmatically, 'We shall probably grow old together'.

When Shirley went on her next European tour the following year, 1968, she couldn't have known that she would not return to her native land until over two years later, by which time she would be a tax exile living in Switzerland. Bernard Hall, who lived and toured on the Continent and was always popping in and out of Shirley's life. He happened to be around in Venice when Shirley fell in love again, but with a man who was very different to Kenneth Hume.

Bernard was appearing at the Fenice Theatre in Venice when he noticed a poster announcing Shirley's forthcoming appearance at the Venice Lido. It was the obvious thing to take a water taxi out to the Lido and see her.

At the hotel they told Bernard that Shirley was out having lunch and explained how to find the restaurant. Shirley out of bed and having lunch? The girl who didn't wake up until midday and then only wanted eggs, was sitting at a table covered with a red and white checkered cloth, a glass of red wine in one hand and the other held by a good-looking man. She looked the happiest woman in the world. Bernard joined them, and as lunch progressed he could hardly believe his eyes. Shirley had changed completely. She ate spaghetti, she drank wine and above all she was enjoying herself over a meal as he had never seen her do before. The biggest surprise of all was her radiance, the sure sign of a woman in love.

Sitting with her was the new man in her life, Sergio Novak. He was one of the most handsome men Bernard had ever seen, not a bit the usual smooth Italian type. He was tall, fair, muscular and very male. There was a Slav look about him, but what Bernard liked most of all was his easy, friendly manner and the way he looked at Shirley. He was head over heels in love with her.

Venice was a very romantic place to be that year. Shirley had come to the Hotel Excelsior to star in their cabaret. Sergio Novak, assistant manager of the Excelsior, was the same charming and helpful person who had looked after Kenneth and Shirley so well on her previous visit. Now that Shirley was alone he could not do enough for her. He had real warmth, there was nothing phony about him. When they discovered that they were in love he seemed surprised how events had overtaken them. He was a modest man, and being the lover of a beautiful woman who was also an international singing star obviously took some getting used to.

Bernard wasn't the only one in Venice who realised that Shirley and Sergio were very much in love. Newsmen came sniffing around. Shirley told them she was willing to answer any questions, but, please, couldn't they see she was having a lovely time – Venice was so romantic, Italy was so wonderful . . . What about Signor

Novak? they insisted. 'He is very kind and helpful,' said Shirley.

She was telling the truth. For the first time for so long here was a man who just wanted to spend time with her, who wanted to look after her. He treated her as if she was an ordinary girl. She was thirty-one and Sergio was thirty-four. They were both young, but not too young, and had the prime of their lives ahead of them.

Back in Cardiff, Shirley's mother was being telephoned by the press. 'Is Shirley going to marry Roberto Vincento?'

'I don't think so. Are you sure you've got the name right.'

'Well, he's an Italian anyway.'

The *Western Mail* still got it wrong: 'Cardiff born Shirley Bassey will marry an Italian. The man she will marry is Roberto Vincento who she met at the San Remo contest this year.

'Last night Shirley's mother told me, "I've known for three weeks that Shirley planned to marry this month.

'"I don't know her future husband but I am delighted at the news. She needs someone to look after her and the children;

'"I shall probably be invited to meet Mr Vincento when Shirley returns to Britain." added Shirley's mother. "It doesn't matter to me what he is like as long as Shirley is happy."'

Although they'd got the name wrong, the facts were right. On 13 August 1968, while Shirley was appearing at the Sahara Hotel in Las Vegas, she and Sergio were married. The ceremony took place at The Little Church of the West in Las Vegas at two-thirty a.m.

Shirley wore a dress of blue and mauve chiffon, specially designed for her wedding by her English dressmaker Douglas Darnell. Sharon and Samantha, aged thirteen and six, respectively were flower girls. The wedding ceremony lasted five minutes but the champagne party afterwards at the Sahara Hotel lasted until four-thirty in the morning.

Shirley said afterwards, 'My daughters adore Sergio. He will be a wonderful father.'

'Mrs Eliza Mendi' reported the *Western Mail,* said that she has never met her son-in-law, but Shirley had promised to bring him over to meet her and send wedding photographs.'

When Shirley's mother did meet Sergio they got on very well. Sergio loved and respected 'Mama' as much as Shirley did. He was a naturally good father and much loved in return. Shirley and Sergio were so much in love that their differences could be overlooked.

This new chapter in Shirley's life was a happy one. The couple lived in Lugano, a lakeside town in Switzerland. On the other side of the lake was Italy and so there was a real Italian feel to the place; a lot of Italians lived in Lugano and spoke their own language there. Sergio himself was from Trieste, on the border of the former Yugoslavia and Italy. There is a great contrast between these two countries, and Sergio looked more like those Italian born on the Austrian border, north of Trieste. His height made him tower over most shorter Italians, He spoke Italian, French, German and English so was perfectly at home in Switzerland.

The Novak apartment was in the Via Sorengo, an ordinary street in Lugano. On the front door of the apartment was a little plate inscribed with the name 'Novak.' Thelma, the nanny from London, had come too, and still looked after Samantha, also acting as housekeeper when Shirley was on tour. Sharon was away at a Swiss boarding school.

Shirley was having a two-year exile from the land of her birth, while financial arrangements were made for her to be officially domiciled in Switzerland. It always helped if you were an international star as far as the Swiss authorities were concerned. The Swiss were renowned for turning down millionaire applicants, and as for buying a house in Switzerland, forget it. But Shirley, with her Italian husband, was welcomed. Earlier, she had inadvertently transferred forty thousand pounds from Britain against Treasury regulations, but eventually the transfer was successfully ironed out. Shirley said, 'I innocently took money that was mine so that I could start a new life.'

Bernard met Shirley and Sergio in Italy after their marriage when the three of them had lunch together. Bernard thought that Shirley looked happy and well. She had even put on a bit of weight. When she stood up to leave, her husband gave her an affectionate little pat on her rear. 'You're putting on weight, baby.'

Shirley was capable of looking after herself. She gave Sergio a very frosty look, then she turned to Bernard, 'Balls,' she said, 'this man! I could kill him sometimes.' As she told Bernard later 'When Sergio suggests that I cook a little pasta for supper, I tell him, listen baby, if I sing for my supper, I bloody well don't have to cook it as well.'

Shirley made it clear to Sergio that if he thought the place for women was in the kitchen he was way out of line. She knew that Italian males were very jealous, but she was earning a lot of money attracting huge audiences and half of the audiences were male.

Sergio did his best to understand. He said in an interview, 'My wife has thousands of male admirers who send her flowers and love letters. I accept this attention from her fans. But if someone flirts with her in front of me my coolness disappears.'

Shirley wanted to stretch herself professionally. The loss of *Josephine* had been a terrible blow, and she knew that Sergio could never be another Kenneth Hume as far as the professional side of things was concerned. However, as time went by, he gradually began to take over the position of Shirley's manager. After Shirley left London, a well-known English agent and manager, Robert Patterson, had looked after her, and his wife Sybil became a close friend. But Sergio though a real beginner in international show business, was anxious to learn the ropes. He knew little yet of the many less appealing sides of the faces of business, the jealousies, the nastiness, the protectiveness, and the unbelievable egos. It was not an easy arena to climb into, and Sergio would not escape completely unscathed.

He said, in all innocence, 'At first I was naïve. For a year people took advantage of me, but after that baby, I made them pay.'

Bargaining was more of a way of life around the Mediterranean and this was one side of the business that Sergio understood well. He could deal with promoters and agents and his views about Shirley's future as a concert artist fitted in with her own: concerts by well-known entertainers were already big business in America, and in the Seventies and Eighties Britain was catching up, building large auditoriums that would hold thousands of fans.

If Shirley could get an engagement at Carnegie Hall in New York and fill it, then year after year she could fill concert halls in all the world's major cities. Not only would it be more financially rewarding than the nightclub circuit but her lifestyle would improve, no more smokey venues and late-night performances that could exhaust her until the early hours of the morning.

Some months after their marriage Shirley and Sergio started off on her usual January Australian–American tour. They were both very happy. Shirley was pregnant, and Sergio was seeing Australia for the first time. In Sydney the booking was as usual for Chequers, the nightclub owned by the Wong brothers, where Shirley always enjoyed an enthusiastic welcome and a great opening night, but then came the first piece of bad luck – Shirley developed a virus infection of the throat. After a week she seemed to be getting over the bad effects when, suddenly and disastrously, in the middle of a performance she felt unwell. She was rushed to the Waverly Memorial Hospital in Sydney where she suffered a miscarriage.

They were both broken-hearted. Shirley was longing to have a baby with Sergio and their disappointment was great. They cancelled the rest of Shirley's bookings in Australia, but as soon as she had recuperated they flew to the United States, for her American tour.

Campione was a beautiful little principality on Lake Como over the Italian border. Almost opposite, on the other side of Lake Lugano was the town of Lugano, where Shirley lived.

Bernard Hall was appearing in a solo act at the high-class Campione Casino. He found Campione a little paradise; a perfect place to work. His audiences were mostly the casino guests. The matinees brought elderly ladies who loved having handsome young men to entertain them; the evening performances attracted a younger, more sophisticated crowd.

At one matinee he noticed that the table right in the front had three unusual occupants, a pretty plump young lady, a little girl who looked about six and a tiny little dark boy of about three or four. The children were wildly excited, and when Bernard finished his opening song and dance, they applauded with gusto. They were Thelma, Shirley's nanny, little Samantha, aged six or seven and Mark Allen. Shirley and Sergio were away on tour and Thelma was in charge. She had seen the Campione poster in Lugano and had brought the two children round the lake in a taxi as a treat.

Bernard beckoned to little Samantha to come on to the stage. She looked very pretty in a ruffled gingham dress and he knew that she was a natural performer. She came running round to the side of the stage and to his surprise the tiny little dark boy, who he didn't know followed, clambering on to the stage after her. Bernard took their hands and led then to the front of the stage. 'Who's the little boy?' he whispered to Samantha. 'He's my bruvver, Mark,' she whispered back.

He told the audience that these were the children of Shirley

Bassey the international singer, and would the ladies like to listen to a song from Samantha? They'd love to. Tiny Mark who clutched a toy ukulele was delighted. In a little yellow tee shirt and shorts he waved to them and blew kisses. The orchestra, on the nod, struck up, and Bernard knew all would be well. The children were good at copying and loved the feeling that they were the centre of attraction. The three of them did a little dance, then Samantha sang, 'I'll Be Your Sweetheart, If You Will Be Mine' to rounds of applause. Tiny Mark insisted on being lifted up, and showered kisses on Bernard's face. He was adorable.

Afterwards Thelma told Bernard the story of Mark. He was the son of one of Shirley's nieces, Barbara Allen, and his father, serving in the American army in Germany, had deserted them. Little Mark had a disability, a rare complaint called malabsorption which needed treatment with an expensive diet which his mother could not afford. Shirley had stepped in and offered to take Mark to Switzerland to help with his recovery. At the age of three he had gone to live in Lugano and Shirley became his legal guardian while he was there. Mark's mother was delighted that her child was to be given a chance and she was full of optimism for his future.

Sharon was away at school in England and little Mark was company for Samantha. Thelma would look after both children. It seemed an ideal solution to the problem. Shirley had lost her baby in Australia, but now she had Mark.

She eventually decided that she would become Mark's legal guardian with a view to adopting the little boy and Barbara Allen was happy with the arrangements. She was aware that she might not see her son again but she knew she had done the right thing for him. She thought Shirley was a wonderful mother.

Both Samantha and Mark took their new stepfather's name, Novak. Every time Shirley came home from a tour, she led a happy and normal life with her children. When Thelma saw Bernard at

Campione she asked him to come round to the flat and have dinner. Shirley and Sergio were going off on tour again and Thelma and the children would love to see him.

It was raining and dismal when Bernard parked his car outside the apartment house in Via Sorengo one evening, and rang the Novak doorbell. There was a rush of small feet to the door which swung open and then he was being kissed and hugged by Samantha and Mark.

The entrance hall to Shirley and Sergio's home looked like most European entrance halls except for the large framed photograph standing on a table. It was the famous autographed picture of President Nixon with Shirley sitting cross-legged next to him. The rest of the apartment had the kind of comfortable ambience where two small children and their nanny would feel safe and relaxed, and was a far cry from the elegance of the house in Chester Square. There was Swiss neatness and cleanliness that was only spoilt by the usual confusion made by small children.

Thelma cooked a very good dinner which the children tucked into while watching the grown-ups with shining eyes. They were good children and made no protest when they where finally marched off to bed and tucked up. Later Thelma and Bernard sat over coffee and gossiped. Switzerland was okay and the Italians adored the children, but Thelma was worried. Samantha and Mark would soon be at school full time, and they wouldn't need a nanny, a housekeeper would do.

Sergio was very nice, Thelma said, they got on very well, he was very good with the children. But she didn't think she would be able to stay.

Bernard asked what the problem was.

Thelma said, 'You know how it is when there are two women. One looks after the children and the other one works very hard for her living. Shirley comes back from a tour tired and exhausted. It makes her irritable. I don't blame her at all, few women could do what she does.'

However, Shirley's temperament didn't seem to bother Sergio then. He said, 'Shirley will argue with me and she can still blow her top. Shirley has had things all her way for the past few years. So I leave her alone, sometimes for eight hours, sometimes a day, then she comes to me and says what a good idea I had . . . and the argument is over.'

Shirley, on her part, once said, 'I'm going to make a real effort to learn Italian so that I shall be able to swear at Sergio in his own language.'

However much he insisted it would not happen, Sergio was forced to change now that his life and altered to dramatically. He and Shirley toured the world in show business, coping with all its ups and downs. It was a very different life to the one he had led behind a desk in the entrance lobby of the Excelsior Hotel at the Venice Lido. He had entered this marriage sure that Shirley would want to settle down in a typical Italian way. He even told the press, 'That is what every woman really wants, a home where the man is boss.' He was determined not to be overawed by Shirley's stardom – he loved her as a person and not as Shirley Bassey the star. But circumstances, slowly but surely, changed everything.

At the beginning, the couple's wedded bliss continued un-abated. Shirley said, 'When I lived in Britain I was always Shirley Bassey and always on show. In Lugano I am Mrs Novak and just loaf around, casually dressed and without make-up – and nobody bothers. Sergio has made me contented and secure and it is about time I was. After all I have been in show business since I was seventeen.' She added that she would be content with growing older out of the spotlight.

For the first time in her life Shirley was taking vacations. She learnt to ski at Christmas time in the Alps. The children were naturals and whizzed up and down the nursery slopes like veterans. Not only did they go to Cortina in the Alps in winter, they went to the Italian beaches in the summer where Shirley played on the sands with the children. She did all the things she'd never done before, which Sergio now encouraged her to try: tennis, boating, water-skiing. Occasionally she'd have a bitter memory of her childhood, of the slag heaps and the docks of Tiger Bay where children used to play with bits of wood, pretending they were canoes, and of the love she needed but never found enough of.

At last she belonged to a proper family, with a loving husband and children, and more money than she could ever spend. She could enjoy the fruits of her career. But despite all this, there were moments she continued to value, and to need, when thousands of people she didn't even know applauded her concerts and screamed, 'Shirley, I love you.'

16

My husband – My manager

In 1970 Shirley's self-inflicted exile ended. She told the waiting journalists that she had celebrated her return to London with a bottle of champagne on the flight over. Sergio said a few words about his new role in Shirley's life, how every woman really wanted the man in her marriage to be the most important partner. He did not tell them that Shirley often found the Italian male culture hard to accept. Shirley had been warned in the past of giving her career to the man she loved, but Shirley was too happy to remember. Yes, said Shirley, she was going to continue living in Switzerland and they were hoping to build a home on the banks of Lake Lugano, it would be called Villa Capricorn.

Meanwhile at Television Centre in White City, the BBC staff and management were all agog. Shirley Bassey was back and her Italian husband was now her fully fledged manager. Round the building floated the words of the management: 'Can you believe it? He must be the luckiest man in London. From hotel desk to manager of an international singing star!'

Everyone was intrigued, watching and waiting to observe this unusual marriage. In Cannes in the early Seventies Bernard met the couple again and he noticed the change in Sergio. He was no longer the wide-eyed young man hypnotised by the glamour of a big star, he'd also discovered the hard slog involved. He was definitely more self-confident, perhaps a little more brusque, but was still very likable.

Shirley was now in her thirties but improving all the time, and working as hard as ever. Rose Neighbour, a dresser from the BBC had often worked with Shirley and admired her very much, 'Shirley,' said Rose, 'is one of the few entertainers who gives as good a performance during the rehearsal run-through as she does for the televised show.'

The BBC were doing a series of shows in Stockholm, presenting the talents of the Young Generation, a group of dancing youngsters. For every show, a big name star such as Petula Clark or Cliff Richard made a guest appearance. This time, when Rose Neighbour went along as dresser, the star was Shirley Bassey.

'I was a bit worried about Shirley,' recalled Rose. 'Sergio had a group of Italians with him, either family or friends, and they seemed to have come along for a treat. They would sit in Shirley's dressing room and chatter away in Italian. I thought this must disturb her although she never made any complaint.' Rose went on to say, 'It was all very different from the old days at Television Centre when there was an absolute rule that no-one should bother her before a performance. It was essential that Shirley had peace and quiet. I knew she wanted to sit there quite alone gathering her strength for the show. Then, my God, she'd go out there and blast apart the studio with her wonderful performance.'

The veto to keep out of Shirley's dressing room applied to

everyone. On one occasion, Bill Cotton, Jnr, the managing director, wanted to talk to Shirley just before a performance. 'Rose,' said Shirley. 'Tell him to piss off.'

I'm not going to do that,' said Rose indignantly. 'He's my boss. You tell him yourself.'

'Right,' said Shirley. 'Bill,' she yelled. 'Piss off!'

Another person thought that Sergio didn't always understand the strict code of not interfering with musicians and other artists before a performance. Steve Crowther was a member of a group in the same concert as Shirley. He recounted how 'This Italian husband was driving us mad saying he didn't like this sound or those notes, making out he know more about the music than us, the professional musicians. There was a bust-up, and Shirley was very angry with Sergio for upsetting us all.' The gossip was that in the Novak household all was not always sweetness and light.

But Sergio did learn all about recording contracts, and Shirley's records were big business in Europe, especially in Italy and France. The Italians loved her singing their Italian songs, though they thought it was more 'simpatico' when she sang them in English.

Way back in 1968 Shirley had recorded 'La Vita,' by Newell, Cantona and Amurri, in Italian. Then, with new English lyrics written by Norman Newell, she sang the song as, 'This is My Life' at the San Remo Festival and, although it did not win, it turned out to be one of the greatest hits in Shirley's repertoire.

In 1970, when Shirley was able to return to England, she had another hit, 'Something' by Beatle George Harrison. She heard the song for the first time in the late Sixties in America, sung by Peggy Lee on the Ed Sullivan TV show. She said, 'I just caught the end of Peggy's performance. I was knocked out of my mind. I have to record that number, I told myself. Everyone explained it was not worthwhile because the Beatles had had such a hit with it. We went ahead anyway.' It was the first time she had been in an English studio for two years, and it turned out to be one of her very best recordings. 'First it was to be an album track,' said Shirley, 'then it came out so good, it had to be a single.'

The 'Something' album turned out to be one of the finest ever made by a female recording star. It became the best-seller of her recording career so far. In Shirley's opinion, 'The recording of the 'Something' album was a major turning point for me. You could even say it made me a pop star.'

Apart from 'Big Spender' Shirley hadn't been in the charts for some time but this was the breakthrough that put her back there.

Although 'Something' was a big hit – it reached number four in the British charts, it didn't reach the magical number three, which would have meant she had beaten the Beatles with one of their own singles. However, it did earn her a fifth silver disc.

Things could not have been better for Shirley's first home-coming after her two-year absence. She couldn't stay too long the bookings had to fit in with the days allowed – but a record-breaking two weeks at the Talk of The Town showed she was as popular as ever. On her final bow in the early hours, the cast of the American rock musical *Hair* leaped on to the stage armed with flowers for her. Shirley joined in their song 'Aquarius', before leading them all off the stage for a champagne celebration.

She promised to come back in November for ten concerts, beginning at the Royal Festival Hall in London and ending in her home town, Cardiff. This was to be the way her life would be programmed from now on. An international concert artist moving from continent to continent, following in the footsteps of the greats – Garland, Sinatra, Streisand, Ella Fitzgerald, Tony Bennett, Lena Horne – whose ranks she had now indisputably joined.

No-one had forgotten her, everyone was glad that she was back in the top twenty charts. She recorded another great hit with, 'Yesterday When I Was Young' by Charles Aznavour and Herbert

Kretzmer, then, in 1971, came 'Diamonds are Forever' by 'Gold-finger's' John Barry.

Back home in Lugano once more, Shirley was having a well-earned rest and taking the odd Italian lesson. Her two children were already fluent in the language, and even Thelma the nanny now spoke Italian. Years later, Shirley stilled talked of how much she appreciated the peace and tranquillity of Lugano.

She even looked forward to the winter and the Christmas break because she could go ski-ing. She says, 'I love ski-ing, she said. 'It's the only sport that I don't mind getting up at nine in the morning for.'

It must have made for an easier existence having Sergio, her husband and her manager with her to look after all the tiresome details of travel, contracts and foreign managements. Easier perhaps, but, as the years went by, Shirley who had a touch of the natural 'loner' about her began to feel that the constant presence of one man, combing both functions didn't, after all, add up to the perfect existence.

The Royal Variety Performance in 1971 had been very successful. Shirley was a hit. She wore a gown so revealing that the millions watching her on television must have wondered how it stayed on. 'People want glamour from their entertainers,' she has said. 'I'm from the old school of entertainers who believe you have to make an impression on your audience. They don't want to see you in any old dress.'

To the press Shirley, and, especially, Sergio, were insisting that she was a happy woman with a happy marriage, but people were noticing that sometimes man and wife were a continent apart – as, indeed, they were that evening in London after the Royal Variety show, when Shirley belted a waiter in a restaurant. 'If someone goads me,' said Shirley, 'the tiger in me still comes out.'

After the show Shirley and a girlfriend had gone to supper in what Shirley described as 'a frightfully chic place. I ordered smoked salmon and asparagus for my main course. The smoked salmon arrived after a long wait, then there was another long wait but no asparagus. I complained to the waiter. He was rude then started walking away. "Just a moment, I haven't finished," I told him, then I belted him.'

'I never got my asparagus,' admitted Shirley, 'but I got some satisfaction from slapping that waiter.' That night Shirley was wearing a gold fertility emblem given to her by Luisa Moore, who was then the wife of Roger Moore. 'It hasn't done me much good,' she said ruefully. 'I haven't had a son so far.' Young Mark, the nephew she had adopted, helped in easing the pain and disappointment of her miscarriage in Australia, but Shirley, who loved having children, always regretted having no son, and no child with Sergio.

In the mid-Seventies Shirley went to Paris to sing at L'Èspace for a week. She had never really taken to Paris, but this time she was given the full red-carpet treatment, and the French paid due homage to a beautiful woman as only then can. She was admired, compliments were showered upon her, and every night for a week *le beau monde* came to listen to her sing.

Couturier Pierre Cardin a friend of Bernard's, had, as a hobby, created an exclusive theatre where only the most talented and attractive performers were invited to appear. If you sang at L'Èspace in the Seventies you were well rewarded.

Shirley had been persuaded by Bernard to accept the engagement. Her opening night was a major triumph and, afterwards, Pierre Cardin entertained a large party of guests at Maxim's in Shirley's honour. There, she was surrounded by admiring Parisians toasting her success with champagne. She changed her mind about Paris and decided that she loved it.

She loved the money she earned and Paris was the place to spend it. Shirley had always loved perfume and beautiful clothes and had longed, since she was a young girl, to be the epitome of elegance. Now she could afford it. She sat in the place of honour at the House of Balmain, whose legendary directrice, Ginette Spanier, made a fuss of her; She went to Christian Dior, where she was told that her 'taille' was superb and that any of the Master's creations would be perfect on her. She bought the kind of exquisite and delicate shoes she loved at Chanel and chose her perfume at Balenciaga. She was pampered more than she had ever been before and very happy.

Afterwards she wrote to Bernard, telling him how much she had loved Paris and the charming Parisians. She added that she and Sergio were starting a tour of Japan in October, followed by a European tour in November to Holland and Belgium and then Paris again. The following week she was off to record in London, before taking a trip to Sardinia.

While the Villa Capricorn was being built on the via Campione at Lake Lugano, Shirley and Sergio had bought another summer holiday villa at Sardinia. Sardinia was suddenly the place to be, full of beautiful people and splendid yachts.

Bernard read between the lines of Shirley's postcard and knew that it wasn't as easy as she made it look. The type of touring that Shirley was undertaking was often soul destroying, completely exhausting. For someone of her slim physique it played havoc with her health. Tempers grew short, rows blew up. Whatever happened, there was always the pressure of the next performance in the next major city, where she must yet again appear relaxed and completely in control.

And Sergio, too, could be having a hard time.

When Shirley returned to Paris – this time for a week at the Theâtre des Champs-Elysèes – for one week, Bernard thought it might be a good opportunity to introduce her, at long last, to Marlene Dietrich. They'd always been interested in each other's careers, although Marlene was forty years older than Shirley. Marlene lived opposite the Hôtel Plaza Athenée, and the theatre where Shirley was to appear was just around the corner from there. A meeting could not be left much longer for Marlene was deteriorating fast; she'd soon be in a wheelchair and then she would allow nobody to see her.

All the parties agreed and a time was set for tea at the Plaza before Shirley's evening performance. She and Sergio arrived at the arranged time, Sergio dashing in a new raincoat he had just purchased at Pierre Cardin. Shirley admired the elegant garment and said airily, 'I'll give it to you for your birthday.' Bernard sensed that all was not too well with them. There was a slight feeling of one partner reminding the other who held the purse strings.

Then came a telephone call for Bernard. Dietrich had decided she didn't have the strength to put on her make-up, without it she could not come. 'Give my apologies to your Shirley.' She had chickened out, probably, thought Bernard, because of an older woman's jealously of the young and successful one.

Disappointed, the three of them had tea and ate English scones until it was time for Shirley to go to the theatre. Whether it was because she was annoyed with Marlene and Bernard, or just annoyed with her husband, she said to Sergio, 'Get me a vodka first.' Bernard watched Shirley knock back the alcohol and was worried that she felt she needed a drink before a performance. He knew it wasn't a good idea even though he did it himself. In the old days Shirley would have scoffed at drinking before a performance, but in the old days Shirley did not have a husband at her elbow.

The marriage between Shirley and Sergio had started so well. On the face of it, all was still well between them but there was conflict now. Sergio could be jealous, and Shirley was usually exhausted after each tour. The child that might have kept them together had not arrived, and the pattern of Shirley's life remained essentially the same as before, work and travel, travel and work. Often happy, often just like old times, but tempers were increasingly frayed as tensions rose more frequently to the surface.

It was always a pleasure to come home to Lugano. Thelma was no longer there, but there was a housekeeper, and the two youngest children, Mark and Samantha, were at day school. It was peaceful and quiet and the family was left alone to live as Mr and Mrs Novak and their children. Every time Shirley and Sergio come back from a tour a bit more had been added to the Villa Capricorn, and one of these days it would certainly be finished.

Sergio finally masterminded the completion of the Villa Capricorn. It faced the lake, with one special glass wall outside Shirley's bedroom so that she could see out but no-one could see in. Her dressing room, the same size as her beautifully fitted bedroom, was lined with walk-in closets. Over the years she had built up an extensive wardrobe of furs and coats and gowns that she could not bear to part with. Shirley's bedroom, as in all the homes she owned, was the most magnificently positioned and luxuriously decorated room in the house.

Shirley's children were growing up. Sharon, now twenty, had already left home. She had quit her Swiss boarding school when she was eighteen and gone back to London. Her first job was selling couture dresses to the wealthy, but she soon found that this kind of life was not for her; she preferred caring for others which was more worthwhile.

Sharon was the only one of Shirley's children who always returned to her roots with the Bassey family. There was a strong bond between Sharon and her former foster parents, Shirley's sister Iris and her husband bill, and she would regularly visit them in

Cardiff. Naturally she would also spend time with Eliza Mendi, her grandmother, who was especially proud of her and the work she had chosen. Sharon loved being with small children and had started training as a nursery nurse in Bristol, working in a school. The following year she would take a college course in order to get a full qualification.

Samantha was now at an expensive Swiss boarding school, but she was having difficulty settling down. Like her mother, she was something of a rebel and didn't adjust well to school. To a school friend Samantha once confided something about her life. She said that with a famous mother you've failed before you've even begun because you can never live up to the glamorous image. A lot of people envy you, but what they don't realise is that you want a Mum and Dad to go home to, a normal easygoing family. Samantha, in fact, wanted and needed something her mother could never give her.

Mark was also at a Swiss boarding school. He too, was finding that life was not always easy.

Shirley's three children did, however, get on well with Sergio. They all called him Dad, and were very fond of him. It was the way of life, the touring and the concerts, the tempers that flared unexpectedly, that didn't always make for a peaceful home life. Now that the children were all at school, Thelma had gone. Shirley later readily admitted that she failed as a mother; show business, still remains number one and she knows she'll go on and on until she's too old to move.

Thelma had always known that when Samantha and then Mark went off to school her job would be over. She returned to London and found getting another job harder than she thought. When she was getting desperate she asked Bo Mills, Shirley's friend, if he could help her find a position. Bo, a generous-hearted man, offered Thelma a job as his housekeeper. Some time later Bernard Hall, who was also a friend of Bo's, was delighted when Bo asked him to dinner cooked by the new housekeeper, Thelma. The surprise guest of honour that evening turned out to be Shirley, and she thoroughly enjoyed herself. She had three good-looking men to entertain her: Bo, Bernard and Yves, who was Bo's partner in the business. They were all making a great fuss of her, hanging on to her every word and laughing uproariously at her jokes. It did cross Bernard's mind that they appeared to him to be behaving rather like three court jesters, whose only wish was to make Shirley, the Queen of Hearts, happy.

But jokes aside, Shirley was going through a difficult time; she was drinking too much and she knew it. Bo Mills and Bernard both worried about her, but Shirley didn't tend to welcome advice.

Eight or nine years after Shirley had made Sergio her manager their marriage had begun to falter. Their son Mark knew this tempestuous marriage was breaking up the day the arguments ended. He thought that all married people fought because his adopted father and mother had fought for as long as he could remember. 'They seemed to live in a boxing ring,' he recalled, 'and when they stopped fighting, that was it, their marriage was over.'

Mark hadn't got it quite right, the marriage didn't collapse as suddenly as all that, but it was going wrong and it was only a matter of time before Shirley decided enough was enough. One of the reasons the marriage was failing was because these two people did not understand each other. Shirley and Sergio came from very different backgrounds and they had widely divergent perspectives on life. Poverty had scarred Shirley, who was still vulnerable under the bravado and feared that one day she might lose all she had worked for.

The Italian personality is not at all like the Welsh. There is sometimes an undercurrent of pessimism in those born near the Welsh hills. From the beginning of her career Shirley had been suspicious of men who looked after her earnings. She has said, 'Moneywise, I've looked after all the men in my life.' She was probably right about the first two. Michael Sullivan always acted as if he was doing Shirley a favour, and Kenneth Hume, although he taught Shirley a good deal about finance, did gamble away portions of Shirley's hard-earned money.

'No man has ever taken care of me and my children,' said Shirley. 'I have paid the bills with my money and it has always been like that.' Both Samantha and Mark could relate to this, they had known Dads who were kind to them but not their real fathers. Only Sharon had been lucky enough to have a permanent foster father and mother in Bill and Iris.

One of the reasons Shirley fell in love with Sergio was, no doubt, because she was always attracted by mature men who represented a protective father figure. Not that Sergio was much older than she, but he was certainly more wise and sophisticated in the ways of the world. Once be became her manager, however, there had been too much close contact. A star and her manager should live apart. Better still, a star's manager should go home each night to another woman who will soothe his nerves which have been pulverised by his close involvement with the star and her demands.

Shirley admitted, 'When Sergio became my manager it did not work.'

Few men could understand the physical strain Shirley was under when she toured. As she put it, 'I need strength. For instance, when I've got a bad cold and I have to go on singing, it's tough. And if it's two shows a night, it's murder. I hate two shows a night anyway because you get yourself all charged up for your first performance and the adrenalin's going and then you need something like two hours to calm down, and just as you're starting to relax, you have to gear yourself up for another performance. It's hell.'

The only man who worked for Shirley and understood what she

went through was another performer, Bernard Hall, and he was a six-foot tall muscular dancer, not a medium-height slim girl. Sergio didn't always have an easy time, not only had he never been a performer himself, but show business was foreign territory for him, and it was impossible for him to understand what Shirley went through.

Shirley always loved going back to Cardiff to see her mother. She had bought her another house, this time a bungalow because her mother was nearing eighty. It was in the same outer suburb of Cardiff called Llanrumney. Eliza hated leaving her little garden with all the bulbs she had planted each year, but she was philosophical in accepting that this happened to everyone when they grew old. As long as Shirley found the time to come and visit her and the rest of the family were still living around her, she was happy.

Shirley arranged that Ella, her older sister who had once lived in Islington, should, with her husband, also move into the bungalow to make sure that Mrs Mendi was well looked after. Towards the late '70s there came a time when Shirley went down to see her mother with a heavy heart. She knew she had to tell her that her marriage to Sergio was on the rocks and she and Sergio were soon to separate permanently. But she knew she had to tell her soon, before she made the formal announcement.

In 1979 Shirley called a press conference at the Dorchester Hotel to announce that she and Sergio were divorcing. The press were, as usual, good-tempered. Shirley agreed with them that she'd made mistakes but, 'I won't make the same mistake again,' she declared defiantly, 'because I shan't get married again.'

One of the journalists at this conference asked Shirley whether, since she was now divorcing Sergio Novak, Kenneth Carter was her new manager.

'Kenneth Carter is my road manager,' explained Shirley. A road manager's job is to keep the show on the road and look after the comfort and well-being of the star. Bernard Hall was once Shirley's road manager and he could have added that the job also entailed being at her beck and call and ducking when the exasperated star throws her shoes at you. The pitfall of becoming too closely entangled with a star is that the road manager often loses his freedom.

Shirley's new road manager, Kenneth Carter, was an Australian who was said to be a strong and silent type. In a picture of the two taken at that time, Shirley looks beautiful and happy and Kenneth towers above her. He had none of the suave good looks of Peter Finch or Sergio Novak. His hair, in the fashion of the time, was longish and his eyebrows were bushy. According to Hilary Levy, who was then Shirley's secretary, he was Shirley's boyfriend.

Now that Sergio was no longer travelling with her, Shirley liked employing people as companions: she referred to them as her family. Kenneth Carter was one and Hilary Levy, another. Touring is an isolated business and according to Shirley the more successful one becomes the worse it gets – and as you grow older it gets even harder.

Hilary Levy met Shirley in 1978 when she was working as PA to a concert promoter. Sergio and Shirley were still together, and Sergio asked Hilary if she would like to accompany Shirley on her winter tour of Britain and Scandinavia. Hilary accepted at once. She was twenty-nine years old, her marriage was over, and she was free to travel wherever she pleased.

By the time the Novaks divorced, Hilary had become a fixture in Shirley's life, as had Kenneth Carter, who quickly learned the ropes as road manager. Every time Shirley came to London for a concert or a recording, her friends, like Soraya Khashoggi, who had a house in Belgravia, arranged parties and social events for her. One of them, unfortunately went disastrously wrong.

One evening in December 1978, Shirley and a party of eight went to the Country Cousins Restaurant in Fulham to have dinner and listen to a new pop group performing there. It was somebody's birthday and Shirley got up and sang Happy Birthday. She was soon the centre of attraction and the evening turned into a party. At three a.m. they left and adjourned to a house in Eaton Square where the party continued until neighbours complained and the police arrived.

One of the women in the house kept singing a song called, 'Quando, quando' and the police told her to keep quiet. When she refused to be quiet the police arrested her. She became distraught and agitated when, reeking of alcohol and her speech slurred, she was led outside. At one point she had pushed a police officer in the back, causing him to fall against another officer.

It was reported that Shirley was then taken to Gerald Road police station and charged with being drunk and disorderly. She gave her name as Shirley Carter, but everyone realised that she was Shirley Bassey.

On December 21 Shirley, soberly and dressed in black and wearing a hat with a veil, arrived at Horseferry Road Magistrates Court. Her barrister said that here was a lady of unblemished character celebrating twenty-five years in show business, and she was extremely sorry that she had disturbed the neighbours. The magistrate bound her over for three months and said he was confident that it would not happen again.

Hilary Levy and Kenneth Carter were learning the hard way that although they travelled first-class, lived in luxury and were very well paid, a twenty-four-hour schedule was often on the cards, and Shirley could sometimes be a very demanding lady. Hilary says that Shirley always insisted that they had adjoining rooms and sometimes, when she couldn't sleep and needed company, she would call out for Hilary to join her. Although their day was supposed to end at two a.m., Shirley's staff found the biggest drawback was their lack of freedom to live their own lives. Kenneth could buy expensive clothes and drive powerful cars for Shirley in Los Angeles, but had scant time to himself. He managed this for three years before leaving.

Hilary found out that a superstar's life can also be lonely and Shirley wanted a friend to confide in, and it became even harder for Hilary when Kenneth Carter left. When all was going well Shirley was charming and the two women got on very well together. Hilary looked a lot like Shirley; she was shorter but she was slim and could get into all Shirley's clothes. Her hair was dark and worn in the same bouffant style as Shirley's naturally curly dark hair or her wigs. People often wondered if they were related.

Touring always sparked difficulties. Sometimes the hotel day would begin with Shirley wanting an unusual breakfast like steamed kippers or, if she was on a diet, just vegetable juice. Then if she felt tired she would spend the hours until she had to prepare for the evening concert, watching television. Hilary was expected to stay within call, or hurry out to do some shopping for her.

Shirley would worry about her children, and whether she was a good enough mother. Sharon had suffered problems in her life, but she had always coped remarkably well. She lived in a little house in Thornbury, a pretty town near Bristol, and she'd had a baby, a little boy, who was just one year old. She was a single parent and called herself Sharon Denning, assuming the name of her foster parents. She was caring for little Luke, Shirley's first grandchild, whilst enjoying her job as a part-time children's nurse.

Samantha, however, was a problem. Shirley recognised that she too had been a rebel, but she'd had no money to rebel with. She often worried that Samantha was spoilt. At school they said she was too independent-minded. Was giving a girl all the things she herself had missed as child bad for her? And Mark, who Shirley wanted to gain a profession, was also having problems as school.

Then something happened that stopped Shirley in her tracks. Eliza Mendi, her mother, died.

Shirley's mother turned eighty in 1981. A young looking eighty, who didn't look a day over sixty-five, according to her daughter, though she did have some blood pressure trouble like most women of her age. As she'd had a hard life and was the kind of woman who would never give in, it was no surprise that perhaps her heart wasn't as strong as it might have been. When she was taken ill, she had all the symptoms of possible heart failure, her blood pressure was low, and she found it hard to swallow anything but liquids. She was admitted to St David's Hospital.

Three days after Shirley's mother's birthday, she died suddenly. Shirley was heartbroken. 'She only wanted to give, never to take. I was the baby of the family and I adored her,' she wept.

Tiger Bay has its own much loved rituals. When someone dies who has been part of The Bay community, a person who is respected by all, they are given a great send off, a loving farewell. No matter how far away Bay people have moved, they will come back to Tiger Bay to walk behind the coffin. Like an Irish village ceremony, where mourners can stretch for a mile or more. The Bay cortège wends its way down the roads and the lanes. It is a ceremony without pomp but still very impressive.

Eliza Bassey was a respected lady who had brought up seven children in Tiger Bay, and her youngest, her baby, had achieved world-wide fame as a great singer. No-one had been more proud of Shirley than Eliza, and no village was more proud of its daughter than Tiger Bay. But Shirley was not the reason the cortège walked behind the coffin, it was for the English girl, Eliza, who had come down from the north and settled in Wales and loved this corner of Cardiff Bay.

Shirley said, 'On the day of the funeral I was in the most terrible state. I felt rootless, as if my life had been torn apart. She had never doubted me, and she has always been there when I needed her.'

Shirley wept without cease. She was led away after the funeral, still sobbing. At a small gathering afterwards for the family and close friends, everyone had a drink or two and the talk turned, naturally enough, to the time when they were all young. However the peacemaker, their mother, who held the strings of the family tight; the one who calmed them down when tensions rose, was not there any more.

An ill-chosen word or a passing recollection at a funeral can often rend a family apart, and this is what happened at the Bassey funeral.

Shirley, who knew that her mother had been the absolute salvation of the family through every trial and torment, was very angry when someone brought up the story of their father's departure. Her mother had carved a new life for herself, she had found peace and happiness again, so why disinter the past like this? What had happened so long ago was one of the worst times in Eliza's life – this was not the occasion to talk about such things. She was in a highly emotional state, holding herself together and trying to keep her feelings of terrible loss under control. At this moment Shirley's composure finally broke down. People took sides and a bitter family row erupted. Shirley suddenly snapped and got up and left. She did not forget easily and remained silent and distant from her family for a long time afterwards.

Marina, her sister, has said about the affair, 'We thought it was because Shirley was so upset over our mother's death. I honestly don't know why all this happened. It was just a tiff. We'd once all been so close. Now Shirley doesn't even exchange Christmas cards or birthday cards. None even arrived for my children or grandchildren.'

Shirley's sisters waited anxiously when she was to sing in Cardiff the following June, 1982, to see if seats would, as usual, be left for them at St David's Hall box office. For some reason no seats materialised, and hurt turned to disappointment and bitterness.

17

SAMANTHA

SHIRLEY HAD TAKEN to spending time in the south of Spain. She was divorced, she no longer had a husband as manager, no man who said with his hand on his heart that he had only her interests at heart. She had learned many lessons in her comparatively short life, and now she wanted to try life on her own without any commitments, apart from her three children. She bought a villa. Her friend Soraya Khashoggi, the divorced wife of arms dealer, Adnam Khashoggi had a villa there, and so did Adnam (whose sister was the mother of Dodi Fayed).

The international set who turned up in Marbella every summer to open up their villas and have fun were a lively lot and they welcomed Shirley with open arms. Between tours she would spend as much as six weeks at a time at her holiday villa. She loved the rackety night life of the town and she had various friends, including the millionaire property developer Roy Boston. He took her dancing one night, along with Soraya Khashoggi and Baron Heinrich von Thyssen, to a new upmarket nightspot, Olivia Valere. Shirley was so carried away that she gave the customers a spontaneous three-hour singalong in the bar.

'The guitar player and pianist were amazed when I jumped up and started singing,' she recalled. 'I found myself doing songs like "My Funny Valentine," which I hadn't sung for twenty years, and I still remembered the words.'

Sometimes, when Mark was on holiday from school, Shirley would dress him up in a white tuxedo and take him out on the town with her.

Drinking had now become part of Shirley's way of life. She admitted that while her marriage to Sergio was breaking up she had started drinking heavily. Sometimes she had two bottles of champagne on ice with her in her dressing room. She said that the men in her life often counted her drinks. This absolutely infuriated her. And Sergio had gone one better, often committing the unforgivable sin of putting her down verbally until he destroyed her self-confidence. All her life Shirley had been shy of making mistakes because of her lack of education. It took years before she realised that her natural intelligence could make her just as witty and clever as the smartest woman in the room. But in the immediate aftermath of Sergio she still needed a glass of champagne to give her confidence.

She has said that her life with men had a ring of the 'Rita Hayworth' about it; it was a reference to how Prince Aly Khan fell in love with, and married, the film star who played the lead in *Gilda*. When he took her to bed he always, according to Rita, expected to find the glamourous, confident Gilda lying at his side next morning; instead, he got a little Spanish dancer from South of the border down Mexico way who'd been discovered and cruelly exploited by Hollywood men.

Sergio, thought Shirley, fell in love with the glamorous Shirley Bassey, a singing star in provocative gowns who held the spotlight at the Excelsior Hotel in Venice. After they married in Las Vegas, Sergio expected to find the tempestuous woman who the press had one called The Tigress of Tiger Bay, sitting in a splendid negligée at her breakfast tray next morning. He didn't. Instead he got, 'Our Shirl from Tiger Bay.' Pretty enough, it is true, but without the luxurious glossy wig on the short brown hair, or the flattering make-up on the complexion. He'd got a star, and stars aren't always perfect.

Soraya Khashoggi, Shirley's close friend in Marbella at the time, was reputed to have received a twenty-million pound divorce settlement. Her Belgravia home in London was famous for the lavish parties she have there. Jack Jones, the American singer, used to be a regular, as were film stars, pop groups and Shirley.

Marbella became a base for Shirley's preparations for her next international tour to the Far East. Well before the departure date, she played tennis, swam, took dance classes and headed for the gym. All this was to keep her body trim and slender so that the revealing gowns she wore on stage would be enhanced by her sensational figure. It was very hard work but, like an athlete, she trained herself into prime condition for the coming ordeal. Towards the end of her training 'the gang,' the people who made up her work force, would be alerted to get ready by Tony McArthur, who became her manager after her divorce from Sergio. He would then telephone Shirley, check all the dates, and discuss the itinerary with her.

Finally Hilary Levy would arrive from London to assist with the packing and generally help Shirley. Hilary was far more than just a secretary. They discussed taking a couple of days off in Los Angeles to go shopping for clothes. Hilary knew exactly which expensive designer clothes would suite Shirley best, though if Hilary arrived from London with something attractive she had bought at Marks

& Spencer, Shirley would ask her next time she was in London to get one for her in every colour.

Once the tour began, the other side of the superstar's life took over. She must not allow herself to become exhausted by accepting the many invitations that poured in, so must settle for loneliness. She is a star, and she must remain at the top and this can cause great stress. There are times when, after a good performance and tumultuous applause, she is very happy, but she must make a quick getaway to her hotel bedroom if she is going to shine again tomorrow night. Writing postcards home is one of Shirley Bassey's touching habits. The pretty scenes of luxurious hotels in splendid surroundings in Australia, Malaysia, Hong Kong and America, sent to her daughters and some in her neat tidy handwriting telling them how much she missed them, concealed a great deal of angst.

She'd write to Sharon and remember the little girl who used to tour with her in Australia and worry about the slight coolness that sometimes existed between herself and her eldest daughter. The nine years Sharon had spent living with Iris and Bill had something to do with it, and yet it was Sharon who had wanted to leave Cardiff and live with her mother in London. She'd write to Mark and tell him that if he wanted to go to University he must work harder and pass his exams. If he did do well he could come out to Marbella on the next vacation. She knew that he'd come anyway. Then there was Samantha. Why had she changed so much since she was a little girl? There was a part of Samantha that Shirley did not understand and that was a constant worry to her. Why did her daughter always dress in those dirty jeans and tee shirts? Why did she act as if those strange way-out friends of hers were the most important people in her life.

And then there was Hilary. She, too, found touring exhausting, and in 1984, when she'd been with Shirley for six years she finally left for a rest. It was an amicable leavetaking. She returned five years later when Shirley asked her to tour Australia.

On her return from the Far East tour Shirley did some television in London and then went to see Sharon and Luke in Thornbury. They were both worried about Samantha. When she left her exclusive Swiss boarding school it was expected that she would do an external course at Bristol Technical College, but after six months she said she wanted no more of it.

Sharon, who had always played the protective big sister role with Samantha, said she'd spent a day with her recently and she seemed happy and full of chat. She loved playing with young Luke and she always made a big fuss of him. Ever since she was eighteen and had left the boarding school there'd been difficulties with Samantha. The school had complained that there had been behavioural problems, which was understood to mean that the girl would not accept school rules.

Sharon knew that Samantha occasionally drank to much, but she wasn't rowdy, she just went home and slept it off. She frequented pubs with a group of friends who were scruffily dressed and stayed until throwing-out time. It may have been Samantha's reaction against expensive schooling in Switzerland, where some of the kids were sons and daughters of dukes or children of very rich members of the international set who just dumped their offspring there.

Sharon hoped it might just be a phase Samantha was going through. After all, she was only twenty and she'd probably grow out of it in time. Sharon knew of an education psychologist who would be willing to take Samantha in as a boarder and tutor her. Would her mother agree to that? She would stay with his family for a year and it would probably settle her down.

Mother and daughter parted with mutual assurances that they would keep a watchful eye on Samantha, and Shirley would go over and see her at her present lodging in Bristol.

*

In August 1985 Shirley was getting ready for her next American tour. She missed Hilary who had left the year before and had not replaced her, but 'the gang' as she called them, the hairdresser and dresser, the tour manager and the musicians, would meet her at Heathrow and they'd all fly into New York together. America had really opened up for her, she sang at Caesar's in Atlantic City now, as well as giving her usual concert at New York's Carnegie Hall and appearing on Long Island.

Through her glass bedroom wall, Shirley could see out over the lake. It was raining cats and dogs as it sometimes did in Lugano in the summer and she wouldn't be sorry to leave it for a while. After her divorce she had decided to keep using the Villa Capricorn as her base. It was, after all, her property. Strangely enough, Samantha had never liked the villa very much, she had once warned Shirley, 'be careful that this house doesn't become your prison.' She reminded herself she must talk to Samantha tomorrow.

Her two daughters were so different; Sharon was so much more level-headed. Although her last relationship hadn't lasted, and she was a single mother, Luke brought them all so much happiness and Shirley believed with all her heart that Sharon would find the right man and there would be a happy marriage in her future.

She knew that Samantha was more like herself; perhaps in the end she would become an entertainer, too. If she was made of the same stuff as her mother she might also have choose between the normal easy life, or plunge into the unknown world of show business.

Shirley had hoped that Samantha's expensive education would help her younger daughter to enjoy a social acceptable life, that she might become a career woman, a barrister, a politician. There was not sign of this as yet but, whatever she became, Shirley would always love and support her daughter as her own mother had done for her.

*

A week later Shirley left Lugano to set off on her American tour. She arrived at Heathrow where, 'the gang' were waiting for her, and waved to her musical director who would start the tour with her at Carnegie Hall. But first she wanted to telephone Samantha. She'd called her the day before from Lugano and her landlady had said that Samantha wasn't there at the moment, but she'd tell her that Shirley had called. For some strange reason she'd started worrying about her daughter yesterday. She thought she'd seen her face on the television screen, but when she looked again she knew she must be wrong.

And then she saw a lovely surprise waiting for her. There was Sharon standing by the waiting group. The two women embraced, then Sharon took her mother by the arm and walked her away from the others. She said something which Shirley did not hear, and led her to a closed door. Sharon opened it as if she'd been there before. They looked inside a strange room and Shirley saw a hospital bed. It was the kind of room where someone suddenly taken ill and unable to walk might go.

Shirley turned to Sharon. 'Why here? You've made a mistake.' Then she saw the tears welling in Sharon's eyes, and the stricken look on her face 'What's happened?' she asked, with a sense of dread. Sharon broke the appalling news that Samantha had been found dead the day before.

'But I phoned yesterday,' Shirley whispered. 'I spoke to her landlady. She said that Samantha was all right.'

Sharon held her hand tightly. 'The police were there. They told her what so say. They had come to tell her that Samantha had been found in the river.' All Shirley, numb with horror, could keep saying was, 'No, no . . . not this, not this.'

She was utterly devastated, flagellating herself with remorse. Why oh why hadn't she come yesterday, or the day before? Why hadn't she come to save her daughter? 'But she told me she was happy, everything was going well.' She simply couldn't begin to comprehend the situation. 'Why this?' she groaned, 'children are meant to bury their parents.'

Sharon told her that no-one knew what had happened. It was a mystery. Samantha had been found about a quarter of a mile downstream from the Clifton suspension bridge. Of course it was not her mother's fault, it wouldn't have made any difference whatever she had tried to do. But Shirley couldn't forgive herself for not being in Bristol with her daughter. She said later, 'Guilt is a terrible thing to carry around. It makes you ill.'

At the inquest, Samantha's last hours were revealed as far as they were known. That last August night, she left her lodgings in Totterdown, a suburb of Bristol, and made for Hotwell's where she always met her group of friends. She was a tall slim girl of twenty-one, with a very pretty face and dark curly hair.

Samantha kept her past secret, never revealing to her friends that she was the daughter of the star, Shirley Bassey. She called herself Samantha Novak, never ever mentioning the name Hume, which she once bore. She went in search of warmth and love of a kind she could respond to, surrounded by friends in a pub. That night she was dressed, as she usually was, in a torn leather jacket, baggy trousers and men's steel capped shoes. She had just £1.65p in her pocket.

What happened in the next hour or so is not known, but three people, a married couple and their friend, were at a pub-restaurant down by the Bristol docks. A girl walked in as they were finishing their meal. Later they recognised Samantha from newspaper photographs as the girl who walked into the pub just as the bar closed. She asked if she could get a drink but was told it was too late.

She asked the people finishing their meal if there was a telephone. They told her where if was and she went off to make a call. One of the men said, 'She was not drunk, but she was definitely not sober,' One of these three witnesses thought the tall, dark girl might be of mixed race.

When they left the pub the girl was standing outside. They had a dog with them and the four of them had a conversation about dogs and then the girl walked off. 'The river was on the other side of the road,' said one of the men at the inquest, 'and there was a high metal railing.' They were the last people to see Samantha alive, and they said she seemed quite happy as she set off along the road by the river. They speculated that she may have had a date and arrived too late, but she didn't seem at all upset. Further along, the high railing stopped and there was a path over a bank that ran steeply down to the river.

That was the last sighting of Samantha, a smiling girl who walked off along a road by the river.

At the inquest, the coroner said, 'It is possible that she may have walked by the river and perhaps tripped. If Samantha was slightly fuddled with drink, she may have slipped down the river bank. Samantha died from the shock of hitting the water. She was an able swimmer but the shock of hitting the cold water killed her. It seems very likely that Samantha's death may have been accidental. There was no evidence that she was unhappy. She was fully clothed when she was found. Samantha's body was spotted by tourists on a passing pleasure boat. She had been in the water for over a week.'

The coroner added, 'There is no evidence to say that she was on the suspension bridge, or that she fell from the bridge. Her injuries were not consistent with her falling from a great height. Thus, that rules out the rumours that she fell from the bridge.' He repeated once again that the cold water caused heart failure and Samantha Novak died from shock.

This was the only comfort Shirley could clutch on to, that her daughter's death was probably an accident. Although the media had blazoned the new of her death as a suicide this theory was disputed and there was no evidence that she was unhappy. There were no suspicious circumstances or any evidence of pre-death trauma.

Shirley would always talk wistfully about Samantha. 'She talked like me. I saw me in her. I thought she'd be an actress and go on the stage . . . but now we'll never know what she was capable of.'

It was revealed after the coroner's verdict that Samantha's friends had been very concerned about her disappearance, but they all agreed that her death must have been an accident. The educational psychologist, Mr Alastair John Williams, with whose family Samantha had lived for the previous nine months, said she had only recently gone into lodgings in Montague Street. She has seemed a happy girl.

Mr Tony MacArthur, Shirley's agent and manager, issued a press statement: 'Miss Bassey is staying with friends in London. It is devastating news but she is handling the situation very well.'

Relatives living in Cardiff were greatly shocked at the news. Mrs Iris Denning of Llanrumney, who had been Sharon's foster mother, said, 'Shirley must have been knocked for six. Although she worked all over the world she was very close to Samantha. She was such a normal happy girl, with everything to live for. We just can't believe it.'

On Wednesday, 12 September 1985, a small crowd gathered outside the Chapel of Rest in Westbury near Bristol waiting to see Shirley Bassey arrive for her daughter's funeral service. When she emerged from her car, she looked ravaged with grief. In one hand she clutched a red rose. On one side, there to help and comfort her, was her friend Soraya Khashoggi, and on the other Sharon, her elder daughter.

Many flowers were taken into the chapel, including a wreath of white lilies from Shirley. There was also a wreath from Dionne

Warwick, and one from Samantha's favourite rock group, The Grateful Dead, Samantha's spikey-haired punk friends were present at the thirty-five minute service. After the prayer, 'The Lord is my Shepherd,' Samantha's friends gave her a rock send-off, playing a tape of her favourite piece of music, Jimmie Hendrix's 'Foxy Lady'.

No other members of Shirley's family were at the funeral. Samantha, with her Swiss education, had had little to do with Tiger Bay or with her aunts or cousins. Marina, Shirley's sister, said later, 'We sent a wreath but none of us were invited to come.' Four years had gone by since the quarrel at their mother's funeral, but it seemed that Shirley had still not forgiven them. Twice now, she had given concerts in Cardiff and twice no tickets had been left for the family at the box office.

Shirley faced a barrage of press photographers when she left the Chapel of Rest. Her manager announced that Shirley would take a brief rest in France before embarking on her American tour, which would begin in New York at Carnegie Hall. The grief-stricken star was driven away in a black Mercedes.

In an interview given much later, Shirley recalled her devastation when she started that American tour: her dread of appearing before an audience and breaking down and being unable to sing. She remembers that when she walked on to the stage at Carnegie Hall, the whole audience rose as one for she didn't know how long. She just stood there, willing herself to stay in control, telling herself, 'If you cry your eyelashes will fall off, your mascara will run, the shadow will smudge. Don't cry. Do you hear me, don't cry!' And then the orchestra started to play, 'When You're Smiling', and the adrenalin began to flow and she was saved.

But she felt the audience were her real saviours, they comforted her, their warmth pulled her along in each song. When she looked back on that night, she said, 'They got me through, but I hardly knew what I was doing. One part of me was quite numb. All my grief was locked away and this wonderful audience helped and comforted me with their understanding and loving support for what I was going through.' Shirley has said, 'To sing has always been my salvation, my closest friend. I never wanted to be a singer, but it seemed to be my destiny. Out of seven children I was the one chosen to sing.'

After a week at Carnegie Hall, she was off for four days at a music fair in Long Island and then four days at Caesar's in Atlantic City. She then flew to Germany for a four-week tour. Shirley believed this was the only way she could cope with the avalanche of grief that had overwhelmed her. If she kept travelling, working, exhausting herself so that she wouldn't spend the long nights brooding about her loss and dwelling on the past to find out where she went wrong, she might get through this misery. If she stopped she knew she would go to pieces.

Her manager, Tony MacArthur, said of Shirley, 'She is handling it all very well, she is going on with her tour.' Then he added. 'But one day the finality of it all will really hit her.'

The months went by, and although the scars of what had happened would remain with her always, she no longer kept demanding of some unseen creator why her baby, Samantha, had been taken from her.

She tried to stop reminding herself that two of the people she loved most in the world, her mother and her youngest daughter, were gone forever. She hoped that this was known as 'getting over it;' that one day she would wake up and feel that life would perhaps be worth living again.

Then, out of the blue, when she least expected it to happen, the secret dread that had started way back when she was a teenager became reality. She had always feared that one day she would stand on a stage facing a huge audience, she would open her mouth and absolutely no sound would come out. It would be a catastrophe. Her voice, after all, was everything.

Shirley always had a special affection for Sydney, Australia. Years before on her very first visit there, the Sydney audience had come to her rescue when the *Daily Sketch* had tried to hurt and humiliate her over her secret baby, Sharon. She went on her usual winter tour of Australia in January 1986, four months after the death of Samantha and knowing it was not going to be easy. Her American and German engagements had taken a lot out of her. Every time she went on stage she had to make a conscious effort not to let go for a single moment. Only when each audience showed they were with her, when she felt they wanted to help her through, could she relax at all. She had always enjoyed singing, it was her life, but all the time it was getting harder.

Her nightmare came true at the Sydney Centre in front of 10,000 people. For the first time in her life her voice dried up. Afterwards she said, 'The amazing thing was that nobody booed.' She knew that they could have done. A lot of the audience had travelled a long way to get to the Centre, they had paid good money for their seats, and now Shirley Bassey was standing in front of them completely mute. Her enormous grief over her daughter's death had finally caught up with her and going on with her work, giving herself no time to stand back and cry, bottling up her misery, had rebounded on her. She had lost her voice, and worse, she couldn't be entirely certain that it would ever come back again as the same glorious instrument.

Her life and her career seemed to be lying in ruins around her feet. She was forty-nine years old, with fifty an approaching and unwelcome landmark. If she'd looked in the mirror she would have seen a vibrant and beautiful woman, but she didn't look in the mirror. Suddenly she didn't want to get up any more, she wanted to stay in bed and cry. When she stopped crying she wanted to drink and she wanted to eat anything that would give her comfort through this bad time. In the middle of the night she would suddenly crave food and find herself with a bar of chocolate in one hand and a slice of cheese in the other.

Sharon stood by and watched it all happening. She had her own problems, she was a single mother with a six-year-old son and was bewildered and angry herself about Samantha's death. Everyone close to Samantha was blaming themselves for what had happened. Could they have done more for her? But how do you stop a girl having a drink and walking merrily along a perilous river bank? How do you stop an accident? Even young Mark, her adopted brother, who was nineteen, was blaming himself. Maybe he should have cared more for his sister.

Sharon, and Shirley's close friends began an unobtrusive campaign to bring Shirley back to life. It would take time to get her to face that some things in life and death have to be accepted. They tried to help her talk about Samantha. One day Shirley said to Sharon, 'Did you know that Samantha was a vegetarian? Did you know that she would never eat meat?' Then, sometime later, she said, 'Samantha really didn't like drinking. I don't like it either. When I was young I didn't drink at all. Do you think one glass of wines all right? I'm going to cut down.' It was as if she couldn't tell Samantha any more that she was drinking too much, but she could be tough with herself and if she put her mind to it, she could stop. Mark said, 'It took Shirley a long time to give up heavy drinking. But she did.'

Sharon helped Shirley reorganise her life and the presence of Luke was a great comfort. Shirley ruefully remarked, 'I make a much better grandmother than I ever did a mother.' The real breakthrough came when Shirley tried on one of her dresses and the zip wouldn't close around the waist. She checked into the Pritikin clinic for eleven days. Shirley had never eaten a great deal, but now she was shown the right food to eat. She was put on a regime of carbohydrates kept separate from protein, an occasional day's fasting on 'cleansing juice', and fruit and rice cakes for breakfast until she reached her desired weight.

She put the Villa Capricorn up for sale – there were too many unhappy memories there – and took up residence in a hotel suite in Lausanne. Then she made her most important decision: how to learn to sing again, how to strengthen her vocal cords so that she would never again suffer the nightmare of losing her voice on a stage. She found a wonderful teacher who gave her confidence. The Opera House in Monte Carlo where she finally settled has some of the best voice teachers in the world. Her voice not only came back bigger than before but she also gained an octave.

Nina Chanel, a former opera singer, was the wonderful teacher who helped Shirley find her voice again, who taught her the vocal exercises that would create an even stronger sound. They were operatic exercises that strengthened her vocal cords and gave her back the confidence to believe that she, alone on that empty stage, could sing her way out of any difficulty, as opera singers are taught to do.

Tapes were made of these lessons and Shirley always took them on tour with her. She would practice in her dressing room every day without fail. If she had an appointment for an interview, if she had to record, she would still find time to do her vocal exercises. She enjoyed doing them. 'Going to Nina Chanel,' said Shirley, 'was the best thing I have ever done and her advice about vocal exercises was the best advice I've ever been given.'

She has often been asked if she'd like to sing opera. Invariably, she has replied in the affirmative, saying it to would be great to sing Carmen, then she tells a little story to make fun of herself. She was invited to hear an opera at the Royal Opera House in Covent Garden. In the interval the director invited her to have a glass of champagne and he said, 'Oh, you would make the most marvellous Carmen.'

'Would I?' replied Shirley.

'Yes, but isn't it a pity that it's for a soprano, the wrong key for you.'

'Couldn't you change the key?'

The director smiled. 'I'm afraid not. It doesn't work like that, here you need the voice to fit the opera.

Hilary Levy who hadn't worked for Shirley since 1984, had a telephone call from her to say that she was leaving on an Australian tour the following week and she wondered if Hilary would like to come along.

Hilary was in a dead-end job and had just broken off with a boyfriend. She suddenly remembered what it was like living in a luxury hotel with someone to clear up after her. She said yes, she'd go to Australia.

After the tour Shirley went to Marbella to relax. She had another interest there now – Mark was living permanently in southern Spain. He had disappointed her very much by refusing to continue with his education and go to university. The reason she accepted his way of life without a fight was because of Samantha's death; the young had a right to do their own thing. Mark had had a brief flirtation with drugs, but he was over that now and he's met a nice girl.

When Shirley was in Marbella, she sometimes took Mark out with her, and she made sure he never went short of money. He seemed to have odd jobs here and there. There were a lot of rich people down on the Costa del Sol. Puerto Banus, the yachting complex next to Marbella, was *the* place to sit at a café and watch the Rolls Royces, Porsches and BMWs drive past, and in the evening you could see Rod Stewart and Jimmy Tarbuck, back from golf, drinking a pint in a local bar.

Patti Flyn, a girl from the good old days of Tiger Bay, had her own show on the local radio and Luigi, a Welsh Italian from Pontypridd ran one of the best bars in the port. It was no wonder that Mark was enjoying himself, dancing in and out of the fringes of the rich at night with his mother and sunning himself on the beach in the daytime. When she'd gone back to work he existed as best he could.

Shirley met Michael Sullivan again in Marbella. He had remarried, and his wife was the French film actress Dany Robin. They bumped at a party given at the Khashoggi villa. She walked up to him, put her arms around his neck and said, 'Hello Mikey, it's good to see you.'

Michael didn't see her again until 1994, when he was seventy-four and in a wheelchair. He and Dany went to the Festival Hall for one of Shirley's concerts. After the show they went backstage to congratulate Shirley, but was unable to see them. He supposed that she hadn't forgiven him after all.

In January 1995 Michael was down on his luck. His health was going, he could hardly walk and he said he was broke. He had always lived it up and spent every penny he made. In the old days when he was building Shirley's career, he was often deep in debt. Fame and fortune came to Shirley and also to Michael. When they parted he became known as the comedian's agent and had many big names on his books. He was prosperous and successful, but the best luck of all was his new wife, Dany Robin. When his fortunes and his health declined, Dany worked to keep him. She was a good and loving wife.

They moved to a one-room flat, a studio, in the Trocadero area in Paris so Dany could find work. When he was given a new publicity photograph of Shirley, he pinned it up next to his chair.

Wonderful news came very soon at the beginning of May. Dany secured a six-month TV contract in Cuba. She would find an apartment and Michael would fly over and join her. Two days before she left, in the middle of the night, there was an electrical fault and a fire swept through the tiny flat. Michael half-paralysed could hardly move and he and Dany both perished in the fire. His new photograph of Shirley the girl he had once discovered, still pinned to the bed drapery also went up in flames.

18

THIS IS MY LIFE

SHIRLEY BASSEY TURNED sixty-one on 8 January 1998. The world's press had not forgotten, particularly not in her home town, Cardiff, where a smiling picture of the star occupied the front page of *The Echo*. Tickets were already on sale for the St David's Hall Concert in June.

It had been a long time – almost five decades – since fifteen-year-old Shirley Bassey started out on the long, hard road to fame and fortune. It would be futile to ask whether she ever dreamed how her life would turn out since, according to people who knew her then, she was certain from the word go that one day she would set the world on fire. Millionaires would court her and Arab shiekhs would want to snap diamond bracelets around her wrist. To impress Elizabeth Taylor, a well-known billionaire would beg Shirley to fly to New York just to sing at his party.

She probably guessed, even before she'd ever heard of Lugano or

Marbella that she'd have homes all over the world; so many, that in the end she'd get so fed up with all these houses that she'd decide one home was as much as she wanted, and it had better be an apartment in Monte Carlo.

But you can't stay too long at a stretch in Monte Carlo. As the natives of the place will tell you, everyone gets 'le cafard', a touch of depression brought on by those high mountains that enclose the principality. Monte Carlo is such a small place and that big backdrop of mountains gives you a feeling of being squeezed tight. So, sometimes Shirley, resting between tours, would fly to London, perhaps for a friend's engagement party at the Savoy Hotel. The TV cameras are always there, so pictures will be in all the tabloids. They'll call her a sparkling butterfly in the papers next morning because of the gold and diamond jewellery glinting around her neck.

From the age of seventeen Shirley was taught that getting one's name and face into the newspaper – or not – is the life or death of a career. Back in the Fifties Leslie Grade told her manager that they'd stayed too long in the sunshine of Australia and the public would soon be saying, 'Shirley Who?' So Sullivan hid Shirley in a Bath hotel and told the police she'd gone missing; Shirley's face flashed on every front page in the land.

Kenneth Hume, her next manager spent a lot of money on a thousand red roses and a 'second time around' diamond engagement ring to get Shirley's face in the papers. At the Pigalle, Shirley was persuaded to sing 'Second Time Around' after she announced to her delighted audience that she was remarrying her manager. But when the next man she married was not Kenneth Hume but Sergio Novak, there were more pages of publicity, and Shirley's new record did well.

Shirley Bassey became completely relaxed about publicity. She loves the camera and the camera loves her, but in the painful moments of her life, she learned that if you really mean it, the press will understand and leave you alone,

She has said that she's become a bit of a loner. She likes to stay in her apartment for days on end. She doesn't want staff to live in any more. 'I don't want a bodyguard,' she says, 'because that would take all the enjoyment out of life. I really like to live out of a suitcase,' and she likes to travel by bus. All the big female singing stars seem to do this and the idea originated in the States; stars go from concert to concert in complete safety with the crew and the star's entourage sitting around them: the road manager, the secretary, the hairdresser and make-up, the dresser with the costumes, and the musicians. The sound and lighting men are there, too, and the publicist with the previous boxes of souvenir programmes. The whole caboodle is there, travelling together. Shirley Bassey has come a long way from the time, forty years ago, when Michael Sullivan and the kid from Tiger Bay travelled economy class.

There are always plenty of fans watching the departure of the bus from a respectful distance. Managements always warn Shirley to be on her guard; for instance, not to bend over from the stage to shake hands with the fans. But she refuses the advice. The only precaution she takes is to remove her rings because the pressure can result in bloody fingers.

Fans, though, *have* frightened her in the past. The worst occasion was when they tried to turn her car over in Liverpool. 'They were shaking the limo,' she reported 'and I was very afraid.' Another time they put a small child on the bonnet of her car to stop her driver moving off. 'I may seem very controlled,' says Shirley 'but off stage I can be very unsure of myself.'

She has said that if she is exhausted after her performance in a big city she does tell her road manager to have a car waiting outside the stage door. This quick getaway, which does wonders for her equilibrium, can upset people. One of them was her old friend, Iris Freeman, the girl who used to slide down the slag heaps at Tiger Bay docks with bare-bottomed three-year-old Shirley Bassey. Iris' story became another Tiger Bay legend. 'So I ran after her car,' she told Tiger Bay,' and I yelled, "I knew you when you had no knickers, Shirley Bassey."'

The legend started as a sad little story of old friends living in another country and hoping to see their old chum again. Three of them, including Iris Freeman, had once been members of The Bay Girls chorus with Shirley. Iris Freeman had been Shirley's best friend and her family lived in 'the nice house' down by Loudon Square in Tiger Bay, where Shirley often stayed overnight rather than go back to Splott. Iris had gone with Shirley to London to audition for that first long-ago touring show, *Memories of Jolson*. She had married an American and left Tiger Bay to live on the West Coast of America. One day she noticed that Shirley Bassey was soon to sing in San Francisco. She knew she'd love to see Shirley again; she hadn't seen her for God knows how many years. She rang up her girl friends she had known in Cardiff. In the end five girls from Tiger Bay arranged to travel to San Francisco and see Shirley's show.

Iris wrote to Shirley, and she wrote and telephoned the management of the theatre to ask them to tell Shirley or her secretary that some friends from Shirley's home town would be in the audience. They'd love to come backstage after the performance just to say hello.

Five excited girls sat in the front row of the stalls. At the intermission Iris went backstage, but she was stopped by a minder and she asked him to give Shirley a note. Part of it was written in Welsh, which they hoped would amuse their old old girlhood friend. They wrote that they were dying to see her after the show.

After the performance the girls went round to the stage door, but this time entry was impossible. No, they couldn't go in and see Miss Bassey. No, they couldn't send a message. She'd be out very soon. Join the rest of the fans. The girls were surprised. But all right, if this was how it had to be, they'd wait. A large limousine drew up and blocked their view of the stage door. Then the fans started to surge forward and there was Shirley getting straight into the car. Iris stared in amazement. Something must have gone wrong, Shirley couldn't have had their messages. She rushed to the car she pressed her face against the back window. 'Shirley, It's me Iris,' she shouted. That was when Shirley looked right through her. 'Drive on,' she ordered the chauffeur. Iris stood in the middle of the road, disgusted and hurt as the car pulled away.

She walked disconsolately back to her friends. She looked at their woebegone expressions. It had been a long trip, a lot of money had been spent.

Although capable of enormous warmth and generosity Shirley can also be volatile and unpredictable and after an unusually exhausting performance might be just too tired to talk. Shirley's apparent indifference can sometimes be due to the pressures of her life on tour.

The people of Tiger Bay were riveted by this account of their one-time heroine's behaviour. In a way it summed up what a lot of them thought. They resented it when Shirley in more recent years swanned down Bute Street, Cardiff in a big limousine with a photographer following in another car. 'Shirley Bassey Comes Home, my eye. The bloody house was pulled down years ago.' There is a brick wall in the middle of a row of little red council houses where it used to be, you'd never know the Basseys had ever lived there.

The history of that community in the Cardiff docks seems to have been tossed aside. Until the bulldozers moved in, Tiger Bay was a real place with its own history, a mixed-race community that had been there for well over one hundred years. Tiger Bay might be compared to the Italian community in Soho, or the Russian and Polish Jews who flooded into the East End of London after the Russian pogroms, who had all arrived as immigrants.

They didn't call it Tiger Bay, the people who once lived there, to them it was just The Bay, but now it has been turned into green lawns overlooking the sea. Only the ghosts of all those foreign seamen who lived in the lodging houses around the docks hover over these new grassy slopes where once stood the seedy, rowdy welcoming, Ship and Pilot pub; the haven where the seamen used to gossip and drink and laugh when their ships were in port all those years ago. Shirley says she feels a stranger when she comes to Cardiff; it has changed so much she feels like a foreigner. When her mother died, she no longer saw any reason to return. Not that she forgets her family any more. When she sings in Cardiff the office now always leaves tickets for her sisters. The quarrel is forgotten, the hurt has been healed.

Sharon no longer lives in the pretty town of Thornbury. Just as Shirley predicted, she fell in love and married, – a builder from Henley-on-Thames. Her wedding day, 11 November 1987, marked the birthday of Samantha who had died two years earlier. It was Sharon's decision to marry on her sister's birthday as a remembrance of the talented little girl who once sang, 'I'll Be Your Sweetheart.'

The press said that Sharon stole the limelight on the day she married Steve Barratt. There were fifty of Shirley's fans waiting outside the quiet little church at Henley-on-Thames. The bride's mother wore a beautiful wide-brimmed hat and a patterned silk dress, but the stars of the wedding day were Sharon and her husband Steve.

Sharon now has two more sons, and the relationship with her mother is close. They talk for hours on the phone though it hadn't always been like that. There was once resentment on Sharon's part because she felt Shirley had neglected her when she was young, but after the birth of her third son she discovered that having more than one child is not as easy as it looks. So she sat down and wrote Shirley a letter. Part of it said, 'I understand after all these years, now that I have children of my own, that it was not your fault.' Shirley says, 'Wonderful letter, how I cried.'

In spite of the fans waiting quietly at Sharon's wedding Shirley Bassey has never had a fan club. It is said that Shirley does not approve of fan clubs, but she has accepted a group founded by an American called The Collector's Club. Not fans, as the president of the club hurries to explain, but people who like to collect memorabilia of the star. This American enthusiast from New Jersey soon found he had over a thousand members in the UK, Europe and the United States.

They travel for miles across continents to attend Shirley's concerts, and usually fill the first two rows of the stalls. The British contingent are dedicated people and look more like a colourfully dressed literary group than rabid fans. After the concert where they have cheered and applauded the star, they will stand in the bars and cafés to discuss Shirley's performance, her past triumphs, concerts, recordings and videos. They are generous in their help to new fans. The 'Chief fan' is a hardworking lady who keeps things together.

They love standing ovations. One of their favourites was Shirley's performance at the Royal Variety Show at the London Palladium in 1994. Shirley appeared in a gown of silver beads and tassels. Every bead and tassel had a life of its own. Tassels have never moved so erotically as they did on Shirley that night.

Shirley has made a career out of entrances. Her opening number must always raise the spirits, then there is the soft song, 'We Never Say Goodbye' No longer belting out the sound her voice had achieved a lyrical quality. For her finale that night as the Palladium she swung into 'Hey Jude' (take a sad song to make it better . . .)

And then, the Bassey magic appeared in full strength, she is up there with the greats, echoing the power and sadness of Judy Garland and Edith Piaf. The song was a 'tour de force'. She had done what her heroine, opera diva Maria Callas, used to do, taken the audience up with her.

The applause from the audience grew as Shirley brushed away her tears. People began to stand up. Over the avalanche of applause the whole of the audience rose. It was the first standing ovation for over twenty years at the London Palladium.

Shirley Bassey had indeed come a long way since she sang in pubs at the age of thirteen where, if they didn't like her songs, they threw things at her. Maybe luck was on her side, but her attitude was always that one day she would sing before vast audiences, just like Judy Garland. Five or ten thousand people would applaud her and her show would be called something like Shirley Bassey in Concert.

Shirley Bassey was in Concert at the National Exhibition Centre at Hampton in Arden outside Birmingham in the summer of 1994. Good tickets started at twenty-five pounds and there were near enough ten thousand takers. The venue has about as much glamour or atmosphere as a giant aircraft hanger: a kind of stable for Jumbo Jets that might have strayed from Birmingham Airport down the road, but the audience poured in. More women than men. Grandmas, grandpas, people in wheelchairs. The volume of people was overwhelming. Down the wide aisles came boys wearing baseball caps and selling popcorn and coke. You had to be a crazed fan to be there – it's togetherness with popcorn and coke and Shirley Bassey. It's raining outside and everyone but Shirley Bassey and the first two rows of the audience are wearing anoraks. The first two rows are made up of fans from the Collectors Club, the men in dinner jackets, the ladies in evening dress.

After the interval on comes Shirley, dashing from the back of the stage as if she's catching a train. It's a very big stage and it's a long way to run. Off comes the dramatic cape and underneath is a dress of black net and ruffles. They call it 'The Pizza Dress' in the Collectors Club because of the two circles of black lace on the bodice. It's an old dress, it's been going for a long time. Unless you're near the front you have to watch everything that Shirley does reflected on a huge screen. Shirley herself is just a little dot on the faraway stage. Even the front rows of 'Collectors' don't see her very well but the songs are good and so is Shirley. For a few minutes one of her songs almost touches the heart. But not quite. This isn't real life but big business; it is the merchandising of product Shirley Bassey. The star smiles from the cover of every large illustrated brochure lining the entrance hall.

Although Shirley had performed as a featured artist or a star in theatres all over the world from the age eighteen, it was probably not until she married Sergio Novak and became a tax-free wanderer that her ambition of taking over a theatre with her own orchestra really took shape. Early in her career in Las Vegas she had disliked the contemptuous way artists were treated, but Las Vegas paid fabulous salaries and it was difficult to refuse.

Sergio Novak has always said that he took her out of the one-night stand and cabaret circuit and made her an international concert star. But it's difficult to believe that this man who knew nothing at all about showbiz until he married Shirley was the mastermind behind Shirley's rise to concert stardom. Shirley's reaction to Sergio's claim was to state that she only wished she had finished with the Novak marriage years before the divorce was finalised. She should have left him much earlier on.

'Neither of my husbands were at all supportive about the children,' Shirley said, bitterly on one occasion, 'I didn't discipline my children, but you know the best mothers and fathers have children that go wrong.'

Shirley admits that Mark has been a bit of a worry for a long time. He still lives in Marbella on the monthly cheque for five hundred pounds which Shirley sends him.

In 1990 twenty-four-year-old Tissa Kimsey went on holiday to Marbella and fell in love with Mark Novak. At that time Mark was working as a waiter and getting over the mess he had nearly made of his life with drugs. He and Tissa lived together for two and a half years and in May 1991 Tatjana was born. Shirley wrote a letter to Mark from Adelaide, Australia, congratulating them both and expressing delight at having a granddaughter.

Tissa first met Shirley at a party at her house in Marbella and found her friendly but not completely approachable. Shirley told her that she loved babies but was always glad to hand them back to their mothers. But there was a happy moment when Mark and Tissa went to London to hear Shirley in concert at the Royal Albert Hall. After the finale, as Shirley stood at the edge of the stage receiving flowers and presents, Mark walked down and held up his daughter for Shirley to see. Smiling happily she lifted her pretty eighteen-month-old granddaughter in the air and showed her off to the audience.

Four years later Tissa and Mark had been separated for some time. Tissa was living at home in Skegness with her family and little Tatjana was going to a local school. It was a sad ending to what had begun as a happy holiday romance. In spite of Tissa's resentment arising out of her belief that the Bassey family don't do more for her daughter, it is not really Shirley's problem; Mark is now a grown man and any girl takes him on at her own risk.

Shirley had always been a generous mother. Sharon's latest house is one of a succession bought for her by Shirley. This one is big enough for Sharon and Steve and their growing family: Luke, Sebastian and Nathan – and Nana if she wants to come.

Anyone expecting to find a calm, sweet, placid person when the meet Shirley might be disappointed. Here is a woman who carries a whole industry on her shoulders, Shirley Bassey Inc. If she wants to give it up, she's going to hurt a lot of people and put a lot of people out of work. She's been working ever since she can remember; she doesn't really know how to stop working.

Hilary Levy rejoined Shirley as her personal assistant and secretary in 1989, and although their first tour together had been a great success, there were subsequent quarrels. The last of these took place in Cape Town, South Africa with dire consequences.

There had been trouble for Shirley before over South Africa. Way back in 1982 she had performed at Sun City, the then fabled and sumptuous casino and hotel complex in Bophuthatswana, the 'independent' homeland on the borders of South Africa that was effectively a satellite state of that country. During the apartheid era, Sun City was not segregated, but Shirley didn't realise the implications of performing in a place with close links to racially segregated South Africa.

However, when she was due to sing in Cardiff later that year things became serious. 'Call off Shirley Bassey's Show' was the first indication of trouble ahead. Then came, 'All trade unions will be asked to picket and demonstrate outside St David's Hall if Shirley Bassey performs there next month – because she has appeared in South Africa.'

On Friday 3 September 1982, the ladies of Cardiff couldn't care less where Shirley had been as they queued for tickets. 'You shouldn't mix politics and entertainment,' said one, 'Shirley sings for everyone, black, white and yellow. Her job is to entertain people.'

Another said, 'I've been drinking coffee to stay awake all night and get tickets. I first saw her at the New Theatre in 1956, she was bottom of the bill, now she's top everywhere. Call the show off? Rubbish!'

Hundreds queued all night, it was Shirley's first appearance there in seven years, 'I've seen her twenty-two times,' said Mrs Mules of Dinas Powys. 'She's fantastic.'

Shirley solved it all. She released a pledge that she would never perform in South Africa or any country which would insist on an audience being segregated for any reason of race, colour or religion. Her manager, Tony McArthur, however pressed home the point that Shirley had not realised that Sun City was an integral part of segregated South Africa – blacks, and whites mixed freely there.

Shirley said, 'I would never perform in Johannesburg, Durban or Cape Town. But I went to Sun City because it was a fantastic project, and they didn't stop blacks from going there. If you are an entertainer, you entertain. I don't like politicians telling us what to do.'

As she said afterwards, 'I'm in good company, Frank Sinatra and Rod Stewart and Elton John all sang there.' And, she might have added, so did Cher, Liza Minnelli and Johnny Mathis among others.

Her name was subsequently placed on the United Nations blacklist of stars who performed at Sun City.

Shirley has never considered herself black. Her mother who had brought her up was white and she professes she does not remember her black father. Her stepfather was black and she loved him, but he was away at sea most of the time and he died early. She was reared by a white mother in the white suburb of Splott.

The end of apartheid meant the end of all barriers to going to South Africa. In December 1993 Shirley, her PA Hilary Levy, and Bo Mills and Yves, her personal managers, went on a South African tour and stayed at the Mount Nelson Hotel in Cape Town. After Shirley's performance there was a party at the hotel were a great deal of champagne was imbibed by everyone.

What happened next became the evidence in a court case.

Hilary Levy sued Shirley Bassey and her trading company, SSM Productions Inc., for alleged breach of contract and seven thousand six hundred and fifty pounds in lost earnings. It appeared that Shirley and Hilary had a quarrel after the party in the early hours of the morning. Part of it was witnessed by Bo Mills and Yves. Hilary said she had been sacked and alleged she had been physically attacked by Shirley. Shirley denied that she had sacked Hilary or that she had hit her. Hilary went home to London the next day and never spoke to Shirley again. It was an unpleasant and worrying time for Shirley. 'It's very distressing,' she said. Both the accused and the plaintiff knew there would be a long wait before the case came to court. They didn't know then just how long it would be.

'You have your down moments,' Shirley commented with an unpleasant court case hanging over her head. 'Call them my vulnerable days, because you never know if people around you want you for yourself or because you are famous. I can count my real friends on one hand. Anyway at this stage in my life I've no time for new friends. They become acquaintances because friendship takes time to build, you need years for that. I don't want to be around phony people so I find myself more alone that ever before.'

'I don't mix much with showbiz people,' Shirley says. 'I hate parties because someone always traps me in a corner and asks me how I became a singer.' And the men in her life have come in for some flack. 'It's hard for a man to live with a successful woman – they seem to resent you so much. Very few men are generous enough to accept success in their women.'

But there is the other side when she thinks she might have found the right man. Shirley has always been enthusiastic about the romancing, the chase, the wonderful feeling of being wanted, the lovemaking. As all her partners confirm Shirley is a good lover.

'The first six months of a relationship are wonderful,' said Shirley. 'I love that intensity, the passion, the "can't keep away from each other", then it all starts to taper off. They don't want to stay home and watch television, they want to go out. They don't want to listen to what I say, they start putting me down and I won't take that.'

She decided that she really doesn't mind not having a man in her life. 'Maybe I'm more comfortable nowadays not getting too close. If I find an older man, then he can't keep up with me; if I take a younger one, they haven't always grown up. They just look good.'

She thinks that perhaps the truth is that she's frightened of being let down and being hurt so it's easier to find a way of ending things before they begin. Shirley sounds horrified at the thought of getting married again. She insists that the idea of getting older on her own doesn't worry her one bit. 'It means that I can please myself and do the things I want.'

In spite of everything that Shirley has said, there lurks that uncertain feeling that suddenly one morning the headlines may read: 'Shirley Bassey gets married.'

But, according to Shirley, 'Only if Mr Wonderful comes along. I tell my life story in songs, the joys, pain, guilt, they all go into my performance. It's my autobiography up there for my audience to listen to.'

In February 1994 Shirley took a few days leave from her American tour and flew to London for an important appointment: on 18 February she went to see the Queen at Buckingham Palace and receive a medal making her a CBE, a Commander of the British Empire. It is the honour given to those of Her Majesty's subjects who have exceeded in good and noble works. Shirley was being recognised for the time and money she had given to charity, especially the Prince of Wales Trust.

Shirley, wearing a wide-brimmed hat trimmed with floating ostrich feathers, was accompanied by her friend and personal manager, Baudouin Mills and her daughter Sharon. She said, 'This honour was the cherry on the cake, it means that all I have done has been recognised not only by Her Majesty but by the country where I was born.'

The Hilary Levy case took five years to get to court, but the trial lasted only two days. The hearing opened at Brentford in 13 January 1998; on 15 January, the headlines blazoned the news that, 'Triumphant Shirley Bassey take the applause after judge throws out allegations that she slapped her assistant in a drunken row.'

Hilary alleged that although the fateful South African tour started well, the relationship between Shirley and herself was deteriorating. The final quarrel came in the early hours of 11 December 1993. Hilary said that Shirley wanted her to go shopping for Christmas presents for her the next morning. Hilary said that meant she would hardly have any sleep as Shirley had to be woken with her breakfast at twelve-thirty. A row ensued during which, Hilary declared, Shirley called her a Jewish bitch, and she told Shirley she was anti-Semitic. Hilary then marched out to her own bedroom slamming the door. She claimed that Shirley followed her, hit her and Hilary fell on to the bed. This was when Shirley shouted, 'You're out tomorrow!'

Hilary was earning eight hundred and fifty pounds a week plus expenses, and agreed that until then she and Shirley had been close friends, 'mates' as Shirley put it. Shirley's evidence was that she had called Hilary, 'a spoiled Jewish princess', and she had not hit Hilary, but only pushed her. She had not sacked Hilary either, and Bo Mills had tried to persuade Hilary to stay but had failed.

Justice Marcus Edwards backed Shirley's version of the events that night. He found Hilary Levy an unpersuasive witness. In contrast, Shirley Bassey was persuasive and Bo Mills also verified Shirley's account of the incident.

Shirley was given a great ovation by the crowd of jubilant fans outside, and accepted a bunch of red roses. She said, 'I've been so tense over the past few days. I just want to have a rest now. I'm so glad it has ended. Hilary accused me of being anti-Semitic, which is untrue. I have been in show business, which is full of Jewish people, for forty-five years, I have a Jewish manager, Jewish friends, Jewish boyfriends. I also have a daughter who is half-Jewish. Hilary thought she would get away with it. But in the end truth wins out, as it always does.'

Shirley hoped that Sharon, her daughter, wouldn't be too surprised to hear the truth about her father at last. She had never told her. As Shirley left she threw each one of the red roses that had been given her to the well-wishers in the crowd. Then she disappeared into her black Mercedes.

Shirleys musical achievements in the past have been prodigious. There are those twenty silver discs for sales in Holland, Britain and France and some fifty plus gold discs for international record sales. In a twenty-year period she was up in the charts in well over three hundred weeks.

She was, and is, one of Britain's best-selling singing stars, with more best-selling singles and albums than any other female performer. The list of her achievements goes on and on:

Voted Best Singles Singer by TV Times in 1973 Awards.

Voted Best Female Solo Singer in the last fifty years of recorded music in the Brittania Award in 1977.

Voted Best Female Entertainer for 1976 by the American Guild of Variety Artists.

Her most recent recordings include, *Shirley Bassey Sings the Songs of Andrew Lloyd Webber* (1993); *Shirley Bassey Sings the Movies*

(1995); *The Birthday Anniversary Album 1997* and *The Diamond Collection: 1958–1998.*

In 1997 she collaborated with Chris Rea to produce the very succesful Clubland hit, 'La Passione'. Then in 1998 her reinvention of herself contrived with The Propeller Heads number 'History Repeating'. The Propeller Heads, so called after their zany headgear, started out as a couple of amateur DJs from Bath, but by the time they met Shirley they had got a group together that had a soaring reputation. They provided backing for the new Bond movie and also the sound track for the film *Lost in Space*. Most of all they had introduced the new 'big beat' music scene and they wanted Shirley for their latest recording.

Big beat wasn't new to Shirley, it was as they said, 'history repeating itself.' She had actually grown up with a variety of it; the frenetic rhythms, the syncopated jazz and the beat of the drums. She loved the recording she made with the Propellor Heads. Shirley, in her Diamond Concert at the Royal Festival Hall on 21 June 1998, invited her London audience to join her beating out the rhythm of 'History Repeating.'

Backed by a superb orchestra and brilliantly lit, she stood there in a dress of silver and gold beads that showed more of Shirley than had been seen for a long time. Her figure was well worth showing off to her appreciative audience, Shirley, with the kind of body she had as a teenager about forty-five years ago, got the whole house on their feet as she belted out,

'The next big thing is here, but to me it all seems clear

That it's all just a little bit of history repeating . . .'

Her audience sings the beat with her as if they are chanting the history of their star. But the voice is better than ever. Shirley gets a standing ovation.

*

Other tempting ideas are suggested to Shirley. Would she do a chat show? Better still, how would she like a chat show of her own? But first she says, she has to get on with her summer open air concerts. After the Royal Festival Hall, she will do her tour of famous castles. Last year they were a great success, Castle Howard was breathtakingly beautiful, and then there was Althorp Park before the tragedy that turned it into a memorial park. Thousands attended the castles with *alfresco* family picnics before the Shirley Bassey concert. There was a touch of street party appeal about these occasions, with everyone enjoying themselves on the rolling lawns, grannies and teenagers, and Mums and Dads with babies and children.

That is what Shirley has said she wants to do, provide entertainment from the top to the bottom of the family. And later on, when the babies are asleep, there is Shirley on the stage under the pink and blue lights, supremely confident in white, feathers from her cape fluttering in the evening breeze. She sings, 'This is My Life'. She has survived a life of much heartache but has been strengthened by it. 'I must have been strong as a child,' she has said. 'I didn't realise how strong until I think of all these things that have happened to me.'

The girl from Tiger Bay has completely vanished; she has grown into a rich European woman, elegant in couture clothes, dining in Monte Carlo restaurants. 'I am a champagne person,' she once said. Her childhood friendships have gone, even her family who once lived in Bute Street, Tiger Bay, are spread out more thinly – some dead, and some long gone elsewhere. Sharon and her family have taken their place. The men who escort the star nowadays are mostly old friends or men who work with her management. She enjoys dates but she also likes being alone.

The fans remain. Hundreds, thousands, millions of fans throughout the world. They worship her, they cry, 'I love you,

Shirley,' as they rush to the stage with their gifts of flowers, teddy bears, champagne and chocolates. This degree of adulation makes Shirley uneasy. 'I feel like I am some goddess, and they are giving up an offering to me,'

Why do they do it? To try and understand one should stand in the foyer of the Royal Festival Hall and watch the audience stream in for a Shirley Bassey Concert. Pretty normal couples, mostly over forty, some young girls and boys, some old people all here to watch a seemingly ageless and indestructible star light up the stage with her presence and their lives with her voice.

Perhaps some of them have been watching Shirley Bassey for thirty years or more and feel they are now part of her family. They clap, they shout, they cheer, they give her standing ovations. At the end of the concert they carry their gifts to the stage to lay at her feet.

Shirley protects her special magic. The fans must not come too close. The magic works better from a distance. Yet, ever complex and contradictory, she sometimes welcomes this kind of love, this torrent of devotion that swells from her audiences, that could consume her but raises her up like a goddess. Shirley Bassey, the diva, sings of love, and from her huge following, love comes back to her. 'It keeps me going,' she says. 'It's my life.'

SOURCES

THERE HAVE BEEN no major books written about the life of Shirley Bassey. I relied upon interviews with people who knew and admired her before she became the international star that she is. Sometimes I was helped by the kindness of strangers, for instance the waitress at the Cardiff hotel who was also from Tiger Bay and lent me a book about her birthplace: *The Tiger Bay Story* by Neil M. G. Sinclair, (published by the Butetown History and Arts Projects, 1993); and also Ifor Harry, Shirley's next-door neighbour when the Basseys lived in Splott. From these and many others I was able to build up a picture of Shirley's young life.

Her steps to fame were helped by Michael Sullivan who included a chapter on Shirley in his book, *There's No People Like Show People*, Quadrant books, 1984. Through the wife of his partner, Sylvia, I learned more about Shirley's personality; Sylvia was always a great champion of Shirley. People who worked

alongside Shirley in show business helped me understand the great pressures of public life. It wasn't hard to find people who knew Shirley.

I offer thanks and acknowledgement to the following newspapers: The Empire News, The Sunday Chronicle, The News Chronicle, The Daily Mirror, The Sunday Mirror, The Daily Express, The Sunday Express, The Sunday People, The Telegraph, The Sunday Telegraph, The Times, The Sunday Times, The News of the World, The Daily Mail, The Mail on Sunday, The Independent, The Cardiff Echo, The Cardiff Post, The South Wales Echo, Wales on Sunday, Cardiff and South Wales Times, The Argus, The Western Mail, *Hello* Magazine, *Ask* Magazine, the *Radio Times*, TV Times, The Sydney Telegraph, The Sunday Telegraph (Sydney), The Melbourne Times, The Las Vegas Sun, *Ebony*, After Dark (USA); and finally the Shirley Bassey Collector's Club, New Jersey.

Picture credits

The plates in this book emanate from the following sources, to whom the author and publishers gratefully offer acknowledgement: Solo Syndication Limited/Daily Mail; P.A. News; Mirror Syndication International; Western Mail and Echo Limited and Redferns Music Picture Library. Also, the private collections of Sylvia Beresford Clarke, Michael Sullivan, Bernard Hall, Wyn Calvin and the author's own collection.

The author and publishers have made all reasonable efforts to contact copyright holders for permission, and apologize for any omissions or errors in the form of credit given. Corrections may be made in future printings.

ACKNOWLEDGEMENTS

I WOULD LIKE to thank Bernard Hall most of all for giving me his reminicences about the years when he knew Shirley Bassey. He walked into my life, drank my whisky and told me about Marlene Dietrich, then he stayed on to tell me about Shirley. We had a very good friendship and I still miss him.

I would like to thank the people from Tiger Bay and Cardiff for their kindness and help in the writing of this book. They include, Glyn Jones, Neil Sinclair, Wyn Calvin, Louise Benjamin, Iris Freeman, Isabella Freeman, Olwen Watkins, Mr. Wesley, Ifor Harry, Bill Barrett, Brian J. Lee, Annis Abraham and Jeanette Cockley.

And then, Emile Ilchuck from Pennsylvania, Brigid McCoffin from Melbourne, Sylvia Beresford Clarke, Kenny Clayton, Silvio Narizzano, Barbara Tieman, Rose Neighbour, Linda Scott, Paula Loveridge, and the staff of Dorking Library.

Finally I would like to thank my editor, Liz Rowlinson.